WOMEN AND HEALTH

WOMEN AND WORLD DEVELOPMENT SERIES

This series has been developed by the joint UN/NGO Group on Women and Development and makes available the most recent information, debate and action being taken on world development issues, and the impact on women. Each volume is fully illustrated and attractively presented. Each outlines its particular subject, as well as including an introduction to resources and guidance on how to use the books in workshops and seminars. The aim of each title is to bring women's concerns more directly and effectively into the development process, and to achieve an improvement in women's status in our rapidly changing world.

The Group was established in 1980 to organise the production and distribution of joint UN/NGO development education materials. It was the first time that United Nations agencies and non-governmental organisations had collaborated in this way, and the Group remains a unique example of cooperation between international and non-governmental institutions. Membership of the Programme Group is open to all interested organisations.

SERIES TITLES – in order of scheduled publication

For full details, as well as order forms, please write to:
ZED BOOKS LTD, 57 CALEDONIAN ROAD, LONDON N1 9BU, U.K.

WOMEN AND HEALTH

PREPARED BY PATRICIA SMYKE

Zed Books Ltd · London & New Jersey

Women and Health was first published by Zed Books Ltd,
7 Cynthia Street, London N1 9JF, UK, and 165 First Avenue,
Atlantic Highlands, New Jersey 07716, USA, in 1991.

Third impression, 1995.

The views expressed in this publication do not necessarily reflect the
views of the United Nations.

Cover and book design by Lee Robinson.
Cover photo: Jean Mohr/UNHCR.
Typeset by Goodfellow & Egan, Cambridge.
Printed and bound in the United Kingdom at The Bath Press, Avon.

The right of the UN NGLS to be identified as the author of this work has been
asserted in accordance with the Copyright, Designs and Patents Act, 1988.

A catalogue record for this book is available from the British Library.

US CIP data is available from the Library of Congress.

ISBN 0 86232 982 5 Hb
ISBN 0 86232 983 3 Pb

CONTENTS

ACKNOWLEDGEMENTS

This book has been prepared by Patricia Smyke on behalf of the Joint UN-NGO Group on Women and Development. The Group wishes to acknowledge and thank the World Health Organization (WHO) for its technical assistance and co-ordination.

THIS BOOK WAS MADE POSSIBLE THROUGH FINANCIAL CONTRIBUTIONS FROM:

- Australian International Development Assistance Bureau
- General Directorate for Development Cooperation, Ministry of Foreign Affairs, Italy
- United Nations Population Fund (UNFPA)

The content of this book has been approved by the Joint UN/NGO Group on Women and Development, which wishes to thank all those United Nations specialised agencies, non-governmental organisations and individuals who generously contributed articles and information towards the preparation of this book. References and credits are to be found wherever these were used. The following organisations have made a special contribution through their participation in the editorial panel formed for this publication:

- Inter-African Committee on Traditional Practices
- International Council on Social Welfare
- International Labour Office (ILO)
- ISIS-Women's International Cross-Cultural Exchange
- Medical Women's International Association
- United Nations Children's Fund (UNICEF)
- United Nations High Commission for Refugees (UNHCR)
- World Association of Girl Guides and Girl Scouts
- World Health Organization (WHO)

Overall co-ordination and management of the Joint UN-NGO Group on Women and Development is provided by the United Nations Non-Governmental Liaison Service (NGLS), an inter-agency unit which fosters dialogue and co-operation between the UN system and the NGO community on development policy issues and North-South relations.

To the women of the world,
without whom none of us
would have developed
into anything.

PREFACE

DO NOT READ THIS BOOK if you are looking for a list of do's and don'ts for specific illnesses. It is not a health care manual.

Do read this book if you are curious to know about the state of women's health globally, why it is the way it is, and what the consequences are—for individual women and for the world.

This is a book about linkages, the linkages between women and health and development. It has two objectives. The first is to inform you about women's health issues, help you understand the root causes of women's health problems, and show what can be, is being, done about them. The second objective is to move you to *action* on these issues.

One of the reasons why the United Nations/Non-governmental Organization (UN/NGO) Group on Women and Development decided to prepare this update of their 1981 publication on Women and Health was (in the words of an author quoted here) 'to make an irresistible case for change'. We do not think you will read the stories of the women on these pages and remain indifferent.

The book is addressed to a wide audience because there is need for action, individual and group action, on many fronts and by many different types of people and institutions. It is addressed to women *and* men, to young people and older people, to development groups, women's groups, human rights groups, teachers, health professionals, and non-governmental organizations (NGOs) in general; to schools and universities, research and training institutes; to government ministries; to concerned individuals.

The case studies, resource guide and suggestions for action are included in the book so that it can be used as a basis for study and planning for action. We hope you will adapt it and use it in your own way in classrooms, seminars, training sessions, formal and informal discussion groups.

As in all books about development, terminology is a problem. The words currently used to describe different regions of the world and different types of countries are all inadequate: developing, developed, North, South, poor, rich, Third World, industrialized countries, and so on. Without getting into the debate as to what development means or should mean (in every country), we stick to the terms 'developing countries' and 'industrialized countries' in this book, except where 'Third World' and other terms are used in quotations or in summarizing documents that use those terms.

This book has been a collective enterprise from the beginning. The UN/NGO Group on Women and Development would like to acknowledge with thanks the many different contributions that have helped to make it a reality, contributions of information, ideas, criticisms, funds and practical assistance.

It is impossible to mention all such contributions, but the UN/NGO Group would like in particular to thank the inter-governmental agencies, NGOs and individuals who offered material for our consideration. Selecting examples of different agency and NGO initiatives for use in this book was a painful process: for every example of action given here, dozens of other equally valuable and interesting initiatives could have been cited. Whether specifically mentioned or not, all the material submitted did contribute to the final result. We are most grateful, also, to those who read the manuscript in draft form and made so many constructive suggestions.

The UN/NGO Group on Women and Development wishes to express its sincere appreciation to those who have given us permission to reproduce articles and graphic materials in this book.

Financial contributions for the preparation of this book were received from the Australian International Development Assistance Bureau and from the General Directorate for Development Cooperation, Ministry of Foreign Affairs, Italy and from the United Nations Population Fund (UNFPA).

UNICEF, WHO, the Non-Governmental Liaison Service, and Webster University in Geneva provided the consultant with invaluable logistic support and technical assistance at several critical stages in the preparation of the manuscript. To the incredibly willing and helpful staff of those institutions . . . our thanks.

Finally, the consultant who prepared and compiled the book would like to thank the members of the Inter-agency/NGO Editorial Panel and the Secretariat of the UN/NGO group for the panoply of support she got from them—intellectual, technical, practical and moral support. It is deeply appreciated, as is the sorely tried but seemingly inexhaustible patience of a long-suffering husband and family. To describe the importance of *that* contribution to this book, there are no words.

PATRICIA SMYKE

1 INTRODUCTION

This has been a harsh decade.

Julius Nyerere[1]

When the first Joint United Nations Information Committee/Non-governmental Organization (JUNIC/NGO) publication on women, health and development appeared in 1981, its tone was one of cautious optimism. Although the state of women's health, especially in developing countries, gave rise to many concerns, there *were* certain grounds for optimism:

- International Women's Year in 1975, the Decade for Women that began in 1976 and the mid-Decade Conference in Copenhagen in 1980 had done much to inform world opinion about women's issues and get people talking about them. There had been 'a number of very pleasing signs of progress for women in terms of legislation . . . perhaps fewer in terms of social and economic relationships'.[2]

- The Primary Health Care (PHC) initiative, launched at Alma Ata in 1978, was called by the World Health Organization (WHO) 'the most optimistic statement of purpose ever made by the world community'. PHC ushered in a new approach to health care that stressed equity, health promotion and prevention of disease. The World Health Assembly's proclamation of 'Health for All by the Year 2000', with PHC as its centrepiece, also held great promise for women—for the masses of women whose health needs were unmet, for the masses of women who, as health care providers, needed recognition and support.

- Women themselves, all over the world, were standing up and speaking out on the issues that affect their lives, families and communities. Women's organizations were growing stronger, networks were forming. Women drawing strength from one another, a phenomenon long apparent at the level of the family and community, was becoming a national and international reality as well.

- Development concepts were shifting from the earlier concentration on economic growth and gross national product (GNP) to a greater emphasis on community development and participation. The role of women in development was at least being given lip service. The aim of the JUNIC/NGO development education materials was to increase awareness of the essential role of women in development and help people translate this into action. Where could that be more 'do-able', where could progress be more indisputably needed and possible than in the sphere of women and health?

A **HARSH DECADE** □ That was 1981. What has happened in the ten years since? There have been inspiring examples of progress on all the fronts just mentioned. But certain obstacles still loom large, and there are new forces that threaten to undo the hard-won progress. For it has been, as Julius Nyerere observed, 'a harsh decade'. One can see the effects on women's health.

Economic recession, debt and adjustment policies have forced governments to make painful decisions about where scarce money will be spent. In *The State of the World's Children 1989* UNICEF reports that:

Over the last few years, a decline in health spending per person has been documented in more than three quarters of the nations of Africa and Latin America, and the decline is almost certainly more widespread than these figures suggest . . . The incidence of low birth weight, a sensitive indicator of the well-being of women, has increased in 7 nations out of the 15 for which recent information is available.[3]

1

'Health' is defined in the Constitution of the World Health Organization as 'a state of complete physical, mental and social well-being and not merely the absence of disease or infirmity'.

While the proportion of malnourished people in developing countries has declined, according to the United Nations Population Fund (UNFPA) the absolute number of persons affected has risen because of increases in population. The situation is similar for illiteracy, unemployment, and people without clean water and sanitation. And always, those most affected by these trends are poor women.

The internal and international armed conflicts that have marked the decade have been especially devastating for women and children. Violence shatters the lives of those caught in the conflict zones and of those who suffer the indirect effects—husbands and fathers are absent, health services dis-rupted and social services cut back because the national budget gives priority to military spending.

Both the economic difficulties and the armed conflicts have caused massive displacements of people as migrants or refugees, again creating special difficulties for women, who are often left alone with families to support. Between 1980 and 1990 the number of recognized refugees in the world doubled. If internally displaced persons are included, the number is probably four times as great now as it was ten years ago.

The end of the 1980s is waking us up to the extent of environmental deterioration and the impact this has on women's lives and health. Women in many countries must go further from home in search of firewood and water, and work even harder to coax a harvest from exhausted soil. Mothers spend more time and energy in order to meet their families' basic needs in even a minimal way. As demands on the mother grow, it

seems reasonable to have more children to help with the work. Or a daughter may be kept home from school for that purpose. 'The mother's burden becomes the daughter's sacrifice—a sacrifice much less frequently demanded of boys.'[4] Finally, the diminishing prospects in the rural areas will add the whole family to the tide of people flooding into cities in search of a livelihood.

Population growth rates came down in the 1980s, but at a slower pace than in earlier years. During the 1970s total fertility dropped by almost 14 per cent worldwide; over the next ten years the fall was less than half as fast.[5] The demographic projections that looked so promising in the early 1980s are having to be revised upward.

Even the apparent improvement in the understanding of women's health issues as a human rights issue has been buffeted by 'the harsh decade'. In many different parts of the world there are renewed signs of intolerance and defence of sex discrimination on the basis of culture, religion or 'economic necessity'. For example, in Mexico, as in many other countries, women are now experiencing greater difficulty in getting into technical education. In some places occupational safety measures that are needed to protect women and their unborn babies are being postponed on the grounds that they are too costly. Women employees are told that they can either forgo child-bearing or quit.

These and other developments of the past decade point to the fragility of the progress that has been made. Nevertheless, as later chapters of this book will show, many of the decade's difficulties have also revealed or created positive elements for women to build on.

❙NSISTING ON THE OBVIOUS □ Anyone who has worked very long on women's issues knows that what seems obvious to some is not at all taken for granted by others. It is necessary to be explicit about the many linkages between women, health and development:

- These linkages are invariably two-way or circular relationships. Cause . . . becomes effect . . . becomes cause . . . Recognizing this is a necessary prelude to understanding how women and girls get caught in a descending spiral of ill health. One illustration is the interaction between women's nutritional state and their reproductive and productive roles. When a rural woman, a subsistence farmer, is malnourished, her productivity falls. Food for the family (or money to buy food) will soon be in short supply, and her nutritional state will get worse . . . along with that of other members of the family. The more numerous and frequent the pregnancies in this scenario, the more rapid her descent down the spiral.

- Many different factors affect women's health, all of them interrelated. While we talk about them separately, an inter-sectoral approach is almost always needed when it comes to action. Effective action on women's health may well involve action in the fields of agriculture, environment, education, commerce, justice, foreign affairs, human development, and so on, not to mention action to change basic attitudes towards women.

- There is a tendency to look at a woman's health at a specific moment in time, for example at the moment she becomes pregnant or becomes ill enough to go to a clinic. It is well to remember that her health status reflects the cumulative effect of all that she has experienced over a lifetime.

- Women have both general health needs the same as the rest of the population, and health needs that are specific to them as women. They need access to health care that enables them to satisfy all these needs.

Total health, having the highest possible standard of health and well-being, is as important and necessary to women as to any other segment of the population. It is a universal human right.

- Women do in fact provide most of the health care in the world. They need to be supported in that role so they can do an even better job, for their own sake and for the good of their families, communities and nations. PHC strategies recognize this.

- The way a country develops has a profound impact on the health of women in that country. That is, the degree of concern for sustainability, the extent of investment in human resources, the possibility for community participation—all of these affect the chances of women improving their health and well-being. This is true no matter what stage of development a country has achieved.

- The level of women's health is one of the major factors determining their ability to contribute, individually and collectively, to a nation's development.

PHOTO: MAGGIE MURRAY-LEE / UNICEF

- Women are often at the critical 'cross-points' of health and development. They occupy the pivotal position between policy and practice in health as in many other domains. In writing about Third World women, Peggy Antrobus has made an observation that could be applied to women almost universally:

Their central role in human survival therefore places them at the centre of the balance between population and land, reproduction and production, between sustainable development and ecological disaster, between a more human world and one which denies a common humanity to the majority of the world's population . . . unless their values, views and vision serve as a central focus for our policy-making we cannot achieve the ultimate goal of peace.[6]

The presumption of an inferior status for women and the persistent devaluing of women's contribution to society shows up in relation to health as in other sectors. One of the most devastating consequences is that millions of women accept poor health as their lot in life . . . and bring up their daughters to do the same.

In the essay that follows, Dr Nafis Sadik, Executive Director of the UNFPA, explains women's central role in development and proposes investment in women as the focus of the 1990s. Her statement that 'change of some kind cannot be avoided' is a good point for readers of this book to keep in mind. Changes of some kind are occurring daily in all the situations we describe here. Someone, something, is going to influence the direction and pace of these changes. It could be you.

INVESTING IN WOMEN: THE FOCUS OF THE NINETIES

Priority for women

Women are at the heart of development. They control most of the non-money economy (subsistence agriculture, bearing and raising children, domestic labour) and take an important part in the money economy (trading, the 'informal sector', wage employment). Everywhere in the world women have two jobs—around the home and outside it.

Much of this work is unrecognized and those who do it can expect no support. Their health suffers, their work suffers, their children suffer. Development itself is held back as a result.

This Report demonstrates some of the costs of ignoring the needs of women: uncontrolled population growth, high infant and child mortality, a weakened economy, ineffective agriculture, a deteriorating environment, a generally divided society and a poorer quality of life for all. For girls and women it means unequal opportunities, a higher level of risk and a life determined by fate and the decisions of others rather than choice.

Many women, especially in developing countries, have few choices in life outside marriage and children. They tend to have large families because that is expected of them. Investing in women means widening their choice of strategies and reducing their dependence on children for status and support. Family planning is one of the most important investments, because it represents the freedom from which other freedoms flow.

Investments in women include, besides family planning, 'social investments' —services such as health and education. The Report demonstrates that such services help women to do much better what they are already doing and open the door to new possibilities.   ▶

But investing in women must go beyond such services, and remove the barriers preventing them from exploring their full potential. That means granting them equal access to land, to credit, to rewarding employment—as well as establishing their effective personal and political rights.

The Report demonstrates that a change in any one aspect of women's lives—for good or ill—affects every other aspect. Increasing the availability of family planning will have its full effect on fertility when both women and men are prepared to use it; improving girls' education will make its full impact when it is accompanied by better employment opportunities; better employment opportunities are irrelevant if women are too burdened by child-bearing and domestic work to take advantage of them.

Making the necessary changes means recognizing women not only as wives and mothers, but as vital and valuable members of society. It means that women themselves must take power in their own hands to shape the direction of their lives and the development of their communities. It means rethinking development plans from the start so that women's abilities, rights and needs are taken into account at every stage—so that women's status and security are derived from their entire contribution to society, rather than only from child-bearing. Few would argue against providing women with better welfare services; but making investment in women a development priority will require a major change in attitudes to development not only by developing countries but by financial and lending institutions. Under increasing economic pressure, in the last four years 37 of the poorest countries have cut health spending by 50 per cent, and education by 25 per cent. This burden falls hardest on the poor, and hardest of all on poor women.

The challenge for those who believe that women's contribution is central to development, and that investment in women should take priority, even in societies under severe economic stress, is to make an irresistible case for the change.

Change of some kind cannot be avoided. In the face of population growth, the urban explosion, the developing environmental crisis, escalating international debt and growing poverty in many of the poorest of the developing countries, many authorities agree that some kind of fundamental rethinking is long overdue. The concept of 'sustainable development', in which human and natural resources are brought into a dynamic equilibrium, is one response. Women have a central part in any system of sustainable development.

Taking the long view, investing in women has a finite if unquantifiable economic value: the return will be an approach to development which will make the most effective use of the world's limited resources; slower, more balanced growth in the labour force; security for the family; and—most important—the possibility of better health, education, nutrition and personal development not only for women but for all people.

Investing in women is not a panacea. It will not put an end to poverty, remedy the gross inequalities between people and countries, slow the rate of population growth, rescue the environment, or guarantee peace. But it will make a critical contribution towards all those ends. It will have an immediate effect on some of the most vulnerable of the world's population. And it will help create the basis for future generations to make better use of both resources and opportunities.

UNFPA

6

1 J. Nyerere, 'Waiting Outside "the Door to Prosperity"', *International Herald Tribune*, 2 March, 1989. Mr Nyerere, former President of Tanzania, wrote this article in his capacity as Chairman of the South Commission.

2 Joint United Nations Information Committee/Non-governmental Organization Sub-Group on Women and Development, *Women, Health and Development Information Kit*, Geneva, UNICEF/WHO, 1981.

3 UNICEF, *The State of the World's Children 1989*, Oxford, Oxford University Press, 1990.

4 UNFPA, *The State of World Population 1990*, New York, UNFPA, 1990, p. 15.

5 Ibid., p. 4.

6 P. Antrobus, 'Women and Development: an Alternative Analysis', *Development*, Journal of the Society for International Development: 1, 1989, p. 26.

OVERVIEW

The health status of women and the disparities in health between the sexes are often critical indicators of equity in a society.

Intersectoral Action for Health,
WHO, 1986

The year 2000! That imposing figure has inspired all kinds of targets and goals as we leave one century behind and start the countdown to a new one. The field of health is no exception. There is the overarching goal of Health for All by the Year 2000. The WHO and UNICEF have worked out 'common goals for the health of women and children by the year 2000.' The 'Forward-looking Strategies' to achieve the goals of the United Nations Decade for Women have 2000 as their target date.

THIS IS NOT JUST RHETORIC. The 1990s, the decade leading to the turn of the century, happen to coincide with the turning points looming in a number of critical areas— geopolitics, population, environment, health, education. The decisions made in the next ten years in these areas will largely determine the kind of world we and our children live in in the twenty-first century.

What is the state of women's health as we enter this critical decade? The report on the subject presented to the 1985 Nairobi Conference on Women summarized the condition of most of the world's women as follows:

Women in developing countries are often in poor health and overburdened with work; they are tired, most are anaemic, many suffer from malnutrition and parasitism and chronic ill health from lack of personal attention and adequate health care, especially during pregnancy and childbirth. Early marriage, repeated child bearing, ignorance, poverty and manual labour all have deleterious effects. Women's special needs have often been ignored by health planners and women have thus had to bear a disproportionate share of unmet health needs.

The extra burdens that women carry in health- and development-related matters can be seen in two ways. First, although women experience the same pressing problems as men—for example, lack of access to resources, under-employment or unemployment, lack of training opportunities—they are almost always the most severely affected. Women are usually the last to be given resources, to be listened to and consulted about their own needs, to be beneficiaries of health and development schemes.

Secondly, many problems are unique to women, for example: in relation to their roles in child-bearing and rearing, and the discrimination against them in almost all social, economic and political arenas, to a lesser or greater extent, in all countries of the world.[1]

Before asking *why* this is so—that is the subject of the next chapter—it is important to have more precision: which women have which health problems, where, when in their lives, and how is the situation changing? This chapter presents some recent findings on women's health that suggest general answers to those questions; more detailed discussion of these issues is found in Chapter 4.

GETTING THE DATA ☐ Answering such questions on a global scale is of course not simple, nor altogether possible, but it is much more feasible now than ten

8

years ago because more health statistics are broken down now by gender. This is mostly due to pressure from women themselves. Significant differences between female and male health patterns are now apparent. Research methods are being changed to ensure that women and girls are no longer under-represented, as they often have been, for example, in studies based only on hospital records or clinic attendance. Research based on household sampling and interviewing may reveal quite a different picture.

But even here, socio-cultural factors can lead to women's voices being muted. Four household surveys in a rural area of Nigeria were analysed for 'don't know' responses. In all but one of the 15 questions examined, the proportion of 'don't know' answers was greater for women than men. On some questions the proportion was nearly twice as large, even though women generally had more experience than men in actually dealing with the health problems concerned. This finding was analysed as follows:

A survey may be perceived as a formal occasion, and tradition would . . . require the husband or elderly father to take on the role of family spokesman. A woman finding herself in the position of survey respondent could therefore feel reluctant to answer questions, fearing that what she said might reflect poorly on her family. Furthermore, when it comes specifically to health, women have a minor role in decision-making. The traditional healers, herbalists and diviners of [the region] are men. Although women can learn much about traditional disease concepts and medical practices while nursing the sick, they may hesitate to speak openly about what have traditionally been areas of male responsibility.

. . . the 'I don't know' formula was a polite way of not answering . . . During informal discussion, women talked more freely and were able to clarify seeming contradictions in survey results.[2]

The recognition that women's well-being has a powerful impact on other parts of the population has stimulated more collection and dissemination of data relating to women. In recent years the annual UNICEF report, *The State of the World's Children*, has devoted more and more space to information on women, their health, education, literacy, social and economic status—all of which turn out to be very

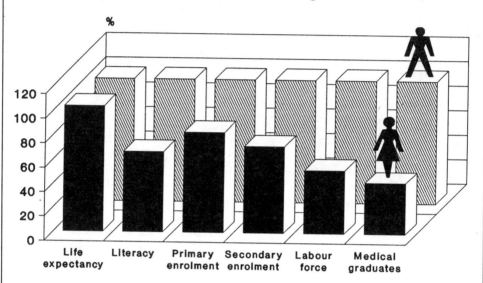

The gender gap
in developing countries
(females as a percentage of males)

%

120
100
80
60
40
20
0

Life expectancy | Literacy | Primary enrolment | Secondary enrolment | Labour force | Medical graduates

Data sources: UN, UNESCO, ILO, WHO
WHO/WHD/90.1

important factors in their children's well-being.

As a sharper picture of women's health status begins to emerge, three observations are inescapable:

1. The data on women show clearly the disparities that still exist in health. These are not just disparities between women and men, but between regions, between countries, and between different socio-economic, ethnic and age groups within a country. Some vivid examples can be drawn from the field of reproductive health:

In the industrialized countries . . . the average lifetime risk for a woman of dying of pregnancy-related causes is between one in 4,000 and one in 10,000. In contrast, for a woman in the developing countries the average risk is between one in 15 and one in 50. These countries commonly have maternal mortality rates 200 times higher than those of Europe and North America, the widest disparity in all public health statistics.[3]

Girls in Jamaica and Nigeria who conceive at 10–14 years are five times as likely to die as a result of pregnancy and childbirth compared with 20–24 year-olds.[4]

In 1984 the Pittsburgh (USA) Black Women's Health Network roused city public health authorities to action when it disseminated a report showing that the black infant mortality rate in the city was 29.7 for every 1000 live births; the

rate for white infants was 10.1. Much of the difference was attributable to socio-economic factors, teenage pregnancies and inadequate pre-natal care.[5]

2. There are important differences between regions in the causes of female mortality and morbidity, but there is a tendency for some of those differences to be reduced:

Cancer of the lung may be the most common cancer in women *worldwide* in 20–30 years, unless effective action is taken. (Emphasis added)[6]

3. For far too long there has been an unconscionable acceptance of *preventable* sickness and deaths among women. Erica Royston and Sue Armstrong, in the introduction to their book, *Preventing Maternal Deaths*, write:

. . . maternal death and injury in developing countries . . . is a tragedy that has been largely ignored by those who set national and international health priorities, because those who suffer generally live in remote places, are poor, illiterate and politically powerless.

. . . It is only very recently that people have started to challenge—loudly and clearly in international forums—the stifling mix of personal fatalism and political disregard for women's needs that has condoned inaction in many poor countries.

Under the spotlight of the United Nations Decade for Women (1976–1985), the sheer scale of the suffering associated with maternity became widely recognized. So, too, did the crucial fact that most of this suffering is preventable, and that Health for All by the Year 2000 is just an empty slogan if glaring inequities in health care provision are allowed to continue.[7]

LIFE EXPECTANCY ☐ Women have certain inherent biological advantages that normally make their life spans between five and seven per cent longer than those of men. (The role of environmental and life-style factors in this difference is still being sorted out.) The difference is less in developing countries, averaging two to three per cent. This biological advantage can, however, be whittled away by discriminatory treatment towards girls and women and by the risks associated with child-bearing.

The 1987 average life expectancy was actually lower for women than for men in Bhutan, Nepal and Bangladesh and very close to being equal in Pakistan, India and Iran, suggesting some imbalance in health risks between women and men in those countries. These are not the only countries where imbalances exist, of course, but South Asia is a region where son preference remains particularly strong, as we shall see in the next chapter. The rising chorus of concern for the health and socio-economic status of women and girls led the South Asian Association for Regional Co-operation (SAARC) to declare 1990 the Year of the Girl Child.[8]

Overall, life expectancy in developing countries has risen for both women and men in recent years: from an average of 51 for men and 53 for women in the late 1960s to 59 and 61 respectively in the late 1980s. The forecast is that life expectancy will continue to rise in developing countries, although probably less rapidly.[9] If these figures are broken down by level of development, the life expectancy in the least developed countries (LDCs) is 49 for men and 52 for women, while in the rest of the developing countries the figures are 62 and 65.[10]

Comparable figures for developed countries show a wider gap between the sexes:

Lung Cancer Deaths for
22 Developed Countries: % Increase

The rate of increase in female mortality far exceeds that for men.

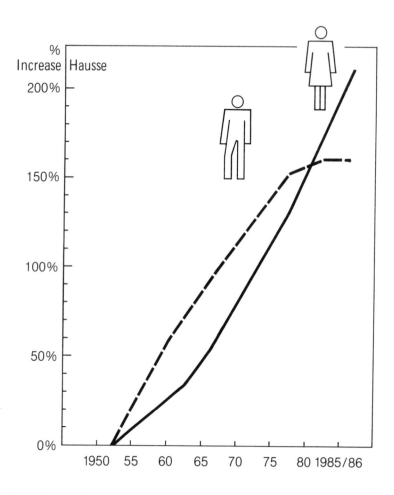

Lung Cancer: Now woman's way of dying too   WHO/20583

women on average have a life expectancy of 77 years compared to 70 years for men.[11] Some observers believe that this gap may narrow 'as more women adopt—or more men abstain from or reduce—such health-threatening behaviours as smoking and heavy alcohol consumption.'[12]

The gains in average life expectancy, however, mask many inequalities in people's chances to live long, healthy, happy lives. Millions of individual and family tragedies still occur when lives are cut short in their prime, and from causes that are for the most part avoidable. Nowhere is this more evident than in maternal mortality . . .

REPRODUCTIVE HEALTH □ Half a million women—wives, daughters, sisters, mothers of families, 'pillars of the community'—die each year from causes related to pregnancy and childbirth. Only a tiny fraction (6,000) of those 500,000 deaths take place in developed countries. All the rest occur in developing countries, where they are responsible for one-fourth to one-third of all deaths of women of childbearing age.

Over half of all maternal deaths occur in South Asia, predominantly in Bangladesh, India and Pakistan. Africa accounts for another 150,000 of the total. It is in Africa, moreover, where women run the greatest

In South Asia each year, 300,000 women die—and many more than this number suffer serious illness or permanent disability—from [pregnancy-related causes]. The region accounts for just 27% of the world's births, but more than one half of all maternal deaths.[13]

risk of dying from any given pregnancy. Maternal mortality rates of up to 1,000 per 100,000 live births are found in certain rural areas. These high rates, coupled with the high fertility rates on the continent, mean that for many African women the chances of dying from causes related to childbearing are at least 1 in 15.[14]

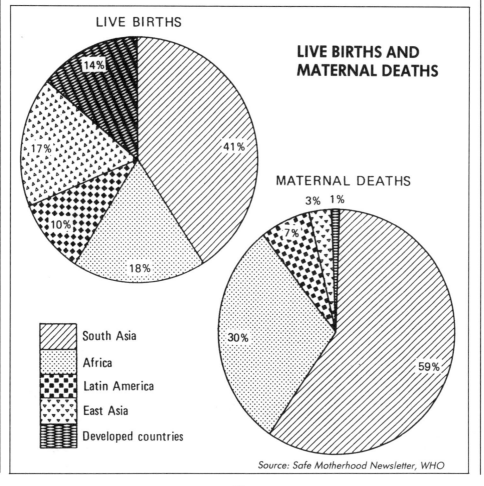

LIVE BIRTHS

LIVE BIRTHS AND MATERNAL DEATHS

MATERNAL DEATHS

- South Asia
- Africa
- Latin America
- East Asia
- Developed countries

Source: Safe Motherhood Newsletter, WHO

Abortion □ Anyone concerned about safe motherhood needs to face the fact that a large part of maternal mortality in developing countries is due to the complications of induced abortion, mostly illegal and clandestine abortions sought by women who are desperate not to have a child. Reliable and complete figures are of course hard to find, but studies that have been done in several countries are indicative. 'The proportion of maternal deaths due to illegal abortion is approximately 29% in Ethiopia, 20% in Bangladesh, 64% in Chile and 86% in Romania.'[15]

Fertility □ If women were able to have only the number of children they say they want, the number of births would fall by 35 per cent in Latin America, 33 per cent in Asia and 17 per cent in Africa. The effect on maternal mortality would be considerable. By conservative estimate the number of maternal deaths would decrease by one-fourth.[16] Other estimates suggest that the reduction would be even greater.

Adolescents □ The figures on maternal mortality and morbidity among adolescents show why it is important to have information on women's health that is broken down by age groups. Bearing children before the age of 18 or so is a very different experience from having children in the 'prime' reproductive years of 20–34. For teenage mothers there is a greater risk of a premature and low-birthweight baby, obstructed labour (because the pelvis is not yet fully grown), and complications that can cause permanent damage and even death. And this is one statement about women's health that holds true across the globe. In developed and developing regions alike, early pregnancy is risky for the health of mother and child, not to mention the social costs if early motherhood reduces the young

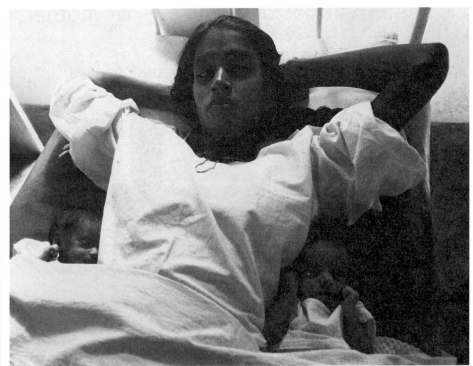

PHOTO: INTERNATIONAL LABOUR OFFICE

woman's chances for education and employment.

The figure below shows how much higher the risk of death is for women giving birth at 15–19 years of age as compared to women 20–34 years old. Similar patterns are found in countries as diverse as Malaysia, Japan, the Dominican Republic and the United States. And yet, early marriage and early pregnancy remain an accepted way of life for vast numbers of women:

In Bangladesh four out of five teenage girls are mothers; three out of four teenagers in Africa as a whole . . . In Africa 40% of teenage births are to women aged 17 or under, compared with 39% in Latin America, 31% in Asia and 22% in Europe. [17]

Older women □ At the other end of the age-scale the health picture for older women is different from that of younger age groups. For example, women who become pregnant after the age of 35, especially those who have had more than three children, are again at greater risk than mothers in the 20–34 age group.

The health patterns of older women differ from those of older men as well. Since demographic trends indicate a 'greying' of the population in almost all regions of the world, it is important to recognize that for some time to come the majority of the elderly are likely to be women.

Further, because women usually live longer and may be considerably younger than the men they marry, there is a good chance that they will spend many of their older years as widows, with all the dangers that that implies for their physical, economic and social well-being. Widows make up 25 per cent of the adult female population in Africa.[18]

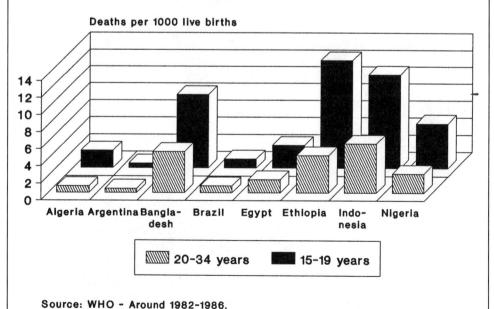

Maternal mortality by age of mother
(selected countries)

Deaths per 1000 live births

Source: WHO - Around 1982-1986.
WHO/WHD/90.2

NUTRITION □ The world produces enough food to feed everyone today—in theory. Yet, in fact, malnutrition affects more than 500 million people. Many factors contribute to this widespread situation, including inadequate distribution of food, poor storage practices, ignorance of nutritional requirements, illnesses and parasites that interfere with the body's utilization of the food consumed. But perhaps the biggest problem is poverty, the inability to earn enough money to assure an adequate diet.

If the problem is poverty, one can be sure that the effects will be felt most keenly by women. (See *Women and the World Economic Crisis* by Jeanne Vickers, the first volume in this series, for an excellent discussion of the 'feminization' of poverty.) This is especially true when poverty is combined with the other factors that undermine women's nutritional status: heavy workload, repeated pregnancies, low social status, discrimination in food distribution within the family, or food taboos.

Between 20 and 45 per cent of women of child-bearing age in the developing world do not eat the WHO-recommended 2,250 calories a day under normal circumstances, let alone the extra 285 a day they need when they are pregnant.

Malnutrition can take many forms. It may be manifested in obesity. There has been a trend in this direction in certain societies, a trend that is especially disturbing, as obesity is seen more and more often among children and young people. For most of the malnourished people in developing countries, however, the problem is undernutrition and nutritional deficiencies.

Anaemia is a particularly worrisome problem for women in the developing world. Women need more iron than men. Nearly two-thirds of pregnant women and one-half of all other women are estimated to be suffering from anaemia. It may be caused by insufficient iron in the diet, particularly when pregnancy and breast-feeding put additional demands on the mother; it may also be aggravated by hookworm or an infectious disease like malaria.

Whatever the cause of the anaemia, the consequences for the woman, her family and community, are far-reaching and serious. Anaemia leads to fatigue and reduced productivity and lowers resistance to disease. In pregnancy and childbirth it means greater risk for the life and health of both mother and child.

Anaemia provides several examples of the two-way interactions that surround women's health and trap Third World women in a vicious circle: unless their additional nutritional needs are met, each pregnancy depletes their supply of iron further, leaving them more vulnerable to infections, diseases and death, and less able to cope with the demands of breast-feeding and the next pregnancy. The low-birthweight babies born to undernourished, anaemic women are likely to become undernourished infants and stunted children. For the girls among them, the cycle leading to another generation of ill-health and low-birthweight babies will have begun.

The outlook for younger women is again rather different from that of other age groups. Dr Loretta Brabin, in a paper entitled 'At risk profiles for young women', points out the dangerous interaction between anaemia and malaria in young women: 'Although the consequences of anaemia become more evident in pregnancy, especially the first pregnancy in malarious areas, anaemia is often present in young women prior to pregnancy. In malarious areas, young women who start their first pregnancy with anaemia are highly at risk, as are their children.'[19] Until the day when it is possible to protect everyone from anaemia and malaria, it is important to bear in mind that both can be identified early and treated, and that young women have a

The Vicious Circle Of Malnutrition

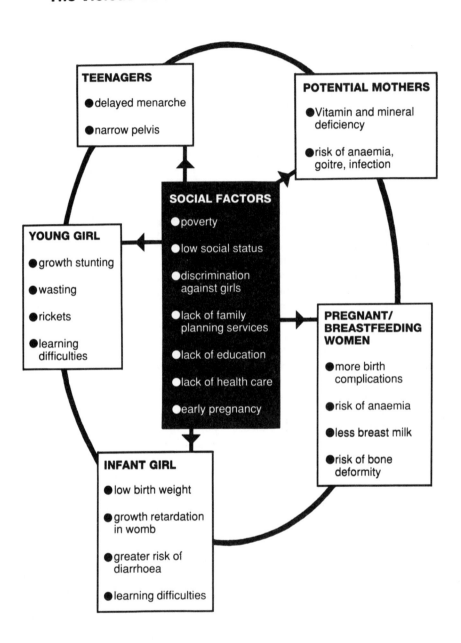

TEENAGERS
- delayed menarche
- narrow pelvis

POTENTIAL MOTHERS
- Vitamin and mineral deficiency
- risk of anaemia, goitre, infection

SOCIAL FACTORS
- poverty
- low social status
- discrimination against girls
- lack of family planning services
- lack of education
- lack of health care
- early pregnancy

YOUNG GIRL
- growth stunting
- wasting
- rickets
- learning difficulties

PREGNANT/ BREASTFEEDING WOMEN
- more birth complications
- risk of anaemia
- less breast milk
- risk of bone deformity

INFANT GIRL
- low birth weight
- growth retardation in womb
- greater risk of diarrhoea
- learning difficulties

Source: UNFPA Investing in Women – The Focus of the '90's

special need to be screened for this purpose.

Other infectious and endemic diseases that present special hazards to women are discussed in the next chapter.

CHANGING PATTERNS ☐ The causes of women's ill-health and death are not static. For a long time the prevalence of communicable diseases in developing countries tended to hide other serious health problems. But now, 'after the first five years of life, cancer, cardiovascular diseases and accidents are the three main causes of death for both developed and developing countries.'[20]

'*Cancer* is a Third World problem, too', says a recent WHO publication. 'If existing trends continue, cancer mortality is expected to rise in the future in nearly all regions of the world. The major reasons for this are a general increase in age of the world population, the control of other major health problems, and an increasing use of tobacco'.[21] The first reason is probably unalterable; the second is something no one would want to change; but women can take action to stop the third! In many areas it is among women that tobacco use is increasing most rapidly.

Already 'cancer is one of the leading causes of mortality in women in both developed and developing countries, especially for those aged 35–55 . . . Cancer of the cervix is the most common cancer in developing countries and breast cancer is the most frequent in women in industrialized countries.'[22]

Cardiovascular diseases account for one-half of all deaths in the industrialized world and for 16 per cent in the developing world. But by the year 2000, these diseases 'are expected to be a major health problem in virtually every nation of the Third World, accounting for 25% of all deaths.'[23] In some countries—the USA is one example—cardiovascular disease is the leading cause

of death in women, accounting for twice as many deaths as cancer.[24]

Women in all regions of the world could perhaps learn from the experience in North America, 'where one of the great myths in American medicine today is that women don't get coronary heart disease. In fact, the same number of women die of heart attacks as men, only a little later in life, at an age about ten years older than men.'[25] As women live to a more advanced age in all countries, it will be especially important that they do not mimic the lifestyle that has led to the heavy toll from cardiovascular diseases in industrialized countries.

CONCLUSION ☐ These are just a few of the elements that make up the patterns of women's health globally. Others are treated in later chapters. Some can only be discovered by people looking at the situation of women's health locally.

The following table permits inter-regional comparison of patterns of marriage, childbirth and life expectancy of women at the birth of their last child. In addition, it shows the patterns prevailing in the more developed countries in the last century as compared to the present, a reminder of the dramatic changes that have taken place in just a few generations.

This chapter closes with a kaleidoscope of facts and figures typical of those that prompted the UN/NGO Group on Women and Development to decide that it was time for an update on women, health and development. Some of the items below are good news, showing the progress that can be made when the will is there. Others deal with new problems that demand our attention because of their impact on women (notably AIDS). And some report on old problems that seem as intractable as ever.

• Women's health coalitions are springing up in cities and countries all over the world, and many regional and

19

Marriage, Childbirth and Life Expectancy for Women in Less Developed and More Developed Regions

Less Developed Regions

	Africa	Asia	Latin America
Age[a] at first marriage	17	17	19
Age[a] at first birth	19	20	20
Age[a] at last birth	37	37	36
Interval between last and first birth (in years)	17	16	16
Number of live births	7	7	6
Life expectancy at birth of last child (in years)	29	36	38

More Developed Regions

	Model Until Mid-19th Century	Recent Model
Age[a] at first marriage	18	23
Age[a] at first birth	18	23
Age[a] at last birth	40	30
Interval between last and first birth (in years)	22	7
Number of live births	6	2
Life expectancy at birth of last child (in years)	23	47

[a] Median age, i.e. the age that divides the population into two numerically equal groups.

Source: *World Population Trends and Policies: 1987 Monitoring Report.*

international networks are going strong. (See Chapter 5.)

- Maternity care saves lives: Sri Lanka has the same per capita GNP as Pakistan but a maternal mortality rate that is one-fifth of Pakistan's. Some critical differences: almost all births in Sri Lanka are attended by trained personnel; there are good family planning services and female literacy is high.[26]

- 'In most developing countries, births to young women below 20 represent an increasing proportion of all births, due to the young age structure of [the population].'[27]

- 'AIDS has become the main cause of death among women aged 20–40 years in some major cities of the Americas, Europe and sub-Saharan Africa. WHO estimates that of the 500,000 people who will develop AIDS during 1990 and 1991, 200,000 will be women.'[28]

- Malaria is staging a 'comeback'. It is found in 102 countries, where half the world's population lives.[29]

- An estimated 84 million girls and women in the world today have undergone some form of female circumcision.[30]

- In the closed camps for Khmer 'displaced persons' along the Thai–Cambodian border, the number of reported violent episodes doubled between June 1987 and June 1988; 40 per cent were related to domestic violence. Ninety per cent of attempted suicides in that period were among young women between the ages of 15 and 30.[31]

- In Southern Asia and Africa nearly 40 per cent of the young girls of primary school age are not attending school. The greatest sex disparity in primary school attendance is in Southern Asia and West Asia where more than twice as many girls as boys are not attending primary school.[32]

- In the Kanghura Community Health Project in the Republic of Korea, only half as many girls as boys were brought for measles immunization after a small fee was introduced.[33]

What does it all mean, not in terms of numbers but of human lives? When the first JUNIC/NGO kit on women and health came out in 1981, it carried a reprint of an article by Vicki Hammer that had appeared that year in the magazine *World Health*. It was entitled 'So many like her'. We reprint it here under the title, '*Still* so many like her . . .'

But that is not the full story in 1990. To round out the picture, '*Still* so many like her' needs to be accompanied by a second portrait of a woman, entitled 'But more and more like Aba . . .'

STILL SO MANY LIKE HER

. . . She's 35 years old. When she was born, her mother was malnourished and over-worked; she was very small and low-weight at birth; she grew slowly. During childhood she had little good food to eat—even less than her brothers. She was malnourished or undernourished most of the time. She could not go to school, as her brothers could, but remained at home with her mother to help with the housework and child-minding.

When she became an adolescent, her pelvic bones were misshapen, and she was shorter in stature than might have been expected. As was the tradition, she was married early, and had her first baby when she was only 14, even before she had fully developed. It was a difficult birth, but she survived. Her second pregnancy was aborted spontaneously. It was a painful event; she was tired and weak afterwards. Her many subsequent pregnancies occurred often, with little time in between to recuperate—to regain her strength or to replenish her body. On one delivery, she had so much bleeding that everyone was afraid she would never recover, and she had a high fever for days. She's been anaemic ever since, a condition aggravated by the hookworm she carries. During another pregnancy, she suffered a malarial fever, and aborted. During later pregnancies her nutritional state was very poor, and her fatigue was draining her. She had so much work—with her children, keeping up the household, fetching the water, working in the local brick factory—she

began to dread the next pregnancy. When it came, she went to a woman in the village for something to end it. She was very sick, but it worked.

She breastfed all of her children, but many times it was difficult and tiring. Once, in order not to lose her job at the brick factory, she bottle-fed her infant. She didn't have enough money to buy enough powder so she diluted the little she had and her eldest daughter had the job of giving the bottle to the baby. The baby died at four months, from diarrhoea.

Like her mother before her, she never went to a health centre when she was pregnant. It was too far away and too foreign. She used the same traditional birth attendant (TBA) who delivered her and who helped her sisters. The TBA, unaware of the importance of cleanliness, used a bamboo blade to cut the umbilical cord, and her unclean hands to extract the placenta. Thus, she suffered serious infections after childbirth.

Though she survived those episodes, today, at 35, she still feels dull pains and soreness in her 'belly' which flare up from time to time.

During her rare menstrual periods she doesn't experience too much pain, but she is anaemic, and sometimes there is infection because she's not able to use clean enough 'protection'. Also, after so many pregnancies, she probably has a partial prolapsed uterus, which often causes her strong discomfort, especially after a hard day's work carrying bricks or large urns of water.

Despite all her hours of work at the factory and helping the family working in the fields, there's never been enough food around. She does all she can to prepare the family's meals, but her husband and children must have the most, and she will manage. She is malnourished.

She is a woman who cares desperately about her family and wants to limit her pregnancies. She heard about family planning from her sisters, but was always too afraid of her husband, who would never allow it. What would people think if she had no more babies, especially after her last son died? Despite these fears she once got some contraceptive pills, yet she felt so nauseated and had so many headaches (this was surely a punishment, she thought), that she stopped.

Vicki Hammer

But more and more like Aba ☐ Aba is 18, in her last year of secondary school and determined to find a scholarship so she can go on for some kind of post-secondary education, perhaps even university. Her father is a civil servant, an administrator in a provincial capital. Her mother, after finishing primary school, had two years of training as a nurse and works now at a local maternal and child health (MCH) centre.

The oldest of five children, Aba has two brothers and two sisters. When they were small their widowed grandmother took care of them while their parents were at work. Grandmother told fascinating stories about the old days when she supported her family by trading. Gradually she accumulated a little property and the family could live more comfortably. In fact the house they all live in now belongs to grandmother.

Most of Aba's classmates expect to get married and start families shortly after they leave secondary school. 'Might as well,' they say, 'why should a girl struggle to get more education when it's so hard to find a job and you are just going to get married anyway and have a husband to support you?' Aba would like to have a husband and children (two boys and a girl) someday, but she wants to wait until after she finishes her education and has worked a while.

She had a teacher in primary school who praised her for her work in mathematics and urged her to take the examinations for secondary school. They were hard, but Aba did well and won a scholarship to cover her school fees. That was fortunate because both her father and mother had their salaries frozen when the price of cocoa fell and the Government had to cut back on spending. With the four younger children still in school, a large part of the family income goes to school fees and related expenses, but her parents say that nothing is more important than education. They are ready to make many sacrifices to keep all the children in school.

Aba's father told her once that with her good results in mathematics she could become an engineer or an architect if she wanted to. Aba thinks, however, that she would rather go into research. She likes statistics. Maybe she will do research in public health.

She talks with her mother about the things they do at the MCH centre to help women and children stay healthy. There are many problems. Most of the women in the city are poor and don't have enough money to buy good food. Some are anaemic. Her mother says they are beginning to see cases of AIDS at the MCH centre, in both mothers and babies.

Sometimes Aba goes with her mother to the MCH mobile clinics in the countryside.

She helps keep the records and explains to the women how to fill in their own and their children's health cards. She shows them how to recognize 'danger signs'. Aba has even done her own small 'research project', an analysis of the MCH centre records to find out what the most frequent health problems are for local women. This was part of some work her mother had to do before going to a meeting in the capital city.

It was a workshop organized by the Ministry of Health and one of the women's associations in their country. Aba's mother and other people from MCH centres talked about what they saw and heard every day in their work. Then they all decided what local branches of the women's association could do to help. Her mother was put in charge of follow-up in their area. The health cards are part of the follow-up.

Aba's mother and most of the women in her country have been circumcised, but after long discussion Aba's parents decided against it for their daughters. This was something her mother had discussed with other nurses and members of the women's association in the capital. Aba doesn't know what position her grandmother took in the family discussion. Once grandmother had said that the girls would never find husbands if they were not circumcised, but she doesn't seem too upset about the decision. She says that times are changing and that 'you can't build a house for last year's summer'. Aba's mother told them that there are groups of people in many African countries who are working to do away with practices like female circumcision. Grandmother looked a little sceptical but said, 'When spider webs unite, they can tie up a lion'.

Aba belongs to an organization of young women who meet regularly to talk about their problems and what they would like to do with their lives. They have had speakers on AIDS and family planning and how to find a job. They carry out community pro-jects like tutoring younger girls and encouraging them to stay in school. Once they organized a protest when the local cinema started showing cigarette advertisements. In one ad there was a glamorous young woman sitting by a swimming pool, cigarette in hand, with the young men in the background exchanging approving glances. The ads were withdrawn.

Aba once went to a meeting in another country where there were young people from all over Africa. She had a wonderful time and was surprised to find out how many other young people are concerned about the same things she is. They all keep in touch now through a little newsletter. From the newsletter she learned that one of the girls she met is going to Dakar to work with a group of African women carrying out a research project on women and the environment. Aba would like to be doing something like that a few years from now, after university. She is willing to work hard for it and sees no reason why she shouldn't succeed.

1 *Report of the Secretary General* to the United Nations World Conference to Review and Appraise the Achievements of the United Nations Decade for Women, Nairobi, Kenya, July 1985, Part Two, Development in Sectoral Areas, *Health and Nutrition* (A/Conf. 116/5/Add.3), 5 December 1984, p. 2.

2 W. Brieger and J. Ramakrishna, letter in 'Readers' Forum', *World Health Forum*, vol. 9, 1988, p. 73.

3 H. Mahler, then Director General of WHO, addressing the International Safe Motherhood Conference, Nairobi, February 1987.

4 *Safe Motherhood Newsletter*, no. 2, March–June 1990, p. 6.

5 *Saving Our Babies*, Pittsburgh Black Women's Health Network, Pittsburgh, PA, USA, 1984.

6 K. Stanley, J. Stjernsward and V. Koroltchouk, 'Women and Cancer', *World Health Statistics Quarterly*, vol. 40, no. 3, 1987, p. 275.

7 E. Royston and S. Armstrong (eds), *Preventing Maternal Deaths*, Geneva, WHO, 1989, p. 9.

8 UNICEF, *Intercom*, no. 55, January 1990.

9 UNFPA, *The State of World Population 1990*, New York, UNFPA, 1990, p. 3.

10 H. Nakajima, Director General of the WHO, addressing the Society for International Development, Geneva, December 1989.

11 *World Health*, May 1989, p. 30.

12 P. Doty, 'Health Status and Health Services Use among Older Women: An International Perspective', *World Health Statistics Quarterly*, vol. 40, no. 3, 1987, p. 280.

13 Data presented to the Safe Motherhood Conference in Lahore, Pakistan, March 1990, as reported in *Population*, UNFPA Newsletter, vol. 16, no. 5, May 1990, p. 3.

14 Royston and Armstrong, *Preventing Maternal Deaths*, op. cit., p. 32.

15 *Safe Motherhood Newsletter*, no. 1, November 1989–February 1990, p. 7.

16 E. Royston and A. Lopez, 'On the Assessment of Maternal Mortality', *World Health Statistics Quarterly*, vol. 40, no. 3, 1987, p. 223.

17 N. Sadik, Executive Director, United Nations Population Fund, *Investing in Women: the Focus of the '90s*, New York, UNFPA, 1989, p. 8.

18 Ibid., p. 5.

19 L. Brabin, Special Programme for Research and Training in Tropical Diseases, WHO, 'At risk profiles for young women', unpublished paper, nd., p. 1.

20 Stanley, Stjernsward and Koroltchouk, 'Women and Cancer', op. cit., p. 267.

21 Ibid., p. 269.

22 Ibid., p. 277.

23 'Heart Attacks are Developing in Developing Countries', Information Kit published by the Cardiovascular Diseases Programme and the Division of Public Information and Education for Health, Geneva, WHO, 1988.

24 W. P. Castelli, 'Cardiovascular Disease in Women', *American Journal of Obstetrics and Gynecology*, Supplement to vol. 158, no. 6, June 1988, p. 1,553.

25 Ibid., p. 1,566.

26 World Health Organization, *Safe Motherhood Information Kit*, Geneva, WHO, 1989.

27 N. Sadik, 'The UNFPA Contribution: Theory to Action Programmes', *Development*, Journal of the Society for International Development, 1990:1, p. 8.

28 *Safe Motherhood Newsletter*, Issue 2, March–June 1990, p. 2.

29 UNICEF and the United Nations Environment Programme, *Children and the Environment*, New York/Geneva, UNICEF/UNEP, 1990.

30 *World Health*, April–May 1990, p. 25, quoting *Women in the World: an International Atlas*.

31 P. Smyke, 'Surviving at Site 2', *Refugees*, no. 70, November 1989, p. 34.

32 UNICEF, *Statistics on Children in UNICEF Assisted Countries*, New York, UNICEF, 1988, p. 38.

33 *Safe Motherhood Newsletter*, Issue 1, p. 6.

3 FACTORS INFLUENCING WOMEN'S HEALTH

1979: *Do you know what women lack most? The knowledge, the deep-rooted knowledge and conviction that they are* **human beings.**

Fathia Al Assal of Egypt[1]

1989: *not for us to be a flower in a stranger's hand*
not for us to be content with half a world
let us unite
let us win back the world we have lost
let us win back our humanity.

Seetha of Sri Lanka[2]

The last chapter posed the question 'What is the state of women's health?' This chapter asks 'Why?' What factors contribute to determining a person's health?

FIRST, EACH INDIVIDUAL IS BORN with a genetic or biological inheritance that predisposes to certain health conditions and reduces the likelihood of others. Second, the environment in which a person lives has a profound influence on what becomes of the biological inheritance (using the word environment in its broadest sense to include physical, social, cultural, economic and other environments). A person's health is influenced also by the availability of health information and health care, both preventive and curative. Finally, the individual's behaviour, or lifestyle, plays a major part in determining the state of her or his health.

There is a tendency to think of lifestyle as a series of options and choices, some of which have an impact on health. It is true that many people can and do make lifestyle choices. They can choose to live their lives in ways that affect their health positively or negatively.

For millions of people, however, there are very few choices. A lifestyle is imposed. Subsistence farmers, the urban poor, refugees, displaced persons—the poorest of the poor wherever they are found—have very little possibility of avoiding health-threatening situations and behaviour. For a long time the women in these groups have had the fewest options of all. But they are beginning to change that!

This chapter examines the major economic, social, cultural, demographic, political and environmental factors that influence people's health. With one exception, these factors affect everyone's health to some extent, but they have particular repercussions for women. The one exception, the factor relevant only to women, is the status of women, and the discrimination that flows from it. This factor underlies, reinforces, causes and is caused by many of the others —again the 'vicious circle'.

ECONOMIC FACTORS ☐ More than one billion people, most of them women, live in extreme poverty. Women are more likely to be poor than men and to be among the poorest of the poor. There is a widening gap between the 'better-off poor' and the 'extremely poor'. (See the first book in this series, *Women and the World Economic Crisis*, for an extensive discussion of the debt crisis and other international economic developments related to poverty and its impact on women.)

Households headed by women, estimated to be one-third of the total worldwide, are many times more likely to be poor than those headed by men, and the number of such households is increasing. An article in

Women in Action speaks of the 'myth of the male provider', pointing out that we have internalized this particular image of the family and accepted it almost universally as a fact. Economic and social welfare policies, development planning, cultural and religious structures are based on it. The reality, however, is very different. In Latin America, for example, 'women head over 50 per cent of families in some countries, and not less than 40 per cent in any country'.[3] Households headed by women tend to have more dependants and fewer members doing paid work.[4]

It would be hard to exaggerate the influence that poverty has on people's health, because poverty restricts choice in so many areas that are basic to good health. Being very poor usually means:

- not having enough food or the right kinds of food;

- not having decent housing, sanitation and water supply;

- not being able to get health care when needed (even if the care is free, the cost of transport or medicine can put it out of reach, or a woman may not be able to take time off from work without depriving her family of income);

- not being able to send children to school or take advantage of adult education opportunities;

- not being able to think or plan beyond today's crisis, today's strategy for survival;

- not being accorded your dignity as a human being.

Those are consequences of poverty at the individual or family level. There may be a corresponding lack of resources or misuse of resources at the national level, leading to an underdeveloped health system, inadequate transport and communication, poor access to water and sanitation.

Poverty, of course, affects the health of everyone, not just women, and all the consequences just mentioned may be present even when poverty is not the cause. But if poverty *is* part of the picture, it will operate with deadly efficiency to make the situation more difficult for women.

Impoverished women spend more time and energy producing food or looking for food that they can afford to buy. They work longer hours if they have paid work or stay longer in the market to trade. Usually unskilled and uneducated, they are obliged to accept whatever work they can find, often the most dangerous, back-breaking and least desirable. The consequences for their health and that of their families can be disastrous. At best they face a slow, inevitable decline in vitality and premature ageing.

The phenomenon of women responding to an economic squeeze by working harder and longer is not confined to developing countries. A study in the United States found that the percentage of working women holding *two or more* paid jobs went from 2.2% in 1970 to 5.9% in 1989. In the same period, the percentage of men holding two jobs went down from 7% in 1970 to 6.4% in 1989.[5]

From the point of view of human resource development, there is an additional cost: when women must work this hard just to survive, there is little question of continuing their education, acquiring new skills or extending their participation in community affairs. On the other hand, there can be some long-term positive effects if their labour creates new respect for women's abilities, even though the burden is heavy for the women concerned. Consider this example:

Women's self-employment has risen drastically during the 80s due to the economic crisis in Tanzania . . . In 1970, 66% of urban women had no source of

PHOTO: ZAFAR / WHO (PAKISTAN)

income but in 1988 the same percentage of women in Dar-es-Salaam worked on different self-created projects. The International Monetary Fund and Tanzanian government adjustment programmes during the 1980s had several direct impacts on urban women. In 1977, wages constituted 90% of household income compared to 1988, when wage earnings made up roughly 10% and informal incomes the remaining 90% of the household income. One of the reasons 'the entire fabric of society did not fall apart was because people, and especially women, took matters into their own hands'. This apparently changed the attitude of both urban men and women step by step towards women's new economic importance in the households.[6]

The economic factor can, of course, work in the other direction: living in an affluent society is very advantageous for the health of women, as most health indicators show. Nevertheless, poor choices in lifestyle can dissipate that advantage. And poor women,

even in the midst of an affluent society, may face many of the same problems as women in poor countries—in kind, if not in degree.

> 'It is women who must cope, and devise survival strategies, when household incomes fall and prices rise.'[7]

STATUS OF WOMEN ☐ If poverty has a direct, dramatic and measurable impact on women's health, there is another factor whose impact is equally powerful and all-pervasive. It operates somewhat more subtly, however, and its consequences are not so readily measured or acknowledged. That factor is the status of women.

It is a slippery concept to define, especially in a cross-cultural context. Perhaps it is better to define it by example, as the International Labour Organization (ILO) did in this well-known sentence:

Women are half the world's population, receive one-tenth of the world's income, account for two-thirds of the world's working hours, and own only one-hundredth of the world's property.[8]

Status has to do with position or rank in relation to others. It implies some judgements about relative value, worth or competence. It leads to conclusions about the right to participate on an equal basis, the right to share in decision-making, the right to do or not do the things that others do. Such judgements and conclusions have become so intertwined with the determinants of women's health and the struggle for an equitable development that we need to look more closely at how the process works.

As part of the status traditionally assigned to them, women, like men, are expected to play certain roles. In most societies women are expected to juggle several roles at once, and they are subjected to a great deal of stress when conflicts arise between their different roles. This happens occasionally in the daily life of every woman but is accentuated in times of crisis or rapid change.

To review some of the roles women have in most societies: they are wives; they are the bearers and rearers of children; they are responsible for caring for the household; they are often food producers and almost always food processors and servers; they are fetchers of water and fuel; they are the ones who care for the sick and elderly; they are breadwinners as part of the paid labour force, as traders, or by selling items produced at home; they are very often the volunteers working on community projects; in some societies they must be hostesses, chauffeurs, and so on; they are in reality the transmitters of cultural and religious traditions, although seldom are they the authority or official spokesman in this realm.

It is usual to divide women's roles into two categories, 'productive' and 'reproductive'. (One might ask why men's roles are not similarly categorized.) Women have long been 'revered' and given at least nominal status in most societies for their reproductive, life-giving roles. Recognition of the value of their productive roles (as farmers, health carers, housekeepers, educators, and so on, as well as paid workers) has been slower, but it is coming. The importance to society of both their reproductive and productive roles would suggest that women *should* have at their disposal the resources, social support and decision-making power needed to do both jobs well. For most women in the world, that is not the case. Listen to the words of Boubacar Diallo, writing about African women:

The paradox is that spiritually the African woman is a superior being, a kind of intermediary between God and men. In practice, however, she uncomplainingly bears the weight of traditions which make of her a sacrificial victim. Many popular songs and sayings state that woman gives birth to prophets, savants, great warriors and rich men, but that a woman may never herself be a prophet, a savant, a warrior or a rich person. In these societies a woman can never act or state her opinions freely, and the work she does, although a tremendous burden, is never paid for. She is guaranteed no property rights whatsoever, neither in her home nor in the community, neither by law nor custom. Her social status is always inferior to the man's . . . Girls are brought up strictly to play their allocated role in life—that of wife and mother.[9]

Varying degrees of status are earned by women for faithfully fulfilling their roles as expected. In societies where large families are the norm, women gain higher status by having many children. There may be few other ways for them to have any status at all. Repeated pregnancies and the responsibility of caring for large families, especially in rural or impoverished households, can put serious strains on mothers' health and nutritional status. They become more 'at risk' as their families grow larger. Yet mothers of large families often regard themselves as blessed and fulfilled, in spite of any costs to their health.

S **on preference** ☐ Recent research on 'son preference' reveals the dynamic by which the status of women can have a profound, even fatal, impact on the health of women and girls. In the opening paragraphs of her paper, 'Health implications of sex discrimination in childhood', Sundari Ravindran gets right to the point:

The low health status of women in most parts of the world, characterized by low life expectancy, high rates of mortality and chronic low grade morbidity . . . arises from a complex combination of factors, and fundamental structural and attitudinal changes are necessary before [their health problems] can be successfully eliminated . . .

Almost all societies have valued sons more than daughters . . . Even where there is no preference for sons, very few cultures actively prefer daughters. Son preference can mean that a female child is disadvantaged from its birth. It may determine the quality of parental care and extent of investment in the child's development. In extreme cases, son preference may lead to abandonment of female infants or even female infanticide, but its most common form is sheer neglect of girls.

Son preference is both a consequence and a cause of the low status of women. It is a consequence because it arises as a result of women being considered as playing only unimportant roles and thus being valued less; and a cause, because this undervaluation in turn leads to lower investment in females as a result of which they are only able to play a peripheral role in society—causing a further lowering of their status. In either case, it

indicates the pervasive prevalence of sexism, where allocation of prestige, power and resources depend on the physical characteristic of sex.[10]

The reasons for son preference vary with the cultures and customs of different societies. In some religions a son is needed to carry out ceremonies for deceased parents. Where the family name is preserved only through male descendants that can be one reason for the preference. Boys may be seen to have a greater economic value if their labour is required on the farm, if only males can own or inherit land, or if they are expected to support elderly parents. Girls, on the other hand, may be looked upon as an additional expense with little return, especially in societies where the tradition of dowry is strong and where a wife goes to live with her husband's family. In some societies boys are highly valued as potential soldiers, heroes, protectors of family and society. Rituals, folk sayings and proverbs reflect the lesser value given to girls. In many places the standard salute to newly-weds is 'May you be blessed with many sons.'

> *Raising a girl is like watering a plant in your neighbour's garden.*
>
> **Telugu saying**

Women themselves are among the firm supporters of those viewpoints. One study based on interviews with widows in India concluded that for these women the value of sons was not so much economic as cultural. Having been conditioned to the values of their society, they found self-fulfilment in having sons. It gave them status in the community.[11]

Whatever the root causes for son preference, wherever it is pronounced the resulting discrimination against daughters begins very early in life. This is not to suggest that

30

daughters are not valued at all or that the discriminatory treatment is deliberate. On the contrary, many survey responses show that girls *are* appreciated for the love and affection parents feel towards them and receive from them, for the help they can give around the home, and for some of the comfort they provide to elderly parents. But girls are perceived and treated differently. Whether the discrimination is conscious or not, if it is strong enough it can have very serious consequences, especially for girls whose families are living a marginal existence.

Studies in different areas where son preference is strong confirm that in these societies:

- girls get a smaller percentage of their food needs satisfied than do boys, and boys tend to get the more nutritious food;

- boys are breast-fed longer (when the baby is a girl, the mother may interrupt

PREFERENCE FOR THE SEX OF CHILDREN

COUNTRY	INDEX OF SON PREFERENCE*	COUNTRY	INDEX OF SON PREFERENCE*
Strong Son Preference		**Equal Preference**	
Pakistan	4.9	Guyana	1.1
Nepal	4.0	Indonesia	1.1
Bangladesh	3.3	Kenya	1.1
Korea	3.3	Peru	1.1
Syria	2.3	Trinidad and Tobago	1.1
Jordan	1.9	Colombia	1.0
		Costa Rica	1.0
Moderate Son Preference		Ghana	1.0
Egypt	1.5	Panama	1.0
Lesotho	1.5	Paraguay	1.0
Senegal	1.5	Portugal	1.0
Sri Lanka	1.5	Haiti	0.9
Sudan	1.5	Philippines	0.9
Thailand	1.4		
Turkey	1.4	**Daughter Preference**	
Fiji	1.3	Venezuela	0.8
Nigeria	1.3	Jamaica	0.7
Tunisia	1.3		
Yemen A.R.	1.3		
Cameroon	1.2		
Dominican Republic	1.2		
Ivory Coast	1.2		
Malaysia	1.2		
Mexico	1.2		
Morocco	1.2		

* Index of son preference = Ratio of the number of mothers who prefer the next child to be male to the number of mothers who prefer the next child to be female.

Source: WHO (based on World Fertility Survey data)

breast-feeding in order to become pregnant and try for a boy);

- boys are more often taken for medical care when they are sick, and more money is spent on doctors' fees and medicine for them.

Inevitably the results of this discriminatory treatment show up on the infant and child mortality charts. Girl babies have a certain built-in genetic advantage over boys, and ordinarily one would expect to find about 117 male infant deaths to every 100 female. But,

in countries where the social status of women is very low, the lack of care received by girls and women is so great that this environmental disadvantage far outweighs their genetic advantage . . . This may result in a complete reversal of the usual trend of higher male infant and/or child mortality in these countries, and a greater proportion of female infants and children die here than male. Excess female infant and child mortality may therefore be seen as a warning signal indicating the serious neglect of girls in the society concerned. [12]

There is some quite dramatic evidence confirming the serious results of son preference/daughter neglect:

In one region of India girls were four times more likely than boys to suffer from acute malnutrition, and 40 times less likely to be taken to hospital. [13]

In Bangladesh the death rate among girls in the one-to-four age group is reported to be 58 per cent greater than for boys. The typical girl receives 20 per cent fewer calories than her brother, is more likely to be malnourished and is likely to attend school for only one or two years. The school drop-out rate for girls is twice as high as that for boys. [14]

It is estimated that 'every sixth death of a female infant in India, Bangladesh and Pakistan is due to neglect and discrimination'. In India alone this would amount to over 300,000 girls per year. [15]

Interview with a doctor working in a hospital in Pakistan's Northwest Frontier Province: 'Female children are hardly ever taken to hospital when they fall ill . . . . In the nursery section, out of a total of 1,233 patients, merely 424 were girls . . .' In the hospital as a whole, 'from a total of 8,900 cases only 2,941 were women'. [16]

Discriminatory treatment is likely to be focused on higher birth order girls, the second, third and fourth daughters faring much worse than the first, regardless of socio-economic status. Even in families with more resources, where food is not really scarce, different feeding practices for females and males are common and the same discrepancies in health care appear. In families where the mother has had some education, child mortality is lower and family size is likely to be smaller, but the discrimination against higher birth order girls seems to be even stronger. [17]

One of the most devastating results of strong son preference is the effect on the self-image of the girls who are treated as less preferred children solely because they are girls. Is it surprising that they grow up to consider themselves as something of lesser value? This has a profound influence on many women's attitude towards their own health and their own bodies. They accept ill-health, pain and suffering rather than finding out if there is something they could do about it.

There are of course other types of discrimination that flow from the inferior status of women and have an influence on women's health. Problems about inheriting and owning land and other property can be obstacles to food production or earning enough to safeguard the family's health. The difficulty for women to get credit can be a factor. Having no part in family planning decisions and in the allocation of family resources—these are examples of status-related factors that have a profound impact on women's health. Many others are pointed out in the pages and chapters that follow.

DEMOGRAPHIC FACTORS ☐ Demographic factors affect women's health status in two ways that are often referred to as 'macro' and 'micro', that is at the level of society as a whole or at the level of an individual or family. At the macro level the continuing growth in population adds to the

If women could choose

This chart shows two projections of population growth in the developing world. The first is the normal UN 'medium variant' projection and the second shows what would happen if the women of the developing world could choose how many children to have.

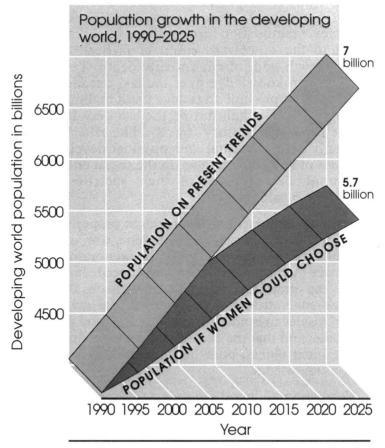

Population growth in the developing world, 1990–2025

POPULATION ON PRESENT TRENDS

7 billion

POPULATION IF WOMEN COULD CHOOSE

5.7 billion

Developing world population in billions

6500 · 6000 · 5500 · 5000 · 4500

1990 1995 2000 2005 2010 2015 2020 2025
Year

Source: Ken Hill, John Hopkins University, School of Hygiene and Public Health, using the United Nations and World Bank Population Projection Models.

strains on the environment and makes it more difficult to keep up with the growing numbers of people needing food, shelter, education, employment, water and sanitation. For women in poorer countries, there is nothing abstract about the consequences of this 'macro level' phenomenon.

'The 1990s will see faster increases in human numbers than any decade in history,' says *The State of World Population 1990* report, and '. . . by and large, the biggest increases will be in the poorest countries—those by definition least equipped to meet the needs of the new arrivals and invest in the future.'[18] Knowing that women are likely to be over-represented among the poor, and knowing how poverty affects their health, this does not brighten the global outlook for rapid improvement in women's health . . . unless some of the more positive trends that are visible around the world can be accelerated.

One demographic trend deserves special attention: if current predictions hold true, there will be around 1,125 million young people under the age of 20 in the world at the end of this decade, roughly half of them girls. They are a critical group, constituting one of the world's great challenges and a great hope.

One in every five people in the world is between the ages of 10 and 19—just over one billion people . . . The choices they make over the next two decades will be decisive for the future of the planet. The challenge is to see that they *do* have choices.

There are indications that many of these young women are open to the idea of planning their families and that on the whole they want smaller families than their parents. But many factors will determine whether those attitudes are turned into practice: how much pressure there is from friends, family and community to marry young and start having children immedi-

ately; what opportunities they have for education and employment; what attitudes their husbands have about family size, family planning or even the idea of discussing it; how accessible family planning information and services are for them.

This brings us to the demographic factor at the 'micro' level, where the decisions about *family size and spacing* that each couple makes, or fails to make, can be one of the major determinants of a woman's, and her family's, lifelong chances for good health. For this reason it is imperative for all women to be aware that this *is* a matter that can be decided and not left to fate, that women have a right and a responsibility to participate in these decisions. Both women and men have a right to the information that will allow them to make informed choices free from coercion. Couples need to be able to implement their decisions safely and effectively.

Migration is another demographic factor with many implications for women's health. Movements of people may be forced, as in the case of refugees and internally displaced people fleeing persecution or conflict; or they may be voluntary, as in the case of migrants who go to other countries in search of work or better living conditions. That distinction is not always clear-cut of course, because migrants may have little choice if economic recession or environmental deterioration makes it impossible for them to earn a living at home.

Both forced and voluntary movements can be hard on women. Families are often separated, with women left as 'head of household', responsible for the support of the children. Or, if the family does manage to remain intact, they may live under very strained circumstances in a different culture. The repercussions on women's health are discussed in Chapter 4.

Urbanization. Perhaps the largest mass movement of our times is the flow of people out of the rural areas and into the

PHOTO: SEAN SPRAGUE / UNICEF (INDONESIA)

cities, especially in developing countries. By the end of this century nearly half the world's population will be city dwellers. In the Americas, this figure is already over 70 per cent.[19] Relatively few of these city dwellers will find the better life and economic opportunity they are seeking right away. Many will be poor, and many of the poorest will be women. Some of the hardships they face and the dangers to their health are shown in the chart overleaf.

POLITICAL FACTORS—POLICY DECISIONS □ It would be naive to think that women's issues, including the right to health, can be apolitical. This does not mean political in a partisan sense, but in the sense that women's health issues soon get down to questions of sharing power and influence, recognizing and bringing into the mainstream a group that has been excluded. The policies adopted by governments and other groups help or hinder that process.

And no policy is worth any more than the political will or commitment behind it.

For a long time there was a tendency not to recognize women's role in development and not to assign any economic value to the work women did as housekeepers, food producers, child minders and the like unless it was paid work. Better understanding of how development takes place, and of women's contribution to it, has forced a change in that policy. The economic and social value of women's work, paid or unpaid, is more widely recognized now and increasingly enters into development planning. Even people not persuaded by arguments based on equity and human rights have had to admit that investment in women is economically sound.

The policies that have an impact on women's health may relate directly to health, or they may be policies in any of the other areas that help determine the status of women.

Habitat

Life in the slums
There are many characteristics common to life in these marginal urban areas

Roots
Most slum and shanty-town dwellers are of rural origin. The majority of migrants are driven to town by poverty and start their urban life in the worst areas.

Youth
The average age of slum inhabitants is very low. Large families are traditional in the countryside, and people continue to have them.

Overcrowding
Population density is the highest in the world. It is common to find a family of 10 members sharing one room.

Women householders
In many slums women – abandoned or divorced – are the only providers for 50% of the households.

Squalor
Overcrowding and lack of drainage and sanitary systems create conditions hazardous to health. Rubbish piles up in the street and is not removed.

No services
In these conditions, the need for water and sanitary disposal services is acute. Most slum households must fetch their water from a standpipe and deposit their waste in open drains. The rate of infection is therefore high; there is a constant risk of epidemic.

Malnutrition
Slum dwellers are dependent for their food entirely on cash. As incomes are very low, children are malnourished.

Premature adulthood
Most mothers earn, and are absent from home. Children fend for themselves, in the care of older ones. Many are abandoned, or leave home, at an early age.

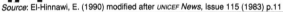

Source: El-Hinnawi, E. (1990) modified after *UNICEF News*, Issue 115 (1983) p.11

Health policies ☐ *Primary health care* (PHC). The near-universal adoption of primary health care policies in developing countries, and in many industrialized countries as well, is good news for women. If the practice matches the theory, PHC has many elements that should promote the status of women:

- the insistence on making health care accessible to all;

- the stress on an intersectoral approach;

- the emphasis on prevention;

- the place given to health information and education;

- the community participation and responsibility;

- the idea that people *can* take action to improve their health.

In addition, PHC recognizes the contribution that women have traditionally made to the health of their families and communities, and calls for measures to support them in this role. Women have been listened to as they discuss the health needs of the community and offer their ideas about how to meet them. Some of the knowledge that women have accumulated from their practical experience in tending the sick has been incorporated into plans of action. PHC training programmes have helped many women acquire new knowledge and skills.

If PHC is carried out as intended, women's involvement in the process can lead them to new awareness of their own health needs and give them new confidence in their own abilities. At its best, PHC can operate as an opening wedge for community development, and in most places women will be at 'the leading edge' of that wedge. More than one woman who started out on a local health committee talking about community health needs has gone on to ask

PHOTO: JEAN-LUC RAY / AGA KHAN FOUNDATION

some searching questions about the state of her own health and how it might be linked to poverty, the right to development or the status of women.

Nevertheless, PHC is not automatically a blessing for women. It is not always carried out as intended. There is a long and diffi-cult road between adopting a policy of PHC and its full implementation, with all the changes in attitude and resource allocation that that implies. Here is what may happen if PHC is introduced without adequate preparation into communities where the status of women is low and their contri-bution to society is devalued. In such communities:

. . . mothers, grandmothers, wives, daughters or neighbours are the usual providers of health care. Nevertheless, women's contributions to health go unnoticed, their working conditions are ignored, and their own health needs are often neglected.

The low status given to women in health care is also one reason for the low status and prestige of primary health care. Because women are its main providers, many people . . . think of primary health care as unprestigious work best left to women.[20]

One point that has particular significance for women: health care at the primary level must be backed up by secondary level insti-tutions that are equipped and staffed to handle the more serious cases referred to them. This becomes very important in the effort to reduce maternal mortality, where obstetrical emergencies demand skilled per-sonnel and well-equipped facilities. Primary level workers must be trained to recognize pregnant women who are at risk and be able to get them to the referral institution quickly and safely. Making sure that this happens is a matter of health policy priori-ties and allocation of resources.

Accessibility. There are other policy issues that determine the accessibility of health

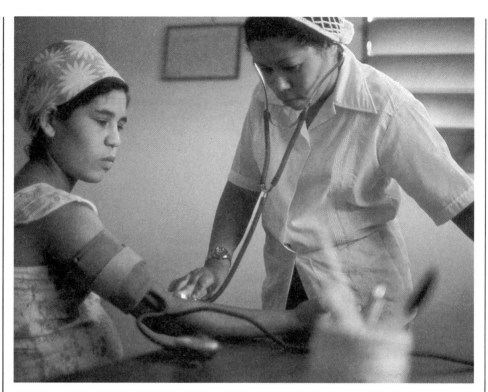

PHOTO: J. LITTLEWOOD / WHO (VENEZUELA)

care for women. Distance from the woman's home is one factor, so equitable distribution of health facilities around a district or nation is important. Having transport available when needed is crucial. The cost of health care or medicine can be a deterrent to seeking help (a sometimes critical point for young girls in families where son preference is strong). The supply of drugs and medicines needs to meet women's particular needs.

Finally, accessibility includes culturally appropriate care. This may mean female staff or separate facilities for women where that is a cultural necessity. Also, women will stay away from a health facility if it is not a comfortable place for them psychologically: if it seems too foreign, technical and impersonal; if they are not treated with respect but made to feel ignorant and at fault; if there are communication problems because of language, ethnic or socio-

cultural differences between staff and clients.

Another policy matter with serious implications for women relates to the availability of modern health *technology*. There are dramatic illustrations in the field of reproductive health. In the poorer countries women die premature deaths because of a lack of equipment and facilities to handle obstetric emergencies. In richer nations some women complain of the 'over-medicalization' of childbirth because health service policy or hospital practice puts pressure on them to have tests and medical interventions they do not want. Other women are profoundly grateful for the modern technologies (*in vitro* fertilization is one example) that have helped them overcome infertility and give birth to healthy babies. Globally, modern health technology raises legal and ethical questions that we have only begun to address.

Technology designed to help women can be diverted from its original purpose. In India, women's organizations and other groups have been fighting to change the policy that permits the use of amniocentesis to realize couples' preference for sons. The procedure is being used to identify female foetuses and abort them.

A study in India found that out of 8,000 abortions following amniocentesis, almost 100% involved female foetuses. Sex-determination testing has become a lucrative business. In spite of the relatively high cost of the procedure, most of the clients are women or couples from the middle and lower classes who say it is better to pay US$20 for an abortion now than to have to find money for a dowry some years from now. The desire for boys ('desire for a balanced family' is the euphemism) is not confined to the South Asia region. In a chain of clinics offering sex preselection services in 46 countries in Europe, America, Asia and Latin America, 248 out of 263 couples selected boys and 15 selected girls.[21]

Family planning policy. There are many policy matters related to family planning that make critical differences for women's health. Some basic questions to ask about any family planning programme are: are information services available to all who want them, not just in theory but in practice? Are the services accessible, and is there a choice of methods that are safe, effective, affordable and appropriate for the culture? Are family planning services integrated with MCH and/or other health services that women need? Does this keep men from being involved and if so are there alternative ways of reaching them? Is there help for women suffering from infertility? Do young people receive family life education? Are young people or unmarried people adequately served by family planning programmes? What is the policy on abortion and what are its effects?

Government backing for family planning programmes has increased in recent years.

Between 1976 and 1988 the number of governments providing direct support for family planning rose from 97 to 125; governments limiting access to family planning fell from 15 to seven.[22] While these figures are impressive, there are great differences in the extent of political commitment behind them. One has to look closely at how policy is translated into action.

Other policies affecting women's health □ In addition to health policies *per se*, there are so many diverse influences on women's health and well-being that one needs to keep a watchful eye on policy in many other areas. These few examples suggest the range of subjects involved:

- In the government of Tanzania strategy for safe motherhood, one of the recommendations is: 'To reduce the risk of septic abortions, school regulations should be changed and expulsion of pregnant school girls abolished.'[23]

- Laws raising the legal age of marriage, if enforced, can help avoid teenage pregnancies and lower total fertility. However, it is clear that laws, while a necessary first step, are not very effective in themselves. Education and employment opportunities for women are actually more effective than laws in raising the average age at marriage. All three together are a powerful combination.

- Legislation and policy on maternity leave and working conditions for pregnant women may make an important contribution to safe motherhood and improve maternal as well as child health. Legislation and policy on day care can make it easier and less stressful for mothers to be employed, knowing the children are well cared for.

- Policies that regulate the promotion, sale

and use of tobacco products help deter young women from starting to smoke and protect non-smoking women and their children from the indirect effects of others smoking.

- Regulations concerning the testing, labelling, import and marketing of pharmaceutical products have their greatest impact on women, the major consumers of these products.

- Laws about accessibility for disabled people in transport, public buildings and the workplace can open the door to employment, and independence, for women with disabilities.

- Laws, policies and practices regarding prostitution sometimes protect women, sometimes expose them to extreme health risks and exploitation.

- Policies on migrants, refugees and asylum-seekers frequently discriminate against women, making it difficult for them to enter a country or have a recognized legal status equal to that of men in the same circumstances. Access to health care and social services is generally difficult for migrant and refugee women unless there is a positive policy to facilitate it.

- Marriage, divorce and inheritance laws, especially customary law, have much to do with a woman's economic, social and psychological status and thus with her health. Laws providing for support in old age reduce the pressures to have a large number of children for this purpose.

- Laws or policies that discriminate against women in the area of civil rights (for example, the right to vote) keep them from having a voice in decisions that are crucially important to them, and keep them from making their full contribution to development.

All policies that raise the status of women and protect their rights contribute to their good health. People who want to press for action on women's health need to be aware that some policies are mutually reinforcing, that is, they are more effective when used in combination with each other. Such a synergistic relationship exists, for example, between raising the legal age of marriage and increasing education and employment opportunities.

There are many issues where policy decisions or modifications in the law can be an important first step in bringing about change: for example, female circumcision, dowry, bride price. Longstanding traditions will not be abandoned overnight, nor the deep-seated cultural values that underlie them. Yet because these traditions have such a profound effect on the status of women, these are precisely the areas where greater awareness and steady pressure for change are needed most.

Women often lack awareness of their legal rights. The civil code in their country may differ considerably from the 'customary law' they live under. For some women, it is not easy to understand the very idea that they have 'rights', especially the right to health. Awakening that understanding is perhaps one of the greatest benefits of the next factor to be examined.

EDUCATION ☐ So much has been written about the benefits of educating women that it is hard to understand how the world tolerates anything less than having 100 per cent of its girls and young women in school. Actually, great strides have been made towards this goal, although in some of the poorer countries the economic difficulties of the 1980s have produced declines in enrolment and increases in the drop-out rates, especially for girls. Another volume in this series, *Women and Literacy*, looks more closely at trends in the education of women.[24]

The education of girls is probably the world's best investment. Nothing else has such power to improve family health, slow population growth, and improve the lives of women themselves—UNICEF, *The State of the World's Children 1991.*

'Today 65% of girls and 78% of boys in developing countries are in primary school, 20 and 11 per cent more than a decade ago. Secondary school enrolment rates are lower, with only 35% of girls and 48% of boys in school—but this is still 29 and 16 per cent more than ten years ago.'[25]

Listed below are some of the many documented results of educating girls and women. Most of these results can be seen regardless of other factors such as socio-economic status and accessibility of health facilities. A woman who has been to school for a few years is more likely:

- to marry at a later age (four years later than an uneducated woman on average);

- to have a smaller family and to use modern family planning methods;

- to seek pre-natal care and have a trained attendant at childbirth;

- to make use of health services generally;

- to have healthy children, and less likely to have children who die in infancy and early childhood;

- to have a larger earning capacity.

These are but a few of the proven results of educating women, and the ones that relate most directly to health.

'In Brazil uneducated women have an average of 6.5 children each, those with secondary education only 2.5. In Liberia women who have been to secondary school are 10 times more likely to be using family planning.[26]

Mothers' education may be even more important to her children's health than flush toilets or piped water or even food intake. Studies put the difference in child mortality (deaths of children between one and five) as high as 9% for every year the mother was at school.'[27]

There are other effects, some difficult to quantify but still quite evident and impor-tant for health. Schooling should help to build up a young women's self-esteem and give her more confidence in herself. School, and especially crossing the threshold of lit-eracy, opens new worlds for many women and exposes them to new ideas, including the idea that they do have choices, that they can make decisions and that they do have rights. The UNFPA publication, *Investing in Women*, traces some of these effects:

Educated women are more likely to stand up for themselves. In Kerala, for instance, educated women—however poor—seem to believe they have a right to good health care. Conversely, lower-class Nepalese women expected and received worse treatment from health staff; illiterate women in Ibadan fared similarly. And detailed interviews with 29 literate and illiterate wives in Uttar Pradesh found that the latter would not take their sick children to the doctor before obtaining permission from their husbands or in-laws . . .

Referring to health care in the industrialized world one expert said: 'The experience of a lower-class person entering the health care system is one which is overwhelmingly bewildering, alien and frightful.' Education helps women go through those doors with confidence. And the result is better health for herself and her children . . .

If women's confidence is higher in clinic and hospital waiting rooms, it is likely to be higher at home too. Research from Nigeria, Bangladesh and Mexico confirms that educated women tend to communicate more with their husbands, to be more involved in family decisions and to be more respected: more able in other words to plan what happens in their lives.'[28]

PHOTO: INTERNATIONAL LABOUR OFFICE

Education does not take place only in schools, obviously. Great changes have been brought about in many communities by adult education programmes, discussion groups, mothers' clubs, agricultural extension work, health worker training. The more women participate, the greater the benefit for themselves, their families and their communities.

But there is no panacea. For example, getting young girls enrolled in primary school, while extremely desirable, is not in itself a guarantee that the changes described above will occur. People working in the fields of women's education and health education have some valuable tips to share:

● Look behind the enrolment figures to check on the reality of women's and girls' participation. Are they attending classes regularly? What is the drop-out rate for females and why do they drop out? Most experts consider four years of regular attendance at primary school a minimum for gaining functional literacy and numeracy.

● Women who have achieved literacy tend to fall back into illiteracy even more rapidly than men unless they have continuing opportunities and motivation to use their reading skills. This is not surprising, given the demands on women's time and energy. But there are successful ways to counteract this tendency.

● Pay close attention to what actually happens to girls in the classroom. Studies in different cultures and school systems show both female and male teachers giving more attention to boys than to girls, expecting less from girls, scolding girls for behaviour that would get approval in boys. In short, both the content of the curriculum and the way it is presented may provide iron-clad reinforcement for the socio-cultural status quo. There is work to be done in teacher orientation, curriculum review (what really counts as 'knowledge'?) and correcting the under-representation of women in ministries of education and school hierarchies.

Education is the starting point for women's advancement in many different fields, whether we are talking about new farming methods, confidence-building, learning how to speak in public, technical skills, or how to handle a budget. Yet access to education in formal institutions has not necessarily empowered all women; like the gaining of the vote, it is a tool with which to work for change, not an end in itself. Formal education may have promoted a few women to positions of power, but for many women it has reinforced their subservient role in society, where they learn that girls are not really very good at science and technical subjects, and will get married anyway, so they don't need education for a career.[29]

- Do not underestimate the possibilities of non-formal learning situations. These can be tailored more closely to the needs of women and girls, with flexible scheduling, creative learning techniques, and content developed by the students according to their idea of what is important for them to learn.

- Uneducated does not mean ignorant. Women have accumulated much experience and knowledge in such vital fields as health, agriculture and child care. Educational programmes must not ignore or undermine those ideas but help people examine them, decide which ones should be preserved, and incorporate them with new knowledge. In the past decade traditional or non-Western medicine has been studied and evaluated in this way. The result is a new appreciation of many traditional skills and remedies, and better use of both traditional and modern medicine to complement each other.

Education is indeed a powerful tool for the advancement of women, but it does not operate in a social or cultural vacuum. As we saw from the studies on son preference, educating women is not enough by itself to overcome the cultural tradition that puts a greater value on male children. Nor does it keep an educated woman from feeling the strong social pressures to conform to the traditional image of 'woman' in a particular setting.

This leads to some paradoxical situations: a successful young female secondary school teacher in Africa, with a Master of Arts degree, told an interviewer that she wishes she had listened to her male classmates at university who said she was 'becoming too educated'. She would like to get married and have a family, but she doubts that she ever will now because she is considered too old, and besides, 'Who could afford my bride price?'[30]

ENVIRONMENTAL FACTORS ☐ It seems to have come so suddenly, the accelerating environmental deterioration that is changing the day-to-day life of every human being on the planet. Awareness has come in different ways: for some it grew from reviewing scientific studies and attending conferences, for others from reading popular magazines and papers, watching television reports or listening to political candidates.

For a woman living in a rural area of a developing country, however, awareness probably came more forcefully and in more concrete terms—when she noticed that she had to walk further each day to get firewood, that it took more time and effort to get water because so many sources had dried up or were too polluted to use. With her growing family she needs to raise more food and keep more animals, but the soil isn't fertile any more and the animals can't find anything to graze on. She would not have to be very old to remember that it was not like this when she was young.

PHOTO: LIBA TAYLOR

A forthcoming book in this series examines in depth the relationships between women, environment and development.[31] Here we point out just a few of the ways that environmental factors have an impact on women's health.

For women living a marginal existence, anything that adds to their burdens adds to the risks for their health. In the case of environmental deterioration it adds to the risks for their children and their children's children as well.

The scarcity of firewood not only drains the energy of the women and girls who must fetch it, it has indirect health impacts too. Food may not be cooked so often or as thoroughly. Drinking water is not likely to be boiled when fuel is scarce.

The relationship works the other way, too; by completely stripping the land of trees in their search for firewood or fodder, women pave the way for soil erosion and floods. Yet they have little choice.

Water □ Over 500 million people have gained access to improved water supplies in recent years and 325 million now have better sanitation. Much of this pro-gress was stimulated by the International Drinking Water Supply and Sanitation Decade, 1981–90. It is a giant step forward in community health, for an estimated 80 per cent of all sickness and disease in the developing world can be attributed to unsafe water and inadequate sanitation.[32]

Another positive benefit from the water and sanitation programmes is the spotlight put on women's participation. Time after time the programmes just did not work if women were not involved in planning and implementing them. Women have been trained to do maintenance on the water pumps and to make sure that the systems function reliably. Women have benefited from education about proper storage and use of water in their homes. They have learned the value of frequent hand-washing to cut the transmission of diarrhoeal diseases, and the reasons for sanitary disposal of excreta. Now it is mostly women who are

'Because women are faced more directly than men with the problems of water supply and sanitation, they can be a substantial driving force behind the installation and maintenance of facilities.'[33]

THE LONG WALK IS OVER

Mwanaisha Mweropia, a 23-year-old mother of six from Mwabungo village . . . used to make seven journeys a day to a well some distance away. There was always a line at the well, even at dawn, and the rule was that no one might draw a second bucketful without joining the queue again. Everyone quarrelled, and women with large families—which was most of them—were constantly tired. Mwanaisha coughed perpetually and had chronic chest problems.

In 1984 her life changed when the Kenyan Water for Health Organization (KWAHO) installed an Afridev hand-pump in Mwabungo—part of a special project to drill 100 boreholes and install pumps in more than 100 local communities. Rainfall in this arid coastal area is seasonal and most streams and traditional wells dry up . . .

Not only is the Afridev handpump much closer to Mwanaisha's home and far less onerous to operate, but the water is safe and her cough and chest pains have disappeared. The local KWAHO community worker, Mwanauba Omar, says that all water-related disease has declined. Before the project, schistosomiasis used to claim around 10 lives a year in Mwabungo alone and cholera was not unknown. Schistosomiasis (*tego*) used to be blamed on adultery. No one has died from it recently. And the number of diarrhoea cases has dropped by half.

The striking feature of KWAHO's programme, which has attracted much international attention during the Water Decade, is the degree to which it is focussed on women. The organization was inspired by women, is mostly run by women, and has fully involved women in the villages . . .

Winnie Ogana/Panos[34]

passing on this valuable knowledge to others.

Nevertheless, *1.2 billion* people are still without easy access to good water and probably *1.9 billion* still live with inadequate sanitation.[35] The implications for women's health are sobering.

In regions where water-borne or water-related diseases are endemic, women may be more exposed to them because so many of their tasks require them to be around water, for example fetching water, washing clothes, working in irrigated fields. The danger of malaria can be increased by ill-conceived irrigation schemes that create breeding places for mosquitoes and by irrational use of pesticides that leads to resistant mosquitoes. (For the effects of pesticides on women working as farm labourers, see Chapter 4.)

The effects of inadequate water supply and lack of sanitation are compounded in an urban setting by overcrowding and the makeshift nature of most slum dwellings. In addition, urban dwellers and their children are exposed to lead from motor vehicle exhausts and the paint in old buildings. Women who work in factories and certain industrial establishments may be exposed to harmful chemicals or radiation, with grave health risks for themselves and their unborn children (see Chapter 4).

The environment within the home, where women spend so much of their time, also helps determine the state of women's health. Half the world's population depends on biomass fuels such as wood, charcoal, crop residues and dung. The smoke from open hearths or stoves using these fuels contains many harmful elements, including

PHOTO: MAGGIE MURRAY-LEE / UNICEF

carcinogens. They have been known to lead
to chronic lung diseases and cancers of the
nose and pharynx. Some of the pollutants
that a woman inhales can harm her unborn
child. The effects are increased if the dwell-
ing is poorly ventilated or the stove is ill-
designed. Simple, inexpensive stoves have
been developed that not only cut the
amount of smoke to a minimum but use
less fuel. In many countries women's health
could be vastly improved by extending the
use of these stoves.

A WHO report from 1984 estimates that women who
cook on open fires in closed rooms are inhaling as much
benzo-a-pyrene (a carcinogen) as if they smoked 20
packs of cigarettes a day. Says the Director of the United
Nations Environment Programme, 'exposure to the
smoke and toxic gases of cooking is probably the most
serious occupational health hazard known today'.[36]

Women are providers and users of food,
fuel, water, money and other basic household and family resources. As such, the role
of 'resource manager' and 'environmental-
ist' has to be added to all the other roles
women play. Women need to be healthy to
do well in this role; they need to do it well
in order to remain healthy. Too often,
though, that circle turns in reverse and
women's health deteriorates along with the
environment. A speaker at the Commission
on Human Rights said:

**Our point is that people living under conditions of
gross inequality, extreme poverty and repression
are likely to use up their environment quickly.
They often have little other choice . . . They [can]
not survive in the present without destroying their
own future.[37]**

FOOD AND NUTRITION ☐ Any discussion of women's health, in any region,
must keep coming back to nutrition. In
industrialized countries there is need for

A woman from Mali using a fuel saving stove.

nutrition education, especially for women, to counteract media advertising and help women understand what is at stake for themselves and their families if they make poor nutritional choices and indulge in junk food, food fads and diet fads.

In developing countries, as we have seen, good nutrition or malnutrition is *the* pivotal factor in many of the circular relationships between women, health and development.

A woman's work-load will certainly not be reduced because she is malnourished. It will just take her longer to do all she has to do, because she is exhausted and lacking in energy. Many millions of women accept this as normal. The case study by Sudhir Varma in Annexe 1 has one very telling paragraph that underlines the irony of women's attitudes towards their own health:

It is well known that most of the members of a household are not interested in the health of the woman of the house unless her condition is near to death. Neglected by the State, a strange sense of well-being has developed among rural woman. During a survey of rural areas of Rajasthan, the author found that women considered themselves healthy if they were able to work at home or on the farm and felt satisfied with their nutritional intake if they got enough food to keep them working. Although their health parameters were extremely poor, most of the women felt they were in good health and were eating sufficient food.[38]

For this reason alone—making women aware of their own nutritional needs and how they can meet them—nutrition education needs to be given much more priority. As does an assured food supply!

In some areas one important task of nutrition education is to persuade people to abandon the food taboos and customs that contribute to malnutrition among women. For example, food taboos in some places keep women from eating chicken, eggs or other foods that they need, especially when pregnant or breast-feeding. The custom of women and girls eating after the men and boys, and eating what is left over, causes serious nutritional problems for them where food is scarce.

Getting rid of these practices requires more than just handing out information to women, obviously. The customs reflect the relative status or value assigned ages ago to different members of the family. Superstitions have grown up around them (for example, that eating eggs during pregnancy will harm the unborn child), making people fearful of violating the taboo. Traditional leaders and the entire community therefore have to have information that will persuade them that there is no foundation for the superstitions and that it is in the interests of the entire community to change.

Nutrition education is important for women for their own sake and because they shoulder such a heavy responsibility for the good nutrition of others. This responsibility starts in the pre-natal period, continues with the breast-feeding of the infant, through the weaning period and the critical early childhood years, and goes on until the young person leaves the family home. Women must know how to select the most nutritious food (if they have the possibility of selecting) and know how to prepare it so that it retains the nutrients and is safe and wholesome to eat.

In poor, urban communities it is common for three-fourths of the family's hard-earned income to be spent on food, with women 'somehow responsible' for making ends meet when food prices soar or a family emergency (most likely an illness) eats up what should have been the food budget.

In many rural communities women do the major share of the work to produce the

family's food, as well as carrying the water and fuel needed to prepare it. In Africa, women are responsible for 60–80 per cent of all food production. Tanzanian women use up 12–20 per cent of their daily calorie intake fetching water. The role that women have long played as food producers, difficult as it has been, is further threatened today by new developments in agriculture:

Changes in agriculture have also tended to undermine women's security. The widespread shift from the growing of subsistence food (mostly grown by women) to the growing of cash crops has often meant that control of the crop passes to men, because agricultural training, credit and technology are routinely given to men rather than women. The women farmers lose an important source of income (and possibly of nutrition too) as well as their chance of benefiting from development. 'Development' ends up as a net loss to the community.[19]

This phenomenon needs to be seen in its global perspective. The demand for cash crops comes mostly from the North; the costs of providing them fall heavily on the women subsistence farmers in the poorer countries of the South. Government policy-makers must take some of the responsibility for this. The South Commission has recently issued a report calling for more self-reliance in developing countries, beginning with greater self-sufficiency in food. Julius Nyerere, in an interview about the report, said that '. . . people are both the purpose and the means of development. Every developing country should adopt a strategy of building the maximum amount of national self-reliance as rapidly as possible by using the nation's human, natural and structural resources to the very maximum.'[40]

That goal can hardly be realized without

more attention to women as food producers and food processors. They need assured access to land and credit, as well as training and appropriate technology to make their work easier, more productive and less time consuming. Felly Nkweto Simmonds stresses the role of the woman farmer in an article about the misleading image of Third World women often conveyed in the North:

There are many aspects of Third World women's lives that are rarely portrayed visually (or otherwise). Even though there is now more documentation of the role of women as farmers . . . visual images are rare . . . Although it is known, for example, that 84% of women in Ethiopia are involved in agriculture, the Ethiopia famine was never portrayed as a disaster for the women *as farmers* and that therefore any aid that tackled the reconstruction of agriculture in Ethiopia would have to be directed at women as well as men. Nowhere in any of the 'famine relief' material did this message come through. This kind of omission misses the opportunity to portray women positively as agents of change in their own society. There is too much concentration by charities and development education on the powerlessness of Third World women.[41]

L**OCAL CUSTOMS AND TRADITIONAL PRACTICES** ☐ Cultural values are translated into 'local custom' in many different ways, but local customs in all parts of the world have strong impacts on women's lives and health, positive and negative. Both the bride price and dowry traditions, as well as the need for certainty about virginity, lead to early marriage and the risks that accompany early pregnancy. Girls are given in marriage as early as eight, nine or ten years of age, invariably to a much older man. Chapter 4 describes the health hazards posed by early child-bearing.

Female circumcision (or female genital mutilation) is a traditional practice that does inestimable harm to the health of women and girls. This is also discussed at greater

length in Chapter 4, but it is important to note it here as an example of the way local customs and superstitions develop. Often, regardless of the surface motivation for a given practice, its ultimate function is to maintain the relative status and power of different groups within a society.

The cultural requirement that women be beautiful and 'desirable' has led to many forms of behaviour that threaten good health, from foot binding to applying unsafe eye-shadow to using carcinogenic skin lighteners. Where womanly beauty and desirability are measured by the size of the waistline, overfeeding and forced feeding of young girls are the result. Where the norm for beautiful women is to be pencil thin, diet pills appear, and anorexia and bulimia are diagnosed among young women. Female circumcision is sometimes defended on aesthetic grounds, as making women more sexually desirable to their husbands.

In a shrinking and interdependent world (and with a little help from the media and the advertising agencies) what was once 'local custom' in one region spreads to other regions with sometimes disastrous results. The next chapter will look more closely at this phenomenon in relation to smoking,

bottle-feeding and other modern 'traditional practices'.

Local customs and traditions also include, of course, many practices that are beneficial to health. Breast-feeding is one of the first that comes to mind. Traditional medicine in some cultures has remedies and ways of administering them that bring great relief and comfort to women when they are sick. The challenge is to discourage the harmful traditions while identifying and preserving the beneficial ones. The policies and attitudes adopted by governments, religious groups, health professionals and women's groups can do a great deal to speed up this process.

LOCAL HEALTH RISKS—ENDEMIC DISEASES ☐ Women are obviously

subject to local endemic diseases just as is all the rest of the population. In some cases, however, they are more at risk. As noted earlier, there is a dangerous interaction between malaria and anaemia, particularly in the first pregnancy. Malaria can also flare up in later pregnancies, putting both mother and child in danger and adding to the likelihood of the mother being anaemic.

Other diseases too exhibit a 'sex bias'

because of women's reproductive function. Pregnant women are more likely to get poliomyelitis. Leprosy and diabetes can become overt during pregnancy or be aggravated by it. Infectious hepatitis becomes more deadly. In any of these diseases, if malnutrition and fatigue are factors, as they often are, the damage to a woman's health is compounded.

Pregnancy and malnutrition are not the only reasons for women being hard-hit by such endemic diseases. As mentioned earlier, research based on hospital and clinic attendance may leave women out of the picture. In the case of malaria, for example, health officials assumed that men were more likely than women to contract the disease because more men showed up at hospitals and clinics for treatment. In fact, house-to-house surveys in Thailand indicate that women are just as likely to be infected, but for a variety of reasons (family responsibilities, constraints on their movement, lack of time or money) they do not go to receive treatment. Mobile clinics that come to them in their villages have increased the proportion of women being treated.[42]

VIOLENCE AND EXPLOITATION ☐
Women are disproportionately the victims of the many types of violence and exploitation raging throughout the world. A continuum of violence affecting women extends from abuse within the family to institutionalized repression and racism to major international conflicts.

In this section we consider four examples of violence and exploitation that particularly affect women and cause inestimable damage to their health: violence within the family; rape; prostitution; and armed conflicts. Women's groups have focused a good deal of attention on these subjects in the past decade precisely because of the need to make people face their real nature (violations of human rights) and accept the need for change.

One difficulty is that the harm they cause is so widespread and so much a part of millions of lives that it is regarded as almost 'normal', something to be regretted, of course, but something to be accepted as part of life. Now women in all parts of the world are coming together and realizing, 'No, we do not have to accept the violence directed against us. Change is possible.'

Violence within the family ☐
Domestic violence is found in all societies and in all social classes, the victims being overwhelmingly women and children. When the violence is between spouses, 98 per cent of the time it is the wife who is assaulted. Societies vary in the extent of disapproval shown towards this type of violence. Where the status of women is low and a woman is considered the property of a man, a husband's right to 'discipline' his wife is accepted. If he is too severe, that is a private matter for the extended family or village elders to deal with. In other societies intra-family violence is condemned and punishable by law, but the law may or may not be enforced. Neither type of social control seems to be very effective in preventing this type of violence against women, as this sampling of statistics will attest:

- In Peru, 70 per cent of all crimes reported to police are of women beaten by their husbands.

- A study in a Bangkok slum found that 50 per cent of married women are beaten regularly.

- In the United States, every 15 seconds a woman is beaten and four battered women die each day.

- In New South Wales, Australia, one in every four homicides occurs between spouses.[43]

These figures are enough to suggest the extent of the damage to women's physical

53

and mental health. Physically, women emerge from these violent episodes with everything from black eyes, bruises and burns to internal injuries severe enough to be fatal. The invisible wounds to the psyche may be just as disabling. Further, there is an inter-generational effect. Children who have been physically or sexually abused or who have grown up in families where they have witnessed domestic violence are more likely to be abusive themselves as adults.

In this domain, as in many others, women tend not to know enough about their legal rights, which may protect them more than the customs and traditions of their society. NGOs have been pioneers in informing women about their human rights (which include the right to be protected from violence) and in supporting them in their claims before the courts. The Women's Federation in Beijing, for example, became concerned about the frequent domestic violence in the three-generation families that make up two-thirds of Chinese households. The Federation organized over 600 legal-knowledge training classes, reaching 90,000 women.[44]

Rape □ Rape represents a special type of violence against women. While the act has not changed much over the centuries, perceptions of it have changed with time. In the past (and in a few societies today) rape was seen primarily as an assault on the honour of the family or on the 'property' of the husband. The father or husband was the aggrieved party. The woman might be punished for bringing dishonour on the family. Later, rape was discussed in terms of lust and uncontrollable sexual impulses. It was reprehensible, yes, but still seen and 'explained' from a male point of view.

Although much of that thinking lingers, over the past decade there has been change. Rape is increasingly recognized as an exercise of power, a violation by force of the integrity of a person's body, a violation of the basic human right to 'security of person'. The perspective is shifting; rape is finally being seen from the point of view of the victim.

This may be one reason why a greater proportion of rapes is reported now, although the vast majority, an estimated nine out of ten, still go unreported. Even allowing for better reporting, the incidence of rape appears to be increasing in many countries. The Asian and Pacific Women's Resource Collection Network found that the 'rape of girls and women by men is increasing in all countries of the Region where data are available'. In Malaysia, according to police figures, reported rapes went from 360 in 1981 to 688 in 1986.[45] A more graphic description was assembled from other sources:

Studies and newspaper reports in the Region have shown that any woman, irrespective of her class, culture, age, clothing, religion and income is at risk of suffering from some kind of violent incident in her life . . . . Women in the Philippines and India who have gone to the police or military authorities for protection against other crimes or who have been detained, have been sexually abused or raped. Women raped have included school children on the way to school or to the shop; nurses travelling to sick patients' homes; rubber tappers working alone in the plantation, and sisters, daughters and wives who were raped by members of the family.[46]

The damage to women's health from rape and the violence associated with it can be extensive, both physically and psychologically. Many women are killed or severely beaten. There may be serious damage to the vagina or anus, especially in gang rape.

Shock, sexually transmitted disease or an unwelcome pregnancy may result.

Equally damaging and disruptive is the emotional trauma of rape survivors. Immediately after the rape many women experience acute fear, anger, guilt, or a sense of powerlessness. These feelings are sometimes accompanied by psychosomatic symptoms like headaches, sleep disturbances, abdominal pain. Some women feel compelled to rearrange their lives after a rape—they move to a new address or a different city, stop going out, find their activities restricted by newly acquired fears and anxieties. A few suffer serious long-term depression.

Prostitution ☐ Another unique, woman-oriented type of violence is inherent in prostitution as it is practised by women in most parts of the world. It is the exploitation of the less powerful by the more powerful. This applies to the pimp who gets the major share of the woman's earnings by threatening or using physical violence or by psychological pressures. It applies to the sex tourist from a rich country whose money allows him to force himself on a child from a poverty-stricken family in a poor country. (It applies as well to the local officials and 'honest businessmen/businesswomen' who make this kind of tourism possible.) It applies to those responsible for the fact that so many thousands of girls and women worldwide are forced into prostitution as the sole means of saving themselves and their children from starvation. It applies to cultural and political leaders who defend prostitution as 'part of our tradition' when in fact it simply reflects and perpetuates the inferior status of women and girls in that society.

The health risks of prostitution are obvious. Prostitutes frequently encounter physical violence. They may contract any of the sexually transmitted diseases, including AIDS, as most of them are not in a position to require their clients to use a condom. They run the risk of becoming pregnant and many have to resort to unsafe abortions. For young girls this sexual activity before their bodies are fully developed endangers their later reproductive health, not to mention their mental health.

Armed conflict ☐ Violence and repression on a large scale are a feature of our times. At least 200 wars and internal conflicts have ravaged the planet since 'peace' came in 1945. Women have died while fighting in these conflicts. Others are among the non-combatants who comprise 90 per cent of the fatalities in modern warfare. Even if women escape death or disability from being caught in the conflict, they suffer many indirect consequences.

Women are raped and tortured as part of political repression, war and factional strife, often for revenge on an opponent (see above, rape as a way of inflicting injury on the male enemy). During conflicts women are subjected to violence because their fathers, brothers or husbands are active in the opposition, because the woman herself is suspected of being sympathetic to the other side, or just for 'being there'.

Women are widowed by war and left alone to care for children and other dependants while men are away fighting. In the chaos that surrounds hostilities, assuring the family's survival becomes a heavy and stressful responsibility. War devastates the environment, sometimes making food production and distribution impossible. The economy may be ruined, sources of income cut off. Still the woman must find food for the family. The health and social services she needs are likely to be totally disrupted, along with the family and community support systems that would ordinarily come to her aid.

Even without open conflict, the arms race drains huge sums of money from national budgets. The need for 'defence' is one of the reasons government officials cite for not giving higher priority to health, education, social services, and other budgetary allocations of prime importance to women. Any attempt to improve the health of women needs to be matched by a parallel improvement in the conditions of justice and equity that lead to peace.

Women react to violence and exploitation □ The one bright side to this picture is the extent to which women have united over the past decade or two to say 'Stop!' to violence and exploitation. They have recognized the need for immediate and long-term action.

The immediate priority is to help the women who are victims or potential victims of violence now. Shelters for battered women are spread across many countries of Europe and North America, Australia and New Zealand. Women's groups and NGOs in more than a dozen developing countries have set up refuges for women who need a place to go to escape from violence. Most shelters offer not only a place to stay for the women and their children, but counselling, material support, and sometimes legal help. Most importantly, the woman in crisis feels the solidarity of other women who have had similar experiences. It helps her gain the confidence she needs to decide about her future.

There are similar centres for rape victims, where they can find sympathetic listeners, counselling, support groups to help them 'get on with their lives again', and assistance in reporting the rape and bringing the case to court.

This last is very important for both abused women and rape victims, especially where police and court officials are not inclined to take the reported violence seriously or to arrest and prosecute the offender. They may, in fact, be more inclined to blame the victim unless someone is there to help her stand up for her rights.

Being arrested sends a clear message to wife-beaters or other perpetrators of violence against women: your behaviour is criminal, society does not condone or excuse it.

NGOs and government agencies have undertaken other actions to help women victims or potential victims of violence. Some have organized courses in self-defence for women, or in procedures for reporting violence. Others have arranged briefings for police and court officials to help them understand the significance of violence against women and enable them to deal more sensitively and justly with the cases that come before them.

'In Brazil a campaign led by the Council for Women's Rights convinced the government to establish almost 30 all-female police stations to provide a sympathetic atmosphere for victims of rape, battering and incest.'[47] Similar steps have been taken in Malaysia and other countries, where specially trained police squads made up of women deal with women who report being raped. In Malaysia 'the number of reported rapes has increased greatly, prison sentences of rapists are longer and public awareness of the severity of the problem (through greater mass media coverage and exhibitions) has grown'.[48]

To counteract the violence and exploitation of prostitution and to provide help for women in need, prostitutes have organized themselves to defend their rights, often with the support of other women's groups or human rights organizations. Many local NGOs, some with international partners, have come to the defence of child prostitutes. They try to offer these young girls and boys education, health care, lodging, and training to earn a living some other way—whatever is needed to get them out of their virtual slavery and open up other options for them and their families. The long-term strategies to eliminate violence against women include:

- as always, measures to raise the status of women and gain recognition of their full human rights;

- research to be able to present a fuller picture of the much under-reported violence against women;

- education of girls and boys from the earliest age in the idea of equality between the sexes, respect for everyone's human rights and non-violent ways to resolve conflict;

- lobbying to reform laws that allow violence towards women to go unpunished, and seeing that the laws are enforced;

- sensitizing police, lawyers, social workers, teachers, religious and political leaders to the issues;

- challenging local customs and traditional practices that incorporate or encourage violence against women, for example, female circumcision, *sati* or burning of widows on their husband's funeral pyre, dowry, and so on;

- working to change public attitudes that tolerate and perpetuate violence against women (see Box on myths).

SIX MYTHS ABOUT WOMEN AND VIOLENCE:

- 'So he beats her . . . it's a family matter, we can't interfere.'

- 'She must like it or she wouldn't stay with him.'

- 'Secretly women enjoy it, they want to be raped.'

- 'She must have provoked it.'

- 'It's human nature . . . (to wage war, to be violent, to get what you want by force, for the strong to dominate the weak).'

- 'We've always had prostitution and always will. There is nothing you can do about it.'

Wrong, 100 per cent wrong, all of them, and the sooner we can dispense with these myths the better.

CONCLUSION □ Reviewing the factors that influence women's health, one is struck by:

- the gap between the *de jure* and *de facto* situation of women, that is, between the principles governments have proclaimed and committed themselves to in international legal instruments, and the reality of women's daily lives;

- the interrelatedness of all the factors and the need to act in several sectors simultaneously;

- the urgency of taking action now if we are not to miss some rare opportunities; change is occurring, for better or for worse, daily;

- the tremendous potential for women, health and development if we *can* learn to use these factors in a positive way.

---

1 As quoted in P. Huston, *Third World Women Speak Out*, New York, Praeger, 1979, p. 30.
2 As quoted in *Women's World*, no. 21–22, December 1989, p. 4.
3 A. Santa Cruz, 'The Myth of the Male Provider', *Women in Action*, 3/88, p. 9.
4 'Bank sets new strategy on poverty', *International Herald Tribune*, Supplement on Asian Development Bank, 25 April 1990.
5 'More and more for American women, one job's not enough', *International Herald Tribune*, 16 February 1990, p. 3.
6 *Compass*, Newsletter of the Society for International Development, no. 43, March 1990, p. 10.
7 D. Elson, 'How is Structural Adjustment Affecting Women?', *Development*, Journal of the Society for International Development, 1989: 1, p. 70.
8 International Labour Organisation, report to the Copenhagen Mid-decade Conference on Women, 1980.
9 B. Diallo, 'The Dream of Domination', *World Health*, April 1985, p. 26.
10 S. Ravindran, 'Health implications of sex discrimination in childhood', World Health Organization/UNICEF document, WHO/UNICEF/FHE86.2, 1986, p. 2.
11 C. Vlassoff, 'The Value of Sons in an Indian Village: How Widows See It', paper presented at meeting of the Canadian Population Society, Windsor, Ontario, June 1988, p. 21.
12 Ravindran op. cit., p. 12.
13 N. Sadik, *Investing in Women: the Focus of the '90s*, New York, UNFPA, 1989, p. 6 (hereafter: *Investing*).
14 UNICEF, *Annual Report 1989*, p. 27.
15 Ravindran op. cit., p. 12.
16 UNICEF, *Intercom*, no. 55, January 1990, p. 7.
17 M. Das Gupta, 'Selective Discrimination Against Female Children in Rural Punjab, India', *Population and Development Review*, vol. 13, no. 1, March 1987, pp. 79–83.

18 UNFPA, *The State of World Population 1990*, New York, UNFPA, 1990, p. 1.

19 Estimate of the World Health Organization, October 1986.

20 United Nations, *UN Decade for Women Bulletin*, no. 10, 1985: 1, p. 9.

21 Information compiled from: V. Patel, *Women in Action*, 3/88, p. 27; ISIS International, Latin American and Caribbean Health Network, *Women's Health Journal*, no. 14, July–August 1989, p. 12; *The Tribune: A Women and Development Quarterly*, no. 44, March 1990, p. 17.

22 UNFPA, *The State of World Population 1990* op. cit., p. 3.

23 'Draft Strategy for Safe Motherhood in Tanzania', document presented at the Third Meeting of Interested Parties, Safe Motherhood Initiative, WHO, Geneva, 18–19 June 1990, p. 10.

24 *Women and Literacy*, prepared and compiled by M. Ballara, forthcoming volume in the Women and World Development Series, UN/NGO Group on Women and Development, London, Zed Books.

25 Sadik, *Investing* op. cit., p. 22.

26 Ibid.

27 Ibid.

28 Ibid., p. 23.

29 J. Goldsmith and M. Wright, 'Women and Educational Alternatives Worldwide', *Links*, no. 27, published by Third World First and World University Service, London, p. 1.

30 D. Van Belle-Prouty, 'Reproducers Reproduced: Female Resistance in a Rwanda Classroom', *Development*, 1990: 1, p. 78.

31 *Women and Environment*, prepared and compiled by Annabel Rodda, forthcoming volume in the Women and World Development Series, UN/NGO Group on Women and Development, London, Zed Books.

32 United Nations Development Programme (UNDP), *Water and Sanitation for Health: Toward the Year 2000*, booklet, New York, UNDP, nd.

33 C. van Wijk-Sijbesma, 'Drinking Water and Sanitation: Women Can Do Much', *World Health*, vol. 8, 1987, p. 28.

34 Extracts from W. Ogana, 'The Long Walk is Over' (Panos), as printed in *New Internationalist*, May 1990, p. 19.

35 UNDP, *Water and Sanitation* op. cit.

36 Department of International Development Cooperation, Government of Denmark, *A Strategy for Human Health*, 1989, p. 15; and *World Health*, August–September 1986, p. 30.

37 R. Barsh, 'Human Rights and the Environment', *UN Special*, Geneva, May 1990, p. 5.

38 S. Varma, 'Policy Planning for Women's Development at Provincial Level – the Case of Rajasthan', *Development*, Journal of the Society for International Development, 1990: 1, p. 97.

39 Sadik, *Investing* op. cit., p. 14.

40 Interview with J. Nyerere by M. Richardson, *International Herald Tribune*, 23 July 1990.

41 F. Nkweto Simmonds, 'Images of Black Women in Development Education', *Links*, no. 27, p. 18.

42 WHO, *Safe Motherhood Newsletter*, no. 3, July–October 1990, p. 4.

43 *Women in Action*, 3/88; *World Health Statistics Quarterly*, vol. 40, no. 3, 1987; and ISIS Latin American and Caribbean Women's Health Network, *Women's Health Journal*, no. 17, January–March 1990.

44 WHO, *World Health Statistics Quarterly*, vol. 40, no. 3, 1987, p. 261.

45 Asian and Pacific Women's Resource Collection Network, *Health*, part of the Asian and Pacific Women's Resource and Action Series, Kuala Lumpur, Asian and Pacific Development Centre, 1989, p. 166 (hereafter: Asian/Pacific, *Health*).

46 Ibid., p. 170.

47 L. Heise, 'Crimes of Gender', *Women's Health Journal*, no. 17, January–March 1990, p. 10.

48 Asian/Pacific, *Health*, op. cit., p. 188.

KEY HEALTH ISSUES FOR WOMEN

In selecting the health issues to include in this chapter we have tried to choose those where, from a global perspective, ▶ women are particularly affected ▶ the need for action is most urgent ▶ the opportunity for action is greatest.

WE RECOGNIZE THAT this *is* an arbitrary selection and that there are many serious health problems for women that are not covered here.

In order to take action on health issues, each individual, group or organization must begin by looking at the situation 'at home'. What are the key issues for you or your group? What are the most urgent health problems for women in your locality? What opportunities for *action* do you have? Perhaps you have the possibility of mobilizing and working with particular groups—health professionals, parents, government officials, workers in a particular industry or profession, one special age, or ethnic, group. If so, your opportunities for action and thus your list of key issues might be quite different.

(To get an idea of the kinds of initiatives people are taking to improve women's health, see Chapter 5. To get information materials and the names of organizations that could help you take action, see the resource guide in Annexe IV.)

This chapter begins with an examination of the wide range of issues related to reproduction and safe motherhood. Then we look at the trends in 'lifestyle' issues, including the use of tobacco, alcohol, drugs and medicaments, where opportunities for education and action are great. Next, cancer, a major cause of death for women, and AIDS and other sexually transmitted diseases are considered. A section on occupational health is followed by a look at the health of three groups of women who must cope with circumstances that leave them open to double discrimination: women with disabilities; elderly women; and refugee and migrant women. Finally, there follow some observations on women's mental health issues and on women as consumers of pharmaceutical products.

PRIMARY HEALTH CARE ☐ Before looking at specifics it is important to repeat that the effective extension of primary health care (PHC) is in itself an underlying issue for women's health. In the quest for 'Health for All' that will include women, there may be no more important issue.

As mentioned earlier, PHC is a strategy that should empower women. It recognizes the value of their activities in the family and community. It should be realized in a way that makes full use of their potential. The philosophy of PHC emphasizes prevention, health education, community participation (not token, but listening to all local viewpoints with respect), the importance of environmental factors, and the need to reach out to even the most remote areas and to all parts of the population, including the poorest. In this, PHC responds to several problem areas for women. To the extent that PHC systems expand and work well, women's health will benefit.

REPRODUCTIVE HEALTH ☐ Women's reproductive health problems, and their right to reproductive health, were brought to the world's attention during the UN Decade for Women, at the Mexico Population Conference in 1984 and at the Nairobi Conference on Women at the end of the decade. Yet:

In contrast to the dramatic decline in infant mortality rates in recent years, there has been no significant reduction in maternal mortality rates in the past two decades.

DR A. PETROS-BARVAZIAN[1]

There are, however, indications that this unhappy situation is about to change. United Nations agencies and NGOs alike are rallying around such global efforts as the Safe Motherhood Initiative. They are stepping up public information activities on this issue and pressing for action at the national level. More and more development groups and human rights groups are hearing about the issues in reproductive health and the unacceptably high maternal mortality rates in developing countries. This is a good start, but the pressures for practical, tangible *action* must continue.

Women's reproductive health is a broad topic. We concentrate here on a few selected issues where the need is urgent and the opportunity for action is great.

Safe motherhood □ It was only in the late 1970s and early 1980s that the data coming in on maternal mortality began to unveil the full magnitude of the problem. And even then it was clear that it was probably being underestimated. There were several reasons for this:

• maternal deaths were so commonplace in many parts of the world that people accepted them as a 'normal' part of life;

• the generally low status of women was another reason, and the fact that most of the women concerned were in remote areas and from socially disadvantaged groups;

• the fact that maternal deaths *could* be avoided, that something could be done about them, was not fully appreciated.

That is not to say that this is an easy health problem to correct. The roots go deep, and there are no quick solutions. But most maternal deaths could be prevented by applying existing knowledge. No technological breakthrough is needed, just the will to give it priority.

At least 500,000 women die from pregnancy-related causes each year, 99 per cent of them in developing countries. For every woman who dies there are countless others who suffer prolonged or permanent ill health and disability. For every woman who dies the risk of one or more of her children dying also increases.

'Two-thirds of women who die in childbirth have at least one other child. Recent analysis of data from Bangladesh on the survival of children under ten [shows that] a mother's death is associated with an increase of almost 50 per 1,000 deaths for sons and 144 per 1,000 for daughters.'[2]

In February 1987, the Safe Motherhood Initiative was launched at a conference in Nairobi co-sponsored by WHO, the World Bank and UNFPA, with support from UNICEF and UNDP. All these agencies are now partners in the Initiative, along with many NGOs and bilateral aid agencies.

The participation of such a wide range of organizations tells us something about the nature of maternal mortality: it has ramifications not only in the field of health, but for people concerned with development, socio-economic progress, population, children's well-being, and human rights. The causes of maternal death are rooted in just as many different domains.

Causes of maternal deaths □ If you ask, 'Why do these women die?' the technical response is: 'The main causes of maternal death are haemorrhage, sepsis (infection), toxaemia, obstructed labour and the complications of abortion.' But looking

61

NEARLY HALF THE BIRTHS IN THE WORLD ARE NOT ATTENDED

BY TRAINED PERSONNEL

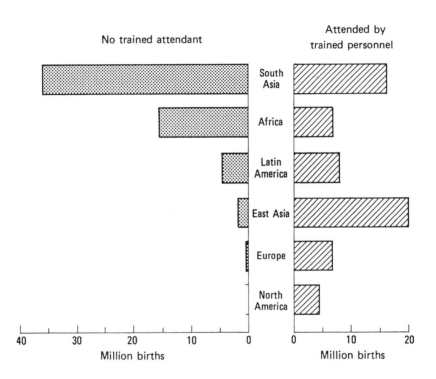

Source: Safe Motherhood Information Kit, WHO

beneath those immediate causes, one must ask why they occurred or why they were fatal. The answer to that is: lack of pre-natal care; lack of trained personnel, equipment, blood or transport at the moment the obstetrical emergency arose, or earlier, when it might have been foreseen and avoided; lack of family planning to help women avoid unwanted pregnancies, too many or too closely spaced births, or giving birth when they were too young or too old; pre-existing conditions like malaria, anaemia, fatigue and malnutrition that predispose to obstetrical complications; problems arising from female circumcision (particularly infibulation).

From that list of intermediary causes, one must go deeper still . . . to identify the cultural and socio-economic factors that put young girls, almost from birth, on this road to maternal death. We have already reviewed some of these factors: low status of women and discrimination against them; poverty; lack of education; local custom; and government policies that give low priority to the needs of women.

All of that tortured causality has been nicely translated into human terms in this statement of the causes of maternal deaths produced by the Safe Motherhood Initiative:

Women die in childbirth because:
- **they received no prenatal care;**
- **they have too many children;**
- **they were afraid to go to the hospital;**
- **they could not afford transportation;**
- **they did not know their condition was dangerous but could be treated;**
- **they were afraid to use contraception;**
- **they were malnourished as little girls;**
- **there is no blood available at the health facility;**
- **the untrained traditional birth attendant thought she could handle the complication;**
- **they live too far from a hospital which can provide emergency care;**
- **they seek illicit abortions to end unwanted pregnancies.**[3]

That list of reasons for dying in childbirth, combined with the following 'call to action' could almost serve as a checklist for people ready to go to work to promote safe motherhood.

Call to Action

SAFE MOTHERHOOD NAIROBI 10-13 FEBRUARY 1987

Maternal mortality is a critical problem that needs to be recognized by all ... The lifetime risk of a woman in a developing country dying in pregnancy or pregnancy-related illness is 1 in 25 or 1 in 40; this contrasts sharply with the one in thousand or several thousand risk for women in the developed world. These measures of maternal death have not been used as part of the quality of health and quality of life index. They should be so used. No country can claim to be advancing if its maternal death rates remain poor.

The causes of these deaths are tragic indeed. Illegal abortion from unwanted pregnancies causes some 25 to 30 per cent of these unwanted deaths, simply because women do not have access to the family planning services they want and need, or have no access to safe procedures or to human and humane treatment for the complications of abortion. For the thousands of women who die in pregnancy and childbirth, millions more are permanently disabled. Many of them are ostracized by their families and communities. For every death, it is estimated that 10 to 15 women are handicapped in one way or another.

There must be a commitment to stop these deaths. We need to mobilize the political will, to mobilize community involvement among men and women, and to implement specific programmes to stop these tragedies from taking place. We must do this for common humanity. We must do this also because women are a major resource to any nation, to any community, and above all to any family. When a woman dies in childbirth, the death sentence of the child she carries is almost certainly written. Often the children she leaves behind suffer the same fate, and the family stands a good chance of disintegration.

The causes of this problem are deeply rooted in the adverse social, cultural, political, and economic environment of societies, and especially the environment that societies create for women. Women are discriminated against in terms of legal status, access to education, access to food, access to appropriate employment, access to financial resources, and to relevant health care, including family planning services. This discrimination begins at birth and continues through adolescence and adulthood, where women's contributions and roles are ignored and undervalued.

These deep-rooted causes need to be addressed if we are to improve the long-term situation of women's health and status. The problems we are discussing will only grow in magnitude with population growth if we do not address these basic causes.

But there are also a number of immediate causes that result in the overwhelming majority of maternal deaths: obstructed labour, eclampsia, toxaemia, infection, and complications from both spontaneous and induced abortion. And there are low-cost, effective and available interventions that can have a major impact.

What is needed now is dedication and action.
- We need to generate the political commitment to reallocate resources to implement the available strategies that can reduce maternal mortality by an estimated 50 per cent in one decade;
- We need to note that the industrialized countries faced this challenge in the past. For some the change has taken place in our lifetime, through dedication and reallocation of priorities; ▶

● We need an integrated approach to maternal health care that makes it a priority within the context of primary health care services and overall development policy;

● We need to reach decision-makers in family and government to change laws, attitudes, and improve the legal and health status of women generally, especially in areas such as adolescent marriage and restrictions on health care delivery;

● We need to mobilize and involve the community and particularly women themselves in planning and implementing policies, programmes and projects, so that their needs and preferences are explicitly taken into account;

● We need to utilize a range of information, education and communication activities to reach communities, women, men, boys, and policy-makers, through the media and all culturally appropriate channels;

● We need to carry out additional studies to gain better country- and locale-specific information on maternal mortality—its immediate causes, which we know, and its root causes, some of which we either do not know or ignore;

● We need to have ongoing operational research and evaluation activities to assess the effectiveness of various programmes;

● We need to expand family planning and family life education programmes, particularly for young people, and make services for planning families socially, culturally, financially and geographically accessible;

● We need to use appropriate technologies at all levels so that women have better care at lower cost;

● We need to strengthen community-based maternal health care delivery systems, upgrade existing facilities and create relevant new ones if necessary;

● We need to ensure that pregnant women are screened by supervised and appropriately trained non-physician health workers where appropriate, with relevant technology (including partograms as needed), to identify those at risk, provide prenatal care and care during delivery as expeditiously as possible;

● We need to strengthen referral facilities and locate them appropriately—hospitals as well as health centres. They need to be equipped to handle emergency situations effectively and efficiently;

● We need to implement an alarm and transport system that ensures that women in need of emergency care reach the referral facilities on a timely basis.

These activities need to be seen within a comprehensive, multisectoral approach . . . need to involve governments as well as non-governmental organizations. They need to stimulate communities themselves.

Perhaps most important of all, this Safe Motherhood Initiative must create an awareness that something can, should—indeed must—be done, starting with the commitment of heads of states and governments.

TRADITIONAL BIRTH ATTENDANTS, THE FIRST LINK IN THE CHAIN IN SOUTHERN ETHIOPIA

In Southern Ethiopia the government is working together with a non-governmental organization in one district to provide a service which involves TBAs in a team effort, and which has succeeded in significantly reducing the incidence of ruptured uterus caused by obstructed labour. Trained by the primary health care team—the first rung of the national health service, which can deal with emergencies like haemorrhage but cannot perform surgery—the TBAs are visited regularly once a month. The TBA's job is to identify all the pregnant women in her village, and to conduct the prenatal clinic together with the visiting midwife. She and the midwife decide who is at risk of a complicated delivery and at what stage this woman should be taken nearer to a hospital for observation.

However, not all problems can be anticipated, so the TBA uses a messenger in the village who will run and walk —for anything up to 3 hours—to alert the sisters at the primary health care post in cases of emergency. The sisters then move out with a landrover to pick up the patient from whichever point it can reach; they do whatever they can and take the patient to the first referral level of the health service.

This scheme works because there is support all down the line. Further- ▶

more, the TBA, who already has the trust of the community, can introduce the women to new ideas about pregnancy and childbirth.

SATELLITE MATERNITY UNITS IN NORTH EAST BRAZIL

In North East Brazil, Dr. Galba Araujo, late professor of obstetrics at Fortaleza hospital, has built a bridge between the traditional and modern practices of midwifery. Believing on the one hand that fundamental change cannot be hurried, and on the other that there is too much interference with childbirth in modern obstetric practice in Brazil, Dr. Araujo set out to improve the quality of care given by the TBAs and to provide back-up from the modern health service only where necessary.

Making use of health buildings abandoned through lack of funds, staff or commitment, he created in the early 1970s a series of satellite midwifery units centred on Fortaleza hospital. He gave basic training to the TBAs and got the natural leaders among them to organise 24-hour coverage at the units for local women in labour. Dr. Araujo arranged for the units to be visited by professional nurses several times a week, and he or one of his fellow obstetricians would generally drop in at weekends. Any TBA who wanted to use the unit to deliver one of her patients could do so. The TBAs were paid by the health service, and funds were set aside to pay for transport to the hospital for anyone in trouble.

The hall-mark of the satellite maternity units set up by Dr. Araujo in the 70s is respect for tradition. Professional staff do not interfere unless problems beyond the scope of the TBAs arise. The TBAs are taught to put up an intravenous drip but otherwise there is no reliance on modern drugs or technology. From the start results were encouraging. Out of the first 5,000 deliveries at the satellite maternity units there was not one maternal death.

True to the principle of picking the best from both worlds, helpful traditional practices—particularly those which respect the dignity of the mother and her sense of control over the process of birth—have found their way back to the modern maternity hospital too. Babies are put to their mother's breast before the cord is cut rather than whisked away to be washed and tagged, and the placenta is expelled spontaneously and without interference.

Safe Motherhood Kit,
WHO

Family planning □ One of the most effective actions that could be taken in support of women's right to safe motherhood would be to assure every woman's right to family planning. The connections between family planning and safe motherhood are examined in the box overleaf

Abortion □ No discussion of reproductive health can ignore the question of induced abortion and the complex moral, social and political issues that surround it. This section looks at the extent of use of abortion, the reasons for resorting to illegal or unsafe abortions, and the consequences.

Induced abortion is one of the oldest and most widely practised methods of avoiding an unwanted birth. It is used to some extent in every country, no matter what the laws regulating it, no matter what the predominant social and moral attitudes towards it and no matter what the percentage of couples

Family planning

The high incidence of complications in pregnancy and childbirth which lead to maternal death, injury, and sickness occurs in the context of poor socioeconomic conditions with scarcity of education, health care and other social services. The incidence of maternal death and ill health is also affected by fertility patterns, and family planning therefore has a crucial role to play in reducing the risk through appropriate timing, spacing and limitation of the number of pregnancies.

Maternal health and unregulated fertility

Not only do women in the world's poorest countries undergo the highest risk of dying from a given pregnancy—due to their own poor health and to the lack of care—but because of unregulated fertility they also undergo this risk more frequently and over a longer period of their lives than do women in the developed world. Without family planning they will continue childbearing for 20 or even 25 years, while women in industrialised countries typically have two or possibly three children spaced over five or ten years. Furthermore, a short interval between births means that the woman will have to care for three or occasionally even four children under five years at the same time—with deleterious effects on herself and her whole family, including an increase in the risk that her youngest children will not survive.

Family planning decreases deaths from illegal abortion

When couples do not have access to effective methods of contraception, women frequently resort to dangerous illegal abortions in order to control their fertility. Illegal abortion kills up to 200,000 women a year and permanently injures the health of countless more.

Early and late childbearing have their dangers

Women who become pregnant while they are still adolescent have a much higher risk of complications during pregnancy and childbirth. These complications can injure their health and even cost them their lives. Postponing the first birth—whether by marrying later or by family planning—will greatly improve a woman's health. Women who are over 35 years run a greater risk of birth defects in their offspring, and in developing countries are approximately two and a half times as likely to die in pregnancy or childbirth as women aged 20–24 years, though there are wide variations from one community to another.

Family planning also serves the intertile couple

In some parts of Africa infertility affects as many as one third of all couples, causing deep unhappiness. The purpose of family planning is not merely contraception, but is to help couples to have the number of children they want, when they want them.

Family planning and the status of women

The status of women and, in particular, their level of education, is closely related with fertility and mortality patterns. But quite apart from the health effects of family planning, the ability of women to regulate their own fertility is one of the keys to greater freedom of choice in how they spend their lives.

The unmet need for family planning services

If women the world over were able to have the children they say they want, the crude birth rate would range between 16 and 28 per 1,000 population rather than the present range of 28 to 40.

About 95% of the people in the developing world live in countries which provide some form of public support for family planning programmes, generally as part of mother and child health programmes. Despite this, it has been estimated that there are about 300 million couples who do not want any more children but who are not using an methods of family planning, chiefly due to inadequate access to services, especially in rural areas and urban slums. To be effectively used, modern methods of contraception need to be relevant to sociocultural beliefs, and to be distributed by health workers who inspire trust and confidence and who are properly backed up by the health services.

The need for improved methods

Many modern contraceptive methods have some side effects, both real and perceived, but the health risk of unwanted and unplanned pregnancies are at least 20 times greater than the risk of the side effects of any contraceptive. Nevertheless, many couples and some health workers are reluctant to use or recommend existing contraceptive methods. There is a need for new and improved methods, including new oral contraceptives, long-acting agents, vaginal rings, new barrier methods, modern male methods and even improved methods for natural family planning.

using contraceptives. When women are determined not to have a child, and if other means of preventing births are not available or have failed, they do resort to abortion, regardless of the risks. Under certain conditions the risks are tragically high, for the individual woman, her family and society.

In trying to look objectively at women's health and abortion, one of the first problems is a familiar one: data on abortion are totally inadequate in most countries, especially on abortions done illegally or clandestinely. Most estimates put the number of induced abortions performed throughout the world at around 50–60 million per year, about half of them illegal or clandestine.[4]

This high proportion of illicit (and therefore mostly unsafe) abortions persists in spite of the fact that three-fourths of the people in the world live in countries where abortion is legally permitted, with few restrictions, and is allowed for social and socio-medical reasons, including the mother's health. However, as Jodi Jacobson points out in the Worldwatch paper on 'The Global Politics of Abortion':

Changes in laws are a necessary but not sufficient condition for widespread access to safe abortion services. Because many national legal codes reflect social ambivalence about abortion, what happens in practice often does not reflect the law on the books . . .

Access to abortion and other family planning services, like health care in general, is determined by four variables: laws, policies and the way they are interpreted, the commitment of public funds to provide services, and personal resources, particularly money . . .

In many countries where women should be able to get an abortion on demand, **they find it difficult to exercise their legal rights for a variety of reasons, including stricter-than-usual medical regulations, burdensome administrative requirements, lack of public funds for services, lack of information or referral networks, lack of trained providers, extreme centralization of services, and local opposition or reluctance to enforce national laws.[5]**

Such barriers to safe abortions have many consequences. At the very least they delay abortions so that the simple, safe procedures that could be used at an early stage of a pregnancy are not possible. Also, these barriers inevitably create inequities. Women with education, those who are informed about their rights, those who have money, those who have the support of family and community in seeking an abortion—these have a much better chance of having a timely, safe, legal abortion.

Poor women, rural women far from medical facilities and skilled health workers, those uninformed about the 'system' and the services that should be available to them, those who are seeking abortion without the approval of their husbands or parents or extended families, those without the possibility of travelling to another state or country where safe abortions are available—these are the women who finally try to terminate their pregnancies in extremely hazardous, exploitative circumstances. Some try to induce abortion themselves with sharp instruments, potions, pressure or blows to the abdomen. Others go to illegal practitioners who perform abortion in unhygienic conditions, with inadequate skills and medical knowledge, and with great reluctance to send a woman to a legitimate health facility if something goes wrong. And very often something does go wrong:

. . . hospitals in many developing countries are literally inundated with women seeking treatment for complications of illegal abortion. Over 30 per

cent of the beds in the gynecological and obstetric wards of most urban hospitals in Latin America are filled with women suffering abortion complications. At Mama Yemo hospital in Kinshasa, Zaire, and at the Kenyatta National Hospital in Nairobi, Kenya, some 60 per cent of all gynecological cases fall in this same category . . .[6]

'. . . restrictive abortion laws are much more likely to have an impact on the *outcome* of an abortion, whether the woman becomes ill or even dies after the abortion, than whether or not she actually has an abortion. Where there's a will, there's a way, whether the "authorities" choose to make the way simple and safe or difficult and dangerous.'[7]

Caring for women with complications due to abortions uses scarce resources—including drugs, anaesthetics, blood supplies, the time of skilled staff—that are badly needed for other patients. 'In Brazil . . . reports indicate that nearly half the national health system's obstetrics budget goes to treating the complications of abor-

tion . . . . Hospital studies from Turkey, where abortion is technically legal, indicate that treating complications following an illegal operation costs four times as much as a safe medical procedure.' The cost of hospitalization and treatment can be catastrophic for patients and their families, as well.

But the heaviest cost is not in money or resources, it is in human lives and suffering. Out of the 500,000 deaths each year from pregnancy-related causes, a large proportion can be attributed to illegal abortion. In addition, for every woman who dies, many more suffer permanent damage to their health and are often left infertile. This is a particularly heavy price for young women to pay.

The demographics of abortion are revealing. In most industrialized countries 'abortion rates tend to be highest among teenagers and women aged 20–24, groups that seek to delay childbearing either because of their marital status (single) or for other reasons, such as the desire to complete their education.'[8] Reliable data are lacking in Africa, but the pattern in urban

Abortion and maternal health

The costs of unsafe abortion, in maternal suffering, risk to health and life, and drain on hospital budgets, is high. In some Latin American countries, 50% of maternal deaths are due to illegal abortion, and more than 50% of beds in maternity wards are occupied by patients with post-abortion complications.

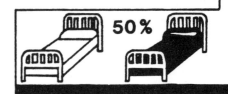

Source: WHO

areas there is not too different. In one Nairobi hospital, 79 per cent of induced abortion patients were young, single women. In Asia and Latin America, on the other hand, abortions are sought most often by older, married women who already have several children.

These patterns probably show where the greatest unmet needs for family planning are, too. 'The growing disparity between low rates of contraceptive use and increasing desires to limit family size—the unmet need for family planning that is evident throughout the Third World—is a sure prescription for even higher rates of illegal abortion.'[9]

To reduce the maternal mortality and morbidity attributable to illicit abortions, the first obvious objective is to guarantee that family planning information and services reach all couples who want to space births or limit family size. Policy-makers should realize, however, that 'Contraceptives reduce, but do not eliminate, the need for abortion as a backup to their own failure: 7 out of 10 women using a 95 per cent effective method of birth control would still require at least one abortion in their lifetimes to achieve a two-child family.'[10]

This combination of family planning for all who want it, plus safe accessible abortion as a back-up, would take us a long way towards the goal of safe motherhood for all women. Whether or not that will happen depends, in Ms Jacobson's plain words, on 'the value placed on women's lives':

Perhaps the most distressing fact about abortion-related deaths and illnesses is that the vast majority of complications are totally preventable. What consigns so many women around the world to death or physical impairment is not a deficiency in technology, but a deficiency in the value placed on women's lives. Technologically simple, inexpensive, easy-to-use tools for safe early abortion are well known, and widely used in some countries. But social intransigence, religious intolerance, economic self-interest, and political apathy all narrow the options for millions of women. Society's message to these women is, in effect, 'carry this unwanted pregnancy or risk your life to end it.'[11]

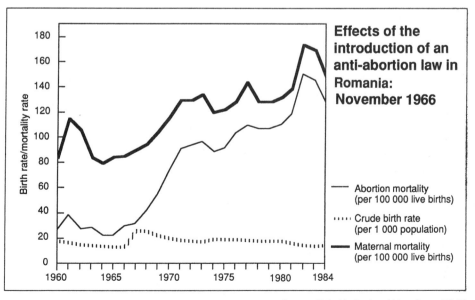

Effects of the introduction of an anti-abortion law in Romania: November 1966

— Abortion mortality (per 100 000 live births)

····· Crude birth rate (per 1 000 population)

▬ Maternal mortality (per 100 000 live births)

Source: Safe Motherhood Newsletter, WHO

Maternal morbidity ☐ If 500,000 women die each year from pregnancy-related causes, many times that number are incapacitated to some extent each year as a result of child-bearing. The long-term damage to their health may range from uterine prolapse and chronic pelvic inflammation to mental health problems and neurological injuries affecting their ability to walk.

One little known trauma of childbirth that occurs most often in young women is the development of an opening (or fistula) between the vagina and the rectum or urethra, which allows urine or faeces to pass through the vagina. Under-age mothers who have prolonged obstructed labour are particularly susceptible to this condition, which is known as VVF (vesico-vaginal fistula). The *Safe Motherhood Newsletter* reports that: 'In Niger 80% of women with obstetric fistula—urinary or faecal incontinence—are between 15–19 years old.'[12]

The impact on these young lives is catastrophic. Smelling of urine or faeces, suffering recurring infections, the young woman is very often abandoned by her husband and family, ostracized by society, and left to survive as best she can, usually in appalling misery. Surgery can correct the condition, but this is beyond the reach of most of the women who suffer from VVF. Dr Halfdan Mahler, addressing the International Safe Motherhood Conference in Nairobi, described obstetric fistulae as 'so devastating to the personal, marital and social life of the woman that many a time she must bitterly wish she had died'.[13]

The following vivid case study by Dr Altine M. Tongo of Nigeria explores the causes of VVF and suggests ways to prevent it.

CASE STUDY—D.A.M.T Vesico-vaginal fistulae (VVF) —the most dreaded condition among the women of northern Nigeria

This paper is dedicated to Jummai whom I will never forget. Jummai was an 11-year-old girl and mother of a dead baby whom I met while I was a medical student working in the maternity ward of Maiduguri General Hospital, Northern Nigeria, in 1984.

Jummai is an orphan whose mother died when she was two years old. Her father did not remarry and Jummai grew up with him. She started menstruating at the age of 10 years and two months later was impregnated by her 'boyfriend'. He disappeared once he discovered that she was pregnant.

Jummai's father ordered her to leave his house because of the pregnancy. Alone, herself little more than a baby, she wandered from one house to another working as a maid or housegirl. When her labour began, her mistress dismissed her with a token 20 naira. Jummai left the house with only her two wrappers (cloth garments) and, still in labour, she went to a half-completed building not far away. But after two days in labour, confused and in pain, Jummai realised that it was necessary for her to begin the long trek to the Maiduguri General Hospital, stopping wherever she could to rest along the way.

I met Jummai at about 10 a.m. in the maternity ward. The baby's hair was already visible but no heart sound was audible. Jummai's labour was then assisted with a syntocinon drip and 45 minutes later a stillborn baby girl was delivered. So before her 11th birthday, Jummai had survived a lonely, painful labour, and had become a mother and then learned that her baby was dead. But her problems were far from over. ▶

A few hours later Jummai noticed that urine was dribbling continuously from her vagina. On examination, a communication was found between her bladder and the anterior wall of her vagina. The condition is known as vesico-vaginal fistulae (VVF).

At that time, VVF repair was only undertaken at the Teaching Hospital and fees were charged for the operation. Jummai needed to eat good food, rest and benefit from a course of antibiotics before her soft tissues would heal and be ready for the VVF repair. But Jummai had no money and little chance of earning very much. She had never been to school.

The social welfare was contacted on her behalf. I do not know what happened to her from then on. I dedicate this paper to her because all that happened to her could have been prevented had the father been sympathetic enough to take care of her, send her to school (government schools are mostly free of charge), and possibly find her a stepmother or maid to take care of her. Jummai's father could have afforded to do that.

What is VVF?

Vesico-vaginal fistulae (VVF) is an abnormal opening or hole between the urinary bladder and the vagina which results in constant involuntary leakage of urine through the vagina . . . Because [the woman] smells of urine, her presence becomes a nuisance to all those around her. She is no longer desirable. Ninety per cent of these patients are divorced by their husbands.

Few medical textbooks give more than a couple of paragraphs to VVF. It is frequently described simply as a genito-urinary tract condition, and no mention is made of the preventable social factors which lead to the development of VVF, nor to the social consequences of the injury on women sufferers . . .

Dr. F. Tahzib has described the typical VVF patient as 'frequently malnourished, anaemic, divorced and rejected'. He says that she often has to travel long distances to seek modern treatment and may wait months before seeing a doctor. She may wait years before it is her turn for the operation.

During this period, in a strange environment, far from her village, homesick and lonely, she has to fend for herself economically. Hour by hour and night and day, the leakage of urine wets, excoriates and pains the victim of this misfortune. Her clothes are ruined, her bed is her nightmare, she is homesick and lonely and shunned by everyone. 'Society has created an outcast', Dr. Tahzib writes. Here [at this hospital] at least 19 VVF cases are recorded each month, the majority of the women are under the age of 20 years. They are mostly Muslims and 98 per cent have no formal education. Over 70 per cent of these young women developed the condition after their first delivery, which was often after a prolonged and obstructed labour at home . . . According to . . . a gynaecologist working here, there are so many VVF cases that, in his opinion, the hospital should open a separate VVF ward.

How could VVF be prevented?

Although the age and height of the mother-to-be is a significant factor in the number of VVF cases, most could be prevented with the help of better maternal health services. Injuries, and even the lives, of mothers and babies could be saved if women who are in labour longer than 12 hours could be taken for hospital care. However, in many countries, ▶

including Nigeria, the maternal services are inadequate, inaccessible and inappropriate. In some cases, the patient is simply unaware of their existence. Another problem is that, in the absence of the husband, no one may be willing to take the decision for the woman to be moved to the hospital—even when she has been in obstructed labour for several days.

Other traditional attitudes such as a belief that a woman's first baby should be delivered at home (*kunya*), the shame and modesty shown in first pregnancies and purdah all contribute to a reluctance to take advantage of modern health services where they do exist. In consequence, these often stoical women spend days in labour at home in an attempt to deliver the baby. Traditional midwives and relatives will try to assist by pressing on the abdomen and applying various traditional mixtures and therapies. Usually, however, the foetus dies while still in the uterus. Frequently mothers cannot survive this ordeal, either, and die during childbirth still in their home.

Those who eventually manage to deliver their stillborn babies are left with serious after-effects. First, the woman is exhausted and semi-conscious due to severe pain and loss of fluid and electrolytes. Her elbows and knees will often be cut and bruised due to the postures adopted during childbirth. Her legs may be paralysed as a result of the pressure of the foetus on the nerves supplying the legs during childbirth. Some time later, her legs will become thin and wasted. Her vagina will be torn, distorted and infected . . .

Although early marriage with consequent prolonged, obstructed labour is associated with about 80 per cent of VVF cases seen in Northern Nigeria, a traditional treatment known as *gishiri* cuts is the second largest cause. (See Definitions of Key Terms.)

What is to be done?

Dr Tongo concludes her case study with suggestions for action to reduce the incidence of VVF. A summary is given here:

- Raise the age of marriage to a minimum of 21 years.
- See that all female children are given free, compulsory and equal education at least to post-primary level. Provide scholarships for university and other educational institutions for women.
- Ensure that modern medical services are accessible to all women and that health education is provided.

Dr Tongo calls on the women's organizations of Nigeria to launch a campaign to raise consciousness about VVF and the fact that its causes are almost entirely social and preventable. Further, she would like to see a fund set up to cover the costs of treatment for VVF patients and to assist them 'during the desperate period before they receive treatment'. She believes Muslim theologians and other leaders should give attention to this problem and the question of divorce, so that women suffering from VVF will not be deserted and left without resources.

Source: *Women's World*, no. 21–22, 1989
ISIS—WICCE

Unmet needs in reproductive health

☐ Sometimes hard-pressed health system administrators feel they have done all they need do for women if they have set up a functioning MCH system. There are two drawbacks to this approach: first, in some places the 'M' in MCH is given minimal attention; second, women have a wider range of reproductive health needs than those usually dealt with at MCH centres.

Infertility ☐ Infertility is a great scourge in many parts of the developing world but is found in all regions. WHO estimates that infertility affects between 35 and 70 million married couples worldwide. It can be the result of untreated reproductive tract infections occurring during childhood, or it may stem from sexually transmitted diseases (STDs), mishandled abortions, and other causes. In societies where *every* woman is expected to produce children as a sign of her womanhood and desirability as a wife, being infertile brings with it social stigma and great difficulty in finding a place in society.

In some instances, of course, the couple's inability to produce a child is traceable to the man. A WHO study of 10,000 infertile couples found a possible cause in the male partner in 33 per cent of cases, in the female partner in 25 per cent of cases, while 20 per cent of couples had possible cause in both partners.[14] STDs and other causes can lead to sterility in men. In the more macho societies, however, many men cannot even entertain the suggestion that they are incapable of producing children, and they may refuse to go for an examination.

Infertile couples need help in an appropriate setting (not an MCH clinic) where the husbands will not be reluctant to accompany their wives and where they can be sure of receiving sensitive, skilled assistance.

Non-mothers and older women ☐ also have gynaecological problems needing attention. Young girls need services and information. This includes, in some areas, girls from age six upward, who are no longer considered children eligible for care at MCH centres but who are not yet mothers either. Many of these young women could profit from screening for anaemia, malaria or reproductive tract infec-

tions. As young adolescents they need information about sexuality and reproduction, STD, and what they can do to safeguard their reproductive health. Boys and girls alike benefit from health education programmes that include this vital information. Those who plan such programmes must be more sensitive to the needs of this age group, which are not often enough taken into account.

Breast-feeding ☐ It was a woman, Dr Cicely Williams, who, in a 1939 speech to the Singapore Rotary Club, first called attention to the fact that children were dying from unsuitable feeding, that is from being given formula in bottles instead of being breast-fed. She called it 'murder'. It took many years and much determined research and advocacy by other pioneers—individual men and women as well as organizations—before the multiple benefits of breast-feeding and the full dangers of bottle-feeding were documented. The successful outcome was due in large part to the innovative action of NGOs like the International Organization of Consumer Unions and the grass-roots groups that joined together in 1979 in the International Baby Food Action Network (IBFAN).

The early 1970s saw the beginning of an international campaign to stop the promotion of breast-milk substitutes. In this campaign UN agencies, especially UNICEF and WHO, joined with NGOs in a worldwide effort to protect the health of women and children by protecting the practice of breast-feeding. One result of this collaboration was the adoption by the World Health Assembly in 1981 of the International Code of Marketing of Breastmilk Substitutes. The Code is designed to eliminate inappropriate marketing practices used to promote products for artificial feeding.

Public awareness of the benefits of breast-feeding has increased over the past decade, but it is a continuing struggle to protect it in the face of many influences that work against it. In most industrialized countries the proportion of women breast-feeding hit its lowest point in the early 1970s and has been increasing in recent years thanks to energetic information campaigns and support groups. In many developing countries, however, large numbers of women are abandoning breast-feeding after a short period or not starting to breast-feed at all. Very often they are women—poor urban women, for example, living in slums—who have little chance of being able to nourish their children adequately or safely by bottle-feeding.

From the point of view of the child, breast-feeding is extremely beneficial, even life-saving, and for the mother, too, it has many advantages:

- breast-milk alone is the best possible nourishment for the first four to six months of life, giving the baby the optimum chance for survival and good health;

- it helps protect the baby against diarrhoea, respiratory infections, allergies and other illnesses;

- it is always clean and pure, always the right temperature;

- it is emotionally satisfying, brings mother and child together;

- there is no danger for the baby from unclean bottles or contaminated water, and the mother is spared the work of preparing formula and bottles. For many women, because of the conditions in which they live, it is almost impossible to prepare and use bottles safely;

- breast-milk is economical;

- nursing helps the mother's reproductive organs return to normal after pregnancy and childbirth and may reduce the risk of breast cancer;

- it helps delay the return of ovulation and

therefore helps in the spacing of births, although breast-feeding is not a reliable contraceptive in itself and needs to be combined with another method by the time the baby is four to six months old.

'... despite all the significant advances made in the development and delivery of contraceptive methods and services, breastfeeding today still accounts for more spacing of pregnancies than any other currently available technique or method.'[15]

Clearly breast-feeding women make an extremely important contribution to the well-being of families, societies and nations. In all fairness we should ask, 'Do they have the resources and support they need in order to do this effectively, and *without* sacrificing their own health and well-being in the process?' In almost all societies, the answer would have to be 'No'.

Here is what women *should have* in order to breast-feed successfully:

- Women need good nutrition throughout their lives, but especially during pregnancy and lactation, so that their own health will not suffer. They need to be well-informed about how much extra food nursing mothers require, and the extra food must be available. Programmes to assure household food security should take the needs of nursing mothers into account.

- Nursing takes time and energy. Nursing mothers need extra rest; they need to be relieved of some of their usual workload.

- Women need good information suited to their specific circumstances about the benefits of breast-feeding and the risks and disadvantages of bottle-feeding and breast-milk substitutes.

- All the knowledge that is important for the breast-feeding woman is equally important for her husband and perhaps other family members so that they can

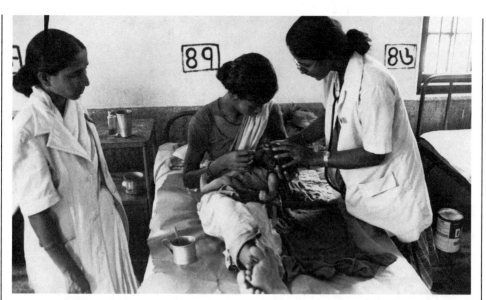

PHOTO: SUPACHAI / UNICEF (BANGLADESH)

relieve her of some tasks, help care for other children, and ensure that she gets the food she needs.

- For mothers who give birth in a maternity facility, everything possible must be done by the staff and administration to encourage breast-feeding: putting the newborn baby to the breast right after birth; keeping the baby in the room with the mother to facilitate bonding and encourage feeding on demand; giving the baby no other food or drink; helping new mothers learn how to put the baby to the breast and how to deal with any difficulties that may arise; not giving out any samples or gifts that suggest that breast-milk substitutes might be needed, are more 'modern' or are as good as breast-milk. Staff of maternity facilities themselves must be convinced about the value of breast-feeding, and trained to assist mothers in getting off to a good start.

- A new mother needs to know that it is important for herself and her child to have an interval of at least 18–24 months before her next pregnancy. She needs advice about reliable contraceptive meth-ods appropriate for nursing mothers, as well as access to the supplies and services required.

- In areas where breast-feeding is declining or is no longer the norm, women need role models and support groups to help them learn the techniques of successful breast-feeding and develop confidence in themselves.

- Mothers who work outside the home need reasonable maternity leaves, crèches at work, and breast-feeding breaks.

- Manufacturers and distributors of breast-milk substitutes have to be held to their obligations as outlined in the International Code of Marketing; governments have to incorporate its provisions in their laws and enforce those regulations. The public, especially young people, need to become more conscious of advertising techniques and know how to resist commercial pressures.

Idealistic? A 'wish list'? Yes. Few nursing mothers enjoy all of this support. They

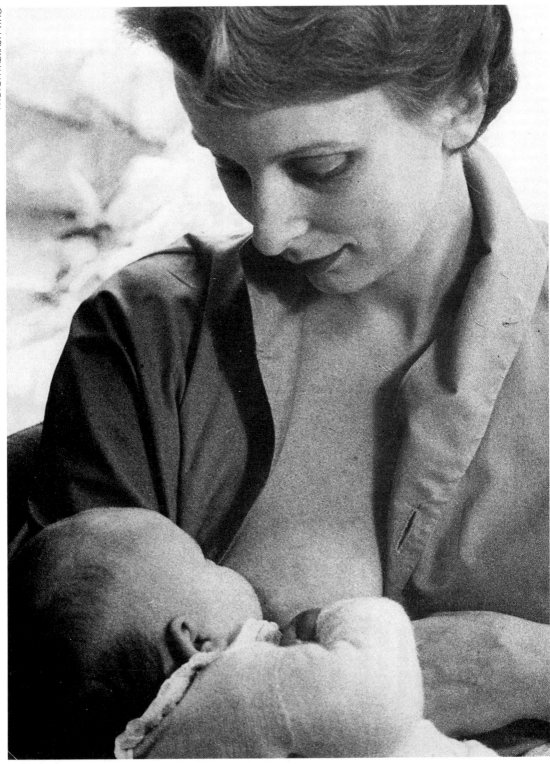

breast-feed anyway, but sometimes at great cost to their own health and well-being. Yet many of these needs *are* being met for a growing number of women, thanks to governmental and non-governmental education and advocacy programmes. School health curricula, nutrition education and parent education programmes have incorporated material on breast-feeding. Health professionals, hospital administrators, social workers and employers have been sensitized to the needs of nursing mothers. Mother-to-mother support groups, which have proved particularly effective in halting the decline of breast-feeding in some countries, are promoted by international organizations like La Leche League and by national groups such as the National Childbirth Trust in the United Kingdom. A very active group of national and international NGOs monitors the implementation of the Code and makes its findings known to governments, WHO and the public.

However, there are still millions of women who are breast-feeding without the resources and support they need, and others who will be forced by circumstances to abandon their attempts to breast-feed. Breast-feeding has to be promoted vigorously in all countries, but without creating guilt feelings in the mother who does not breast-feed. If women are expected to breast-feed, then all the other groups who should be providing the resources and support described above must meet their responsibilities too.

Female circumcision □ *Eight-year-old Halima had never had so much attention. For three days relatives and friends had been bringing her gifts—clothes, jewelry, money— singing and dancing and celebrating the fact that she was about to 'become a woman'. She was excited. She had looked forward to this day for so long. She could just imagine herself in the new red dress with the beautiful bracelets jingling on her arm. But suddenly she felt*

a catch in her throat and wondered what 'becoming a woman' would really be like. She remembered how her older sister had looked afterwards and how she wouldn't talk about it.

Then they came in, her mother and four friends and Aisha, the old woman from the next village who helped women who were giving birth. They were all smiling and saying kind, happy things to Halima. But when they pinned down her arms and shoulders and spread her legs apart, their grip was like iron. Aisha approached, murmuring reassuringly . . . with a razor blade in her hand.

★ ★ ★

So Halima joins the estimated 80 million other girls and women living today with the results of genital mutilation. Female circumcision is current in some 26 African countries and is found also in Malaysia, Indonesia, Yemen and in scattered parts of Brazil, Mexico and Peru. The operation has also been performed in European countries by immigrants from areas where it is practised.

Female circumcision, which should more properly be called 'excision', involves the removal of parts of the external female genitalia. There are three types:

1. *Clitoridectomy*: removal of the skin over the clitoris or the tip of the clitoris. This is known as 'sunna' and is the mildest form.

2. *Excision*: removal of the entire clitoris and the labia minora, but without closing up the vulva.

3. *Infibulation*: removal of the clitoris, the labia minora and parts of the labia majora, stitching together the sides and leaving just a small opening for urine and menstrual fluid to pass through.

There are many variations in the way the operation is carried out today. In primitive settings the TBA may use a razor blade, knife or piece of broken glass, stitching the sides and holding them in place with thorns. At the other extreme, a few well-to-do parents now have the operation done under anaesthesia in a modern health facility with skilled health professionals in attendance (a practice strongly disapproved of by WHO, medical associations and health ministries).

What motivates such a wide diversity of people to cling tenaciously to a practice that inflicts pain and suffering on the children they love? Overwhelmingly the answer given is 'tradition', the reluctance to break with an age-old part of their culture. For some women and men it is a symbol of the shared heritage of a specific ethnic group and satisfies a deep-seated need 'to belong'. The second frequently cited reason is that female circumcision is required by religion, particularly Islam. But no-where in the Qu'ran or the Bible is there any such requirement, and this has been stated by both Muslim and Christian authorities who have spoken out against the practice.

In addition to tradition and religion, more specific reasons are also given for circumcising girls:

- it safeguards the woman's virginity until marriage;

- it protects family honour and ensures legitimacy of descendants;

- it reduces the woman's sex drive and makes her a more docile and contented wife, less likely to become promiscuous;

- it enhances the man's pleasure in intercourse;

- girls will not be accepted as wives if they are not circumcised;

- it is necessary for cleanliness;

- it is more aesthetic;

- it is better for the woman's health and guarantees fertility.

In spite of all the contradictory evidence, these ideas are firmly held beliefs and do cause parents to have their daughters circumcised in large numbers every year, convinced they are doing the best thing for the child. In the western part of Sierra Leone, where circumcision is part of the initiation into the women's secret societies, a survey found that 90 per cent of women were circumcised. The desire 'to belong' was a strong factor.[16]

Age at circumcision varies from infancy up to the sixth month of the first pregnancy. The latter practice is found in communities that believe that if the first-born baby's head touches the clitoris during childbirth the child will die.

In reality the effects of circumcision are often quite different from what was intended. But the resulting health problems, unless they occur immediately after the circumcision, may not even be connected with it in the mind of the parents or the patient. Many women seen in health clinics years later for a gynaecological, obstetrical or urinary problem are surprised to learn (and reluctant to believe) that it is related to circumcision.

The hygienic conditions under which the operation is performed, the skill of the circumciser, the general health of the girl or woman being circumcised and the amount of struggling she does all influence the outcome. The effects appear at different points in time: immediately after the operation, during later years, at the time of marriage and first intercourse, at the first birth, after giving birth.

Immediate effects include: pain, shock, haemorrhage, retention of urine, infections and fever, tetanus. Death is not uncommon, especially if the child or woman lives far away from medical help. Over the ensuing years many circumcised women experience pelvic infections, sometimes severe enough to block the Fallopian tubes and cause infertility. Urinary tract infections are common. Cysts and hard scar tissue form. Menstrual discharge may build up inside the vagina.

Inevitably the first intercourse or consummation of marriage is an ordeal for an infibulated woman. If the vaginal opening is too small for penetration the husband or traditional birth attendant may cut the scar to enlarge the opening. The small opening and scar tissue create even more difficulties at childbirth. The obstructed labour may result in haemorrhaging, tearing of perineal tissue, urinary or rectal fistula (see Maternal Morbidity and VVF, pp. 70–2), and eventually prolapsed uterus. For the baby, such a prolonged, difficult labour is life-threatening. The infant may be stillborn or suffer brain damage from lack of oxygen.

And when it is all over, most circumcised women ask to be stitched up again. Few wish to discuss sexual matters, but among those who do there are many reports of frigidity, anxiety connected with intercourse, and depression. From the results of one study in West Africa, it was estimated that 83 per cent of circumcised women had a circumcision-related condition requiring medical attention at some time in their lives.[17]

It is difficult to quantify the dimensions of the health problems caused by female circumcision. However, midwives, nurses and doctors who have been dealing with the results in Africa for many years all testify that they constitute a major public health problem, especially in areas where infibulation is practised and virtually all women have been circumcised. African women in the health professions were among the first to call for the eradication of the practice and to begin to work for change.

Over the years African women's groups, NGOs, governments and intergovernmental agencies have joined forces to raise the issue with national policy-makers, key groups in the health care system, opinion leaders and the general public. Says one African woman:

Education is the key element in changing the attitude of the public. When we consider the reasons advanced for the persistence of female circumcision we realize that they are all based on ignorance and lack of scientific information on the part of the parents. Mothers subject their daughters to this ritual with the best of intentions, unaware of its dangers. They attribute sickness and death to supernatural powers. The remedy for this misapprehension is intensive, relevant education, which should be aimed at parents, schoolchildren, teachers, health workers, religious leaders, traditional chiefs and others concerned. The message on the harmful effects of female circumcision and other such practices can be transmitted in literacy programs and included in national health education initiatives. Physicians can play an important role in convincing their patients to discontinue the practice.[18]

Needless to say, in dealing with a practice as deeply embedded in culture and tradition as this one, sensitivity is required. 'Sensitivity' should not of course become an excuse for inaction, but it does mean that the main thrust of the campaign must come from within the countries and communities concerned, especially from the women. Any suggestion that local traditions are being attacked from outside creates resistance.

African women approach this issue with great good sense and clarity of vision. The Kenyan women's magazine *VIA* has commented: 'There is nothing "African" about injustice or violence, whether it takes the form of mistreated wives and mothers, or slums, or circumcision.' It adds, rather irreverently: 'Often the very men who . . . excuse injustice to women with the phrase "it is African" are wearing three-piece pinstriped suits and shiny shoes.'[19]

The Inter-African Committee on Traditional Practices Affecting the Health of Women and Children (IAC) was established in 1984 to unite and strengthen Africans who were working to abolish female circumcision and other harmful practices. IAC is composed of representatives of national groups in 20 African countries who are involved in education and training, legal and policy reform, and meeting the health needs of women already circumcised. IAC initiates and supports local seminars and training sessions (e.g. for TBAs and for 'trainers of trainers'). It produces educational materials and a newsletter where national groups can share experiences.

Representatives of IAC bring the concerns of their national and local groups to international forums, presenting female circumcision as both a health issue and as a human rights and child rights issue. The president of the IAC has pointed out the complementarity between the Safe Motherhood Initiative and the work of the IAC, saying, 'A careful and honest evaluation of traditional practices is a prerequisite for attaining a certain degree of Safe Motherhood in Africa.'[20]

Female circumcision is a sensitive issue, there is no doubt. But with the proper approach it is possible to be effective in discouraging it. The Egyptian affiliate of the World Young Women's Christian Association reports on their experience thus:

As a matter of fact, we were very hesitant to approach this topic even here in Cairo, let alone elsewhere. But we at last took courage and held the seminar in our vocational training centre, in a very overpopulated suburb of Cairo. The two speakers who came from the Family Planning Association spoke so well—gave the information in a clear, simple, decent and convincing way, so much so that the reaction during and after the meeting was very satisfactory. Everybody was fully attentive. Someone said she was intending to 'harm' her girl in the near future, though she was very apprehensive about her going through the bitter process she herself had experienced at her age. 'But now I will change my mind.' Others asked questions. Bashful young girls went up to the speakers for other side questions, and so on. We now intend to offer the same programme in Upper Egypt . . . .[21]

Reproductive health—a question of **rights** ☐ For a long time health planners, development experts and government priority-setters saw women primarily through the prism of their reproductive role. Solutions to women's health needs tended to emphasize the expansion and improvement of maternal and child health systems. Welcome and necessary as this has been, it is not sufficient in itself.

Over the past decade the vision of woman has broadened. It has gone from that of a person with a reproductive role to that of a human being with reproductive rights among many other human rights. In this broader perspective reproductive rights include:

- the right to safe motherhood;

- the right to plan one's family;

- the right to assistance in preventing and overcoming infertility;

- the right to full and timely knowledge about all aspects of reproductive health and sexuality.

The last point is especially important for young women so they can learn about and exercise their reproductive rights and safeguard their own reproductive health.

LIFESTYLE ISSUES ☐ Most noncommunicable diseases are closely associated with choices we make in our lifestyle. For example, too much saturated fat in the diet contributes to heart disease, too much salt to hypertension and stroke, too much sugar to obesity and diabetes, too little fibre to cancer, and so on. Smoking, too much alcohol or too little exercise cause some health problems directly and contribute to many others, combining with the dietary and other factors to put people at risk of poor health and premature death.

These facts have been publicized for some time in many of the industrialized nations and measures have been taken to encourage people to develop good health habits. Norway took decisive action to make its citizens' diet more nutritious. A growing number of countries regulate tobacco and alcohol promotion. They put high taxes on these products or restrict their purchase and use to certain places and certain age groups. Many countries have seen real improvement in the health of their citizens as a result of these measures, the educational campaigns that have accompanied them, and the wise choices that individuals have made.

In developing countries there has been a time lag in the appearance of most of the 'diseases of modernization', but now they are showing up with a vengeance! One must, of course, bear in mind that countries vary greatly in their rate and style of development, from the newly industrialized countries (NICs) to the least developed countries (LDCs). They vary in the standard of living achieved. Their health problems could be expected to vary accordingly.

For a long time the major causes of mortality and morbidity in most developing countries were infectious and parasitic diseases and malnutrition. As the first two at least are brought under control, as people live longer and as the lifestyle of large groups of the population changes, the noncommunicable diseases are becoming prominent in developing countries, too.

These trends have great significance for women's health. In developing countries, the better treatments now available for the communicable diseases will have a very positive impact, provided women have access to them. There is one positive aspect, too, in regard to the noncommunicable or 'lifestyle' diseases: in both industrialized and developing countries there is something of a time lag in the picture for women as compared to men, which means that there is still some time for preventive action.

In industrialized countries women lagged behind men in taking up tobacco and alcohol, but as their use of these products began to approximate that of men, female death rates from lung cancer, heart disease and cirrhosis of the liver began to go up. The rates for men have begun to stabilize or turn downward as more of them give up smoking, get more exercise or otherwise adopt healthier lifestyles.

One hopes there will be a similar turn around for women, but there are disquieting signs. For example, smoking is increasing among young girls in many countries, even as it is decreasing among young boys. In industrialized countries, heart disease is now the leading cause of death for women, and it is on the increase throughout the developing world.

Women and tobacco □ In developing regions there is a ray of hope in the time lag for women: for the most part women have not yet adopted the more health-threatening behaviours in great numbers. There are exceptions: in Papua New Guinea the proportion of adult women who smoke or use tobacco in some form is 80 per cent; in Swaziland, 72 per cent; and rates range from 50 to 60 per cent in Bolivia, Nauru, Nepal and Brazil.[22] But in developing countries as a whole, it is estimated that only about 5 to 7 per cent of women smoke now.

Therefore there is an opportunity to help millions of women avoid health-destroying, addictive behaviour. But with no time to spare! A glance at cigarette advertising in developing countries makes it clear that two groups have been singled out as targets: women and young people. And it is among young women that the proportion of smokers is rising most rapidly.

Chances that a first-time cigarette smoker will become addicted: nine out of ten. Chances that a first-time cocaine user will become addicted: one out of six.[23]

PHOTO: WHO

Advertising for alcohol and tobacco targets women and young people.

In the article that follows Drs Amanda Amos and Claire Chollat-Traquet look at the trends concerning women smokers in different parts of the world, the effects of smoking on their health (and that of their children before and after birth), and the measures needed to help women remain, or become again, non-smokers.

WOMEN AND TOBACCO

When smoking amongst women was not as widespread as it is now, women were considered to be almost free from cardiovascular diseases and lung cancer. Unhappily, the situation has changed, and smoking kills over half a million women each year in the industrialised world. But it is also an increasingly important cause of ill-health amongst women in developing countries.

A recent WHO Consultation on the statistical aspects of tobacco-related mortality concluded that the toll that can be attributed to smoking throughout the world is 2.7 million deaths per year. It also predicted that, if current patterns of cigarette smoking continue unchanged, the global death toll from tobacco by the year 2025 may increase to eight million deaths per year. A large proportion of these will be amongst women.

Despite these alarming statistics, the scale of the threat that smoking poses to women's health has received surprisingly little attention. Smoking is still seen by many as a mainly male problem, perhaps because men were the first to take up the habit and therefore the first to suffer the ill-effects. This is no longer the case. Women who smoke like men will die like men. WHO estimates that, in industrialised countries, smoking rates amongst men and women are very similar, at around 30 per cent; in a large number of developed countries, smoking is now more common among teenage girls than boys. In most developing countries, where it is generally estimated that 50 per cent of men and five per cent of women smoke, the epidemic seems not to have reached women yet. But as cigarettes become more widely available and more heavily promoted, trends are changing.

As women took up smoking later than men, the full impact of smoking on their health has yet to be seen. But it is clear from countries where women have smoked longest, such as the United Kingdom and the United States, that smoking causes the same diseases in women as in men and the gap between their death rates is narrowing. On current trends, some 20 to 25 per cent of women who smoke will die from their habit. One in three of these deaths will be among women under 65 years of age. The US Surgeon General has estimated that, amongst these women, smoking is responsible for around 40 per cent of heart disease deaths, 55 per cent of lethal strokes and, among women of all ages, 80 per cent of lung cancer deaths and 30 per cent of all cancer deaths. Over the last 20 years, death rates in women from lung cancer have more than doubled in Japan, Norway, Poland, Sweden and the United Kingdom; have increased by more than 200 per cent in Australia, Denmark and New Zealand; and have increased by more than 300 per cent in Canada and the United States.

There are dramatically increasing trends in respiratory cancer among women in developed countries, and the causal relationship of smoking, rather than air pollution and other factors, to lung cancer is very clear. In the United States, for instance, the mortality rate for lung cancer among female nonsmokers has not changed during the past 20 years. In the same period, the rate among female smokers has increased by a factor of five. Smoking is already an important cause of cancer in many developing countries. In South-East Asia, more than 85 per cent of oral ▶

cancer cases in women are caused by tobacco habits.

Smoking also affects women's health in ways that are specific to women, and that put them at added risk. Women smokers have higher rates of cervical cancer, while those who smoke and use the oral contraceptive pill are several times more likely to develop cardiovascular diseases than those who use neither. Smoking affects women's reproductive health, increasing the risks of earlier menopause, miscarriage and low birthweight babies—a major concern in those developing countries where a baby's health is already jeopardised by poverty and malnutrition. Smokers are more prone to osteoporosis, a major cause of fractures in older people, particularly post-menopause women.

Women's health is also affected by the smoking of others, that is, by passive or involuntary smoking; for example, it has been shown that non-smoking wives of heavy smokers run a higher risk of lung cancer. In addition to these direct effects, we should not forget the indirect ones such as the additional burden in economic and non-economic terms that must be carried mainly by the mother as a consequence of morbidity and mortality of other family members from tobacco-associated diseases.

Protection, education, support

What can be done to halt and reverse the tobacco epidemic amongst women? The challenge is twofold: to reduce the already high level of smoking among women in the industrialised world and to ensure that the low level of smoking in developing countries does not increase. In order to achieve these goals, all countries need to develop comprehensive anti-tobacco programmes which take into account and address the needs of women. Whilst these programmes should be culture-specific and tailored to meet the local situation, experts agree that to be successful they must contain three key elements: protection, education and support.

Tobacco is a multinational, multi-billion dollar industry. It is also an industry under threat; one-quarter of its customers, in the long-term, are killed by using its product.

Young girls and women need to be protected from inducements to smoke—smoking is declining in many industrialised countries. To maintain profits, tobacco companies need to ensure that at least 2.7 million new smokers, usually young people, start smoking every year. Women have been clearly identified as a key target group for tobacco advertising in both the industrialised and developing worlds. Billions of US dollars each year are spent on promoting this lethal product specifically to women. 'Women only' brands, widespread advertisements depicting beautiful, glamorous, successful women smoking, free fashion goods, and the sponsorship of women's sports and events (such as tennis and fashion shows), are all part of the industry's global marketing strategy aimed at attracting and keeping women smoking.

This strategy has been highlighted by several tobacco journals which have carried articles on 'Targeting the female smoker' and suggesting that retailers should 'look to the ladies'. Among the 20 US magazines that received the most cigarette advertising revenue in 1985, eight were women's magazines. In the same year, a study on the cigarette advertising policies of 53 British women's magazines (read by more ▶

than half of all British women) showed that 64 per cent of the magazines accepted cigarette advertising, which represented an average of seven per cent of total advertising revenue.

Research in industrialised countries has shown the subtle methods used to encourage young girls to smoke. The impact of such methods is likely to be even greater in developing countries, where young people are generally less knowledgeable about smoking hazards and may be more attracted by glamorous, affluent, desirable images of the female smoker. This is why WHO, together with other national and international health agencies, has repeatedly called for national legislation banning all forms of tobacco promotion, and for an appropriate 'high price' policy which would slow down the 'enthusiasm' of young women for tobacco consumption.

Resisting the pressures

Young girls and women have a right to be informed about the damage that smoking can do to their health. They also need to acquire skills to resist pressures to start smoking, or to give it up. Several countries have developed integrated school and pre-school health education programmes which have successfully reduced girls' smoking rates; but this education should not be restricted to what happens in school. There are many other examples of effective cessation programmes in the workplace and primary health centres. Unfortunately, many women do not have the opportunity to be involved in such programmes, and programmes have generally been less successful with women than men. In countries where smoking has decreased, the rate of decline has been usually lower in women than men, and least amongst women

with low education and income. This suggests that educational initiatives ought to be more sensitive to women's needs; they also ought to cover issues of particular significance to women—such as the gain in weight that sometimes occurs after they stop smoking.

They need support

In order for women to become, and remain, non-smokers they need support. Support over these difficult days when the addiction cycle is broken. Support to help them deal in other less damaging ways with the reasons that caused them to smoke. Many women use smoking as a coping strategy, for example to create a 'space' in a day filled with the stress of bringing up children and having to face different types of work, often with little social support and on a low income. Environments need to be created which enable them to break free of this health-damaging behaviour, to make the healthy choices the best choices.

Smoking amongst women has already reached epidemic proportions and will continue to escalate unless action is taken now. Delays can only cause further suffering and deaths of women; this is why WHO's new programme on Tobacco or Health is giving high priority to action to protect women and children.

But what can be done to tackle this problem? Community health workers can develop health education programmes for young girls. Primary care workers can ensure that all women receive information, advice and support to help them give up the habit. Governments, national and international non-governmental organizations, and WHO in particular, can act as advocates for women's health to ensure that the issue of women and tobacco is put high ▶

on the health and political agenda, by pressing for action to protect women. Strategies to this effect should involve health and educational services, community and women's organizations, the media and even the employers.

Only by exposing the previously hidden problem of women and tobacco, only by putting women in the picture, will we be able to secure major improvements in the health of women worldwide.

Amanda Amos and *Claire Chollat-Traquet*, WORLD HEALTH, April-May 1990

FACTS ON SMOKING AND REPRODUCTIVE HEALTH

- Women who smoke are three times more likely to be infertile than non-smokers
- Women smokers have more difficulty conceiving than non-smokers
- Smoking during pregnancy causes higher rates of spontaneous abortion (about 10,000 spontaneous abortions each year in the United States are attributable to smoking)
- Smoking during pregnancy shortens gestation (in the USA more than 10 per cent of all premature births are attributable to smoking)
- Smoking during pregnancy increases chances of infant death during the first month of life
- Women who smoke during pregnancy have more frequent complications of labour and delivery than non-smokers
- Babies born to women who smoke during pregnancy weigh significantly less than babies of non-smokers (so have a lower chance of survival, and are more susceptible to infections). Low birthweight is the major factor associated with the death of infants in the first month of life
- Children 6–24 months old, of parents who smoke, tend to have more ear infections and respiratory problems (from 'passive' smoke breathed in the home)
- Women who smoke undergo earlier menopause and in general are relatively deficient in the hormone oestrogen
- Women over 30 who smoke and use oral contraceptives have an increased risk of developing cardio-vascular problems
- Smoking may impair the ability of intrauterine devices (IUDs) to prevent pregnancy, and
- Women who smoke more than double their risk of contracting cervical cancer.

Source: Family Health International 'Conference on Smoking and Reproductive Health'

Women and alcohol ☐ Research has confirmed that women are more sensitive than men to alcohol effects. Adjusting for differences in body size, a woman absorbs more of the alcohol she drinks into her blood stream due to a biochemical difference in the stomach lining.

Heredity plays a role too, but this greater physiological vulnerability, added to changing social attitudes and the increasingly stressful lives of many women, may account for the increasing number whose health is jeopardized by addiction to alcohol.

Women pay a high price for this addiction. Physically, women who drink heavily are more likely than men to develop cirrhosis of the liver. Consumption of alcohol also correlates with certain cancers (mouth, pharynx, larynx, oesophagus and liver).

Socially, women alcoholics tend to become totally isolated. The shame and guilt they feel—most societies are hard on women drinkers—cause them to stay at home, drinking in private and denying or 'hiding' their drinking problem. Working women go to elaborate lengths to conceal their drinking habits from colleagues. When their addiction can no longer be

LOOKING FORWARD WITH HOPE: INDIAN ANTI-ALCOHOL MOVEMENT INITIATED BY WOMEN

In Oakland, California, two Blackfeet women, mother and daughter, are at the apex of this new Indian movement. Betty Cooper is director of the Native American Alcoholism Program and her daughter Theda New Breast is a pioneer in the field of Fetal Alcohol Syndrome (FAS) prevention.

Betty Cooper has been working in the Bay Area Indian community for many years. It was during her years as a social worker that she first experienced the effect that alcohol was having on the Bay Area community. She believes that most of the problems that families confronted then originated from alcoholism in the family.

While working at Inter-tribal Friendship House in Oakland she saw the devastating result of alcoholism: people who didn't have food, babies with no milk, no gas for the car, no place to live, evictions, teenage problems and every type of health problem. She next worked for the *Urban Indian Child Resource Center*, also in Oakland, where she says, 'We had child abuse and neglect, more neglect than abuse. It was probably 99 per cent alcohol related.'

It was in the 1950s when alcohol was no longer restricted from the reservation that it began to be sold openly. The results were immediate and devastating. It seemed that everyone began to drink, including grandmothers who had never used alcohol. Small children were left sitting outside the bars crying for their parents who were inside drinking. Even babies were left alone in cars while the parents drank. She saw a pattern of arrests, spouse battering, and fragmented families emerge as a result of alcohol.

Within her own family her brothers developed severe drinking habits and the problems that came with it. After she and her husband moved to California he also became an alcoholic. After what she had seen and experienced personally she decided to become involved in the field of alcoholism treatment, recovery and prevention . . .

Cooper's work with entire families has given her insights into what happens in many homes where one or both parents are alcoholic. The whole family must find ways to cope with the chaos and unpredictability of daily life. One of the ways this coping manifests itself is to pretend there is nothing wrong. This is denial.

Cooper adds, 'You know there is family denial but our communities also deny that there is an alcohol problem and I think our communities have to begin to look at themselves. . . .'

Learning to have fun without drugs and alcohol [requires] role models. Cooper adds, 'We have more clean and sober events here (Bay Area) than we used to . . . each year we have an event we call "Running is my high", and we invite everyone out to run, walk or stroll. We ask all family members to come back to the lodge and we have a brunch. Instead of saying don't drink, don't drug, don't do this or don't, don't, don't, we have a strong positive message about natural highs.

'. . . if we can reach the children from the third to the fifth grade and teach them not to use alcohol and drugs and how to cope with it if it's at home, then we're looking at the year 2000 having young people, young Indian people, who have never "used or abused".' ▶

Theda New Breast has been involved in the field of FAS prevention and education for ten years. She focuses her attention on women and youth. FAS, she says, is very high among Indian women: 'In some Indian communities it is seen in as many as one in 100 births.'

Fetal Alcohol Syndrome is a birth defect that is caused by drinking alcohol during pregnancy. It is probably the second most common birth defect and probably the number one cause for mental retardation. FAS manifests itself in both physical and mental development delay. Facial deformities and deformities of the limbs, heart and central nervous systems are often FAS related.

According to New Breast, FAS is 100 per cent preventable and 0 per cent curable. A women does not have to be an alcoholic to have an FAS child. There is no known 'safe' level of alcohol consumption for a woman while pregnant.

She also stresses that, 'Indian women have been ignored in alcohol literature. Alcohol abuse has become the single most serious health problem . . . among American Indians.' After reading studies [showing] that most women who are pregnant spontaneously decrease their alcohol consumption, she '. . . saw that pregnant women were a prime source for intervention'.

New Breast has developed an innovative training program and . . . a training manual that has an Indian focus, talks about Indian culture and gives any kind of caregiver or community person ideas on what to do about FAS education. 'We try to get them [community workers and officials] involved because they are the ones who are making critical decisions over Indian people with either incarceration or taking the kids away or whatever. They need to know about Indian people and we try to sensitize them.'

The overall purpose of the three-day training cycle is to provide personnel of the Indian alcoholism programs, Indian youth and other key 'gatekeepers' in California with the knowledge and tools to conduct training seminars on the prevention of alcohol related problems, with the emphasis on Fetal Alcohol Syndrome and Fetal Alcohol Effects. . . . Each trainee who attends a session must sign an agreement to return to the community and train a minimum of 25 people.

Theda also works in the rural areas of California. She has designed a youth alcoholism prevention program on the Tule reservation, the second largest in California. Focusing on girls between the ages of 11 and 19, the program teaches them about the physiology of women, traditional midwifery, and how to deal with contemporary issues, choicemaking and how to be a traditional woman in contemporary society. 'A lot of the choicemaking is just simple skills. It is teaching our young women the ideas of a support system, especially for raising kids.

'We do a lot of cultural things, outdoor things, showing them they can still have a good time and alcohol does not have to be involved.'

They also bring women speakers to talk with young women. These women serve as positive role models because they are doing things with their lives and it doesn't include alcohol. Now [the young girls] say things like, 'Hey, I want to grow up and be like that. . . .'

Extracts from an article appearing in *Women in Action*, 3/88. ISIS International. Original source: *Native Self-Sufficiency*

hidden, women usually experience a total, crushing loss of self-respect. They are less likely than men to seek treatment or get into a self-help group.

Family life suffers, marriages break up. In Paraguay a group promoting education on alcoholism found that nine out of ten husbands in that society leave their addicted wives, but it is the reverse when the man is the alcoholic: only one of ten wives leaves her addicted husband.[24]

There are very few reliable figures on the number of women addicted to alcohol, especially in developing countries. It is certain, however, that the production and consumption of alcohol has soared in the past two decades. Beer production has increased by 124 per cent throughout the world, but by 500 per cent in Asia, 400 per cent in Africa and 200 per cent in Latin America. It is safe to assume that what was produced was consumed and that some of that increased consumption is by women. We do not know enough about this, but we should make greater efforts to find out, because the alcohol producers, like the cigarette producers, are targeting women and young people in their promotion campaigns.

Alcoholism in women is also a problem that could be aggravated by the strong trends towards urbanization in the developing world. Alcohol is readily available in the city and there are fewer of the social controls that might exist in a rural community. Also, women are drawn into the production and sale of home-made alcoholic beverages as one way to earn income.

The increasing consumption of alcohol

'Between 1970 and 1980, the alcohol conglomerates . . . increased sales of beer, wine and spirits in developing countries from US$325 million to $1.3 billion a year. This . . . is the cutting edge of a $2 billion-a-year alcohol promotion campaign aimed at previously untapped markets, including women and youth.'[25]

may affect women's health indirectly even if they do not drink to excess themselves, for example if someone in the family or household drinks heavily. Much violence against women is associated with alcohol and many family problems arise, ranging from the wasting of scarce income to physical and emotional exhaustion from trying to cope with all the family responsibilities.

In many industrialized countries and in a growing number of developing countries, people are taking action to prevent more harm to women's health from alcohol. The following article shows what two determined women can do, in this case a mother and daughter, members of the Blackfeet Indian tribe in California. In their fight against alcoholism and foetal alcohol syndrome, they use Indian cultural values and traditions to help young women build up good attitudes towards themselves and their health. Although this case study is drawn from a particular ethnic group and culture, the principles are applicable in any of the many societies where alcoholism is a problem.

DRUGS AND MEDICAMENTS ☐ From the earliest times women and men have used plants and other substances to treat diseases and reduce pain, as well as to experience pleasure, relieve anxiety, or induce a state of ecstasy for religious ceremonies. Modern use of drugs can be roughly divided into the same two categories: when needed for the treatment of health problems; and when used to experience the pleasurable effects or the escape afforded by the 'psychotropic', or mood-altering, drugs. In general it is the second category of drug use that people have in mind when they speak of 'the drug problem', that is abuse, addiction, lives ruined and lost. But the line between the two categories of use is not always clear, and this has particular consequences for women's health.

Minor **tranquillizers** ☐ Women's health networks, first in the industrialized countries, but soon after in developing regions, have become increasingly concerned about the use of legally prescribed 'minor tranquillizers' among women. In several countries and regions women have mounted successful campaigns against the misuse of these drugs. The information below is summarized from an article in the *Women's Health Journal*, a publication of ISIS International, Latin American and Caribbean Women's Health Network.[26]

The psychotropic drugs that are the main concern of these campaigns are the minor tranquillizers that have a sedative effect on the brain. They include the benzodiazepines and all other sedative, hypnotic and anti-anxiety drugs. Sold under the brand names of Valium, Librium, Ativan, Mogadon, Normison, and so on, the benzodiazepines in the mid-1980s accounted for more than half of all tranquillizers sold in the world. At one point Valium became the world's most prescribed drug.

About 40 million doses of minor tranquillizers are taken each day throughout the world, most of them by women. A study in Europe in the 1970s found that the proportion of women among users of anti-anxiety sedative drugs ranged from two-thirds to three-fourths, depending on the country. More recent figures from the United States show women twice as likely as men to use tranquillizers and sleeping pills. In Australia, four to seven per cent of men and 7 to sixteen per cent of women were found to be daily or almost daily users of psychotropic drugs. In industrialized countries the women who are using psychotropic drugs regularly tend to be poor, less-educated urban women, with a high proportion of housewives, the unemployed and the elderly.

The *Women's Health Journal* article comments on women's use of minor tranquillizers as follows:

These drug use patterns have very much to do with doctors' attitudes about women and with advertising by drug companies . . . Studies have shown that when men and women report similar psychological or psychosomatic symptoms, men are more likely to be given physical and laboratory tests, and women are more likely to be given drugs. Women are also more likely than men to be given a repeat prescription once they have been prescribed a minor tranquillizer.

One study showed that drug companies in some countries spend almost a quarter of every sales dollar on drug promotion and advertising . . . This literature frequently shows women using these drugs rather than men . . . Because many doctors lack training in dealing with problems of anxiety and depression, they are very susceptible to information provided by drug companies about how to 'treat' them.[27]

The article explains that these tranquillizers work by damping down the activity of the brain 'so that the effect of naturally calming substances is increased and [that of] naturally arousing substances is stopped. In the long term, the drugs seem to turn off the brain's own built-in control mechanisms so that it becomes difficult to function without them. After months or years of "damping down", the brain's own mechanisms for controlling anxiety and tension can no longer function.'

What is the effect on the user? Benzodiazepines were originally welcomed as being safer than barbiturates, but observed side effects include 'drowsiness, sedation, blurred vision, unsteadiness and uncoordinated movements, difficulty concentrating and remembering, depressed mood, irritability and anger, changes in sleeping patterns'.

If minor tranquillizers are combined with alcohol, as they frequently are, the side effects can be very severe. Furthermore, tranquillizers taken during pregnancy increase the risk of birth defects ranging from cleft palate to mental retardation. If taken in late pregnancy they may cause the baby to be born in a drugged state and have to go through withdrawal.

The misuse of tranquillizers has other serious, long-term consequences for women. It keeps them from tackling and solving the underlying problems that cause them to turn to drugs. The tranquillizers mask the misery and allow women to put up with situations that should be intolerable and should be changed. Or they keep the user from fully experiencing emotions that need to be dealt with. For example, grief over the death of a family member needs to be expressed in order for the bereaved to get over the bereavement.

The article points out that when women express anxiety, stress, anger and other reactions to the lives they lead, it may be a normal and appropriate response, given the situations many women face in their roles as housewives, mothers and breadwinners. However, they are not encouraged to take steps to change the situation, as a man might be, and their reactions are not accepted as normal and healthy. Instead, their problems are medicalized, and drugs are prescribed to treat the 'illness'. Women tend not to argue with their doctors, especially the groups of women described above as typical users of minor tranquillizers. Some women become convinced that they are sick and cannot cope, that they are incapable of taking control of their lives . . . a reaction that is reinforced if they find that they have become dependent on the drug.

For this is the most serious effect of the use of minor tranquillizers: dependence. 'Many doctors, health workers and people who take minor tranquillizers are not aware that dependence can occur fairly quickly—sometimes within four weeks of regular use.' The article lists three signs of dependence:

1. [when the user] relies on the tranquillizers to carry out her normal life;

2. when 'tolerance' has developed, i.e., the person needs more and more of the drug to have the same effect;

3. when withdrawal symptoms occur after stopping the drug.[28]

For women who are determined to break free from this dependence, the article tells them what to expect in withdrawing from different types of minor tranquillizers. It stresses the need for gradual withdrawals and the support of family, friends and a qualified health professional. It passes on practical suggestions as to how women can make the withdrawal process easier for themselves and others, *inter alia* through support groups.

What can be done to prevent these situations that cause women so much unnecessary suffering? The article gives the name and address of several groups working on prevention. Their strategies include providing information about the problem and calling it to the attention of the public and medical authorities; talking to doctors, pharmacists, nursing home administrators, and health centre staff about the changes that are needed; approaching policy-makers and politicians (lobbying is more effective if you represent the views of a group); encouraging publicity about the extent of the problem and the need for more appropriate services.

Women need to be more involved in the planning and implementing of such services, which must first of all ensure that women get clear, simple and accurate information on all health problems and what

they can do about them, including mental health and emotional problems. It may mean '. . . a move away from a "medical treatment" model in which all problems are automatically treated with drugs'.

Ultimately, of course, as with so many other health problems affecting women, these strategies must be combined with an attack on the underlying causes that push women to use minor tranquillizers. The article mentions poverty, lack of child care, inadequate housing, poorly paid jobs, low status and discriminatory treatment as problems that 'need to be addressed, rather than being masked by minor tranquillizers'.

The campaigns against the misuse and overuse of minor tranquillizers have had an effect. In many countries usage has declined from the peaks reached a few years ago. People have become more aware of the dangers. Also, many countries have put stricter controls on the prescription and sale of minor tranquillizers. In 1984 the United Nations Commission on Narcotics and Drugs put the benzodiazepines on the list of controlled substances.

Nevertheless, there has been a reaction similar to the one that occurred with tobacco and alcohol. As the market in industrialized countries shrank, manufacturers turned to marketing their products more aggressively in the countries where controls are less strict or not enforced. This is the case in quite a few developing countries, where psychotropics are often self-prescribed and bought over the counter. Women in developing countries are now prime targets.

A group in Lima, Peru, investigating the use of tranquillizers by middle-class women aged 25–50 found that Lima accounted for 67% of the tranquillizers sold in the country and that women were given twice as many prescriptions for them as men.[29]

Action now could spare many women in developing countries from having to learn for themselves the bitter lessons faced by women in the industrialized countries. Support groups, education, publicity and lobbying for stricter regulations nationally and internationally are effective strategies for reducing the use of minor tranquillizers. Now is the time to expand these strategies in developing and industrialized countries alike.

Other psychotropic drugs □ The abuse of other psychotropic drugs, such as marijuana, hashish, cocaine, crack, heroin, LSD and glue-sniffing, has had dramatic consequences in all parts of the world and has been the subject of daily headlines for some time. Few readers of this book could be unaware of the crime, violence, misery, ill-health and death associated with the traffic in these drugs. This section will be limited to some of the special implications for women.

First, a reminder that drug abuse is both a worldwide phenomenon, and an ancient one. But the drug problems we see today, with powerful global production and distribution networks, aggressive 'pushing' of drugs, incredible profits, are more recent. Everywhere women and girls are among the victims and consumers, from the street children sniffing glue in Rio to the well-to-do matron in Philadelphia trying to hide her addiction. Women and girls are involved in every step of the supply process, from production and harvesting of raw products to serving as couriers and pushers. In the exploitative world of the drug trade, women and girls are among the easiest to exploit. They are most likely to be poor and desperately in need of income, easier to intimidate by physical force, more likely to be submissive to male demands. In some countries very young girls as well as young boys are used as couriers to deliver drugs, because minors are less severely punished if they are caught.

'It has been estimated that there are about 48 million drug users in the world, a large proportion of whom are children aged 10–15.'[30]

As consumers of 'hard drugs' like heroin, cocaine and crack (a cheap and very addictive cocaine derivative), women and girls are subject to all the well-known health risks connected with these drugs: death from overdose, physical and mental deterioration, infections and disease from impurities in the drugs and from the use of contaminated needles. Both hepatitis and AIDS are transmitted by needles.

Women may pay two additional heavy penalties when they become dependent on these drugs. First, many turn to prostitution as the only way to earn enough money to support their habit. Prostitution invariably exposes them to violence, exploitation and disease, but their addiction or dependence drives them to take the risks. Second, women who use drugs during pregnancy, especially crack, run the risk of producing infants with serious birth defects. 'Crack babies' show heart-rending withdrawal symptoms after birth, and a high percentage suffer permanent damage, including physical and sensory problems, learning disabilities and personality disorders.

At present the problems linked to drug abuse are more prevalent and better recognized in certain Western societies where they have reached epidemic proportions and where reasonably good figures are available. In general, there are more men using hard drugs than women, but for some drugs the gap is closing. There are indications, moreover, of similar trends in developing countries, especially the producing countries and among urban populations throughout the developing regions. It is vital to reverse these trends and to reach young women and girls before they are drawn into the world of drugs.

Young people give many reasons for starting to use drugs.[31] It is useful to ask which ones might be especially strong motivations for young women and girls. One reason usually mentioned is curiosity; almost all adolescents want to know 'what it feels like'. A second important reason is peer pressure. Adolescents long for the approval of their peer group and need to find ways to gain status within the group. Girls often have fewer ways open to them to gain status. If experimenting with drugs is one way to do it, they may accept. Lack of full information about the risks of drug use is another factor. Lower levels of schooling and literacy reduce girls' chances of receiving such information. Poverty, marginality, changing social norms, immigration, urbanization and unemployment are other social factors that have been linked to drug use among young people.

On a more individual level, research shows drug use to be higher among young persons with low self-esteem and self-confidence, and in persons seeking escape from both inner conflicts and intolerable external situations. One has to ask how much the low status of women and girls and the discriminatory treatment they receive contributes to this set of motivations for their use of drugs. One thing that helps young people *avoid* being drawn into drugs is practice in decision-making. They need to develop the ability to make wise choices and feel confident that they can exercise control over their future. For many young women, this is not an area where they have had a lot of prior experience.

CANCER ☐ As we saw in the overview, the proportion of deaths from cancer is expected to rise in all regions of the world (because of the ageing of populations, control of other major health problems and changes in lifestyle). There are 14 million cancer patients in the world today,[32] the majority in developing countries, with men slightly outnumbering women. Little more than ten per cent of global spending for cancer treatment and research takes place there.[33]

There are different patterns in the incidence of cancer between women in industrialized countries and those in developing countries. For the most part the differences reflect differing lifestyles; but these patterns change rapidly. In industrialized countries lung cancer is replacing breast cancer as the top cause of cancer deaths among women; in some countries it has already done so. An article in *World Health Forum*, reporting these findings, comments: 'Lung cancer is a self-induced avoidable and preventable tumour, and these WHO findings clearly indicate the need to establish new priorities and strategies in cancer control.'[34] As noted earlier, there is still time to avert a similar rise in lung cancer cases among women in developing countries, where the proportion of women smokers is low. However, the rising pressures on young women to smoke (advertising, celebrity models, false notions of sophistication) need to be counteracted quickly.

> Richard Peto, a leading Oxford epidemiologist, has predicted that 'of all the children alive today in China under the age of 20 years, 50 million will eventually be killed by tobacco'. This is a powerful statistic in a country with a one-child policy.[35]

Cervical cancer ☐ In developing countries the most frequent cancer for women is cancer of the cervix. It is estimated that there are more than 350,000 new cases each year.[36] Cervical cancer can almost always be treated successfully by surgery or radiotherapy if detected early, before symptoms appear. Therefore large-scale screening programmes (by taking vaginal smears) are the only way at present to prevent sickness and death from cervical cancer. Where such programmes have been functioning effectively and treatment is available, mortality from cervical cancer has fallen 50–60 per cent.[37]

Setting up effective screening programmes in developing countries presents many challenges: there is a shortage of the technical skills, resources and laboratories needed, and they are clustered in the urban area. The same low-risk women tend to get screened repeatedly while the vast majority in the most high-risk categories are not screened at all. It has been suggested that existing health structures such as the MCH and family planning (FP) systems could be used to collect the smears, but the age focus of MCH/FP programmes is on younger women, not the older women who most need screening.

More than 60 per cent of the cervical cancers in developing countries now are not detected until they are at a rather advanced stage. Screening programmes are therefore to be encouraged wherever possible, making sure they are effectively organized to reach the most at-risk groups of women and with clear responsibility for follow-up. Studies on screening show that where coverage was good and women were screened once every three years, there was a 91 per cent reduction in risk. Even screening each woman every ten years resulted in a 64 per cent reduction in risk.

The other opportunity for taking action on cervical cancer is to get at the causes. The risk of cervical cancer is greater in women who begin sexual activity at an early age (yet another reason for doing away with early marriages). That risk is increased by having multiple partners or by having a partner who has had multiple partners. Barrier method contraceptives (diaphragm and condom) offer some protection. Smoking also appears to be a risk factor, although a causal relationship has not been clearly established.[38]

Breast cancer ☐ Breast cancer is the leading cause of cancer death among women in most developed countries and in many developing countries. Treatment is less successful than for cervical cancer. There has been an increase of 22 per cent in breast cancer mortality over the past two decades. Again, early detection is vital. Three methods are used: examination by a trained physician; mammography (X-ray screening); and self-examination. A 1988 article in the WHO publication *World Health* offers these recommendations:

Women over twenty years should examine their breasts regularly every month. Periodic examinations by a physician, in combination with an annual mammogram for women over fifty, are also recommended where possible. Women with a family history of breast cancer should consider a more intensive screening programme.[39]

The combination of examination by a physician and regular mammograms has proved effective in reducing mortality from breast cancer, but screening programmes of this type are expensive and not yet available to the vast majority of the women in the world. While we work towards that goal, all women could benefit from learning the techniques of breast self-examination.

Although self-examination is reported to be less effective than mammography or examination by a trained physician, it is a valuable approach, particularly in countries which cannot afford sophisticated screening services for the entire female population at risk. Breast self-examination is simple, inexpensive, non-invasive and non-hazardous. It also encourages women to take responsibility for their own health.[40]

Cancer pain relief ☐ Looking at the totality of cancers that affect women, one-third of cancers could be *prevented* if women were armed with the right knowledge, had access to proper diets and could avoid environmental hazards and the use of tobacco (smoking and chewing of tobacco quids). Another one-third of all cancer cases could be *cured* if detected and treated early enough.

The remaining one-third of cancer patients could and should benefit from recent advances in cancer pain relief. The knowledge and methods exist, yet an estimated one-third of suffering cancer patients in the developed countries do not get adequate relief. In developing countries that is the case for the great majority. This is especially regrettable since most cancer patients in developing countries are incurable at the time of diagnosis.

The obstacles to more widespread relief of cancer pain are: lack of physicians and health workers trained in pain control; scarcity of drugs; drug legislation that unnecessarily restricts the use of certain drugs; lack of public awareness that pain can be controlled. Cost is also a factor in some places. (See the Resource Guide in Annexe V for information on the WHO booklet, *Cancer Pain Relief.*)

SEXUALLY TRANSMITTED DISEASES –AIDS □ Amongst the many sexually transmitted diseases (STDs), the AIDS epidemic—with its high media profile—is the subject of most controversy and public concern.

In the context of HIV and AIDS, special attention should be given to the human rights of women. This is justified by the reproductive role of women, and a subordinate role in some societies which makes them particularly vulnerable to HIV infection, as well as affecting their access both to knowledge about AIDS and the steps they may take to protect themselves.
HUMAN RIGHTS NEWSLETTER[41]

The emergence of HIV/AIDS in what are already health-compromised populations highlights not only the vulnerability of mothers and children, but

also the concomitant social stresses that have traditionally been imposed on them . . .
WORLD HEALTH ORGANIZATION[42]

To put it simply: the AIDS epidemic could just erase whatever progress has been made in women's health over the past decade. We are all familiar with the ever-rising figures. Now it is clear that the number of HIV-infected women will surpass the number of men within a few years. By the end of 1992, over 600,000 cases of AIDS will have occurred among women. More than three million women are now infected with the virus. About 25–30 per cent of babies born to HIV-positive mothers will also be infected with the virus.[43]

If there can be any bright side to the AIDS epidemic, it is perhaps what is reflected in the two quotations at the beginning of this section: the impact of AIDS on women and children has forced large sectors of the public to recognize not only the 'vulnerability' of women but the socio-cultural, economic and status factors that keep them that way. It is all played out with dramatic effect around AIDS. From the point of view of women's health, AIDS has been a grim but effective attention-getting device.

In an article explaining why AIDS is a special threat to women and why it is particularly difficult for them to protect themselves against it, Dr Rosmarie Erben writes:

The condom is seen at present as the only effective preventive measure against sexual transmission of HIV. Yet, for many women—whatever the cultural context—to suggest to their husband or partner that he use a condom is seen as evidence of the woman's infidelity or is felt by the man as defiance or insolence. This results at best in painful discussions and a breach in the relationship, or at worst in the woman being beaten and

abandoned. In cultures where the married woman is traditionally expected to bear many children, insisting on safer sex or refusing to engage in sexual relationship is impossible.[44]

From the latest WHO figures, 'It is estimated that, during the 1990s, AIDS will kill 1.5 to three million women of reproductive age in Central and East Africa, producing several million orphans.'[45] Such large-scale social disruption will put an unprecedented strain on families and social services alike. Even in regions where the extended family support system is strong, and where relatives could always be counted upon to care for orphans, some communities are beginning to find themselves overwhelmed by the sheer numbers of parentless children and sick adults.

It is clear that AIDS is putting additional burdens on women in their role as health care providers. Dr Renée Danziger, in an article in *World Health*, points out some of the effects on women individually and as professional health care providers: 'Called upon to care for family members and friends with AIDS, they face physical, emotional and social stress from watching a loved one, often in the prime of life, weaken and then die. Professional care providers working with people with AIDS are subject to similar pressures, as testified by the cases of "burn out".'[46]

The article by Elizabeth Reid that is reprinted on the following pages focuses on young women and is valuable in identifying the many background factors that put women at risk of HIV infection.

Other sexually transmitted diseases □ The other STDs tend to be overshadowed by the drama and media coverage surrounding AIDS. This must not be allowed to happen. The dimensions of this problem are enormous. An estimated 250 million sexually transmitted infections occur each year, and the number is increasing.

More than 20 disease agents are transmitted sexually, and all can have serious repercussions on women's health, as well as the health of their children and sexual partners. For one thing, the ulcerative conditions often associated with STDs facilitate the transmission of the AIDS virus. STDs contribute to the incidence of blindness, brain damage, pelvic inflammation, spontaneous abortions (miscarriages), ectopic pregnancies and cervical cancer. They are a major cause of infertility.

'Some 17% of women who have pelvic infection for the first time and are treated for it subsequently develop tubal obstruction and infertility. This figure rises to more than 50% if the woman has three or more episodes of infection ... In England and Wales an annual total of 83,000 cases of pelvic infection in women can be expected to result in about 8,600 cases of infertility due to tubal obstruction and 2,750 cases of ectopic pregnancy ... In sub-Saharan Africa up to 85% of primary infertility in women and 20% of infertility in men can be attributed to previous genital tract infection, and the rate of tubal occlusion is three times that in developed countries.'[47]

THE ANNUAL TOTAL OF SEXUALLY TRANSMITTED INFECTIONS: 250 MILLION NEW CASES

DISEASE	1990
Trichomoniasis	120 million
Genital Chlamydia	50 million
Genital Papillomavirus	30 million
Gonorrhoea	25 million
Genital Herpes	20 million
HIV infection	1 million
Syphilis	3.5 million
Chancroid	2 million

Source: *World Health Organization, 1990*

YOUNG WOMEN AND THE HIV EPIDEMIC

Elizabeth Reid looks at how women increasingly are affected by the HIV epidemic. Sharp increases in new infections are occurring among women and youth. It is estimated that over one-third of those presently infected are women and over one-half are youth under the age 25. A large proportion of these youth were infected during adolescence. She examines the factors which make young women vulnerable to infection—poverty and homelessness, social and geographical mobility, sexual assault, civil unrest and, in particular, the way societies construct gender, masculinity and femininity.

The HIV epidemic is a women's epidemic: women are particularly vulnerable to infection and increasing numbers of women are becoming infected. It is estimated that one-third of all those thought to be infected—about 2 million —are women. It is also estimated that the number of infected women may overtake the number of infected men by the mid-90s. Already in sub-Saharan Africa there are more women than men infected. Studies in Central African Republic, Equatorial Guinea and Gabon show nearly three times as many women infected as men. In Honduras, Haiti, the Dominican Republic, the Bahamas and Trinidad and Tobago, the male to female ratios of reported AIDS cases, the last stage of HIV infection, have dropped rapidly in the last three years from over 6:1 to under 2.5:1.

It is also an epidemic of youth. At least half of all those infected are under the age of 25 and a large proportion of these young adults were infected during adolescence. Recent studies indicate that the infection rate in some teenage groups is far higher than that for adults. The number of reported AIDS cases in teen-agers has increased rapidly over the last two years.

Data are not available on the number of young women infected. However, women are constituting an increasing proportion of all AIDS cases and often women become infected at a younger age than men. A Zairian study reported that among young adults aged 15 to 30 years, HIV infection was four times more common in women than in men. These are bleak and disturbing facts. Infection rates in pregnant women in high incidence countries in Central and Eastern Africa range from 10 to 25 percent. High infection rates in women will cause a sharp increase in maternal and child morbidity and mortality rates. Maternal mortality rates in developing countries are already 12 times higher than in the developed world, the greatest gap in any human indicator.

The overwhelming majority of infected young women do not know they are infected. Most young women are diagnosed during pregnancy or at birth. To the shock of discovering their own infection status is added the fear that their baby might be infected, guilt and grief at having brought all this about and the desolation of motherhood in these circumstances.

TRANSMISSION

The HIV virus may be transmitted sexually through anal, vaginal or oral intercourse with an infected person. Sexual transmission can be prevented through the proper use of a good quality condom. Young women in most parts of the developing world are sexually active. Data on adolescent sexuality in developing countries indicate that the initial sexual contact occurs before age 17 for half of the population and by age 15 for ▶

one-third of adolescents. In Jamaica, Nigeria and Sierra Leone, more than four out of five single women aged 20 years are sexually experienced. In Mexico and Costa Rica, from about one-fifth to one-fourth of single adolescents are sexually experienced by age 20. Condom use is not common. Studies show that in four countries (Costa Rica, the Gambia, Jamaica and Zimbabwe), the condom was the most frequently used contraceptive at first intercourse. However, in general, use at first intercourse is very low. Condom usage in unmarried women aged 15 to 19 years in 15 countries studied is low but second to the pill in most African countries and in Jamaica, Peru and Thailand. Thus there are in the developing world, many young women at risk of infection through unprotected sexual behaviour.

HIV transmission may also occur through the sharing of drug-using equipment with an infected individual. Protection can be achieved through not sharing needles, through the cleaning of shared needles or through changing the mode of use away from intravenous administration. Fewer young women than young men are at risk of infection through drug injecting since, in almost all drug-using communities, men predominate. Young women are however at significant risk of infection through an unprotected sexual intercourse with infected current or past drug users. It is virtually impossible to know whether another person is HIV infected, certainly during the long period of infection before symptoms appear. Even HIV testing only tells the infection status of a person at an earlier period of time and not at the present. In the case of sexual behaviour and intravenous drug use, only each individual can take the necessary steps to protect themselves from infection. The responsibility of governments is to make people aware of the epidemic and the modes of transmission of the virus, to ensure that the means of preventing infection—condoms, sterile needles, bleach—are affordable and of easy access, and to minimize the possibility of iatrogenic and occupational transmission.

Young women can also become infected iatrogenically through the medical use of non-sterile needles, through the trans-fusion of contaminated blood or blood products and rarely, through the use of infected human tissue or organs in surgical procedures. In many parts of the developing world, needles are commonly used in both the modern and traditional health sectors, without any or sufficient sterilization. Adolescent pregnancy can place young women at further risk of infection from blood transfusion or unsterile needles. The extent of iatrogenic transmission has not been adequately studied, but women and young children are at high risk from this form of transmission.

VULNERABILITY TO HIV INFECTION
There are many factors affecting the lives of young women which make them vulnerable to HIV infection while there are few data available to determine the extent of that vulnerability; the following discussion can serve to indicate areas for further research in this area. Prevalence patterns of HIV infection are known to be a factor of poverty, social and geographic mobility, commerce, tourism, social disruption and civil unrest.

Sexually transmitted diseases and adolescent pregnancy
The presence of sexually transmitted diseases, particularly ulcerative ▶

99

conditions, increases the likelihood of infection in both men and women when intercourse occurs with an infected partner. STDs are common amongst young women, particularly in Africa, the Caribbean and Latin America. They are not easy to detect in women and so most women remain unaware of their presence. Studies in Central Africa have shown that in some communities up to one-third of women in their child bearing years are infertile, with 80 per cent of that infertility being caused by STDs. Drug use is also increasing in some parts, particularly in the Caribbean. The incidence may be much lower in sub-Saharan Africa; however, this epidemic carries within it the seeds of violence. Although rape is traditionally uncommon in sub-Saharan Africa, there are increasing reports of the rape of young women by older men in high HIV-incidence countries. This is clearly associated with the belief that the younger the woman, the more she is likely to be free from HIV infection. The raped young woman, however, is at high risk of infection, particularly since reports indicate that the attackers are usually either sexually promiscuous men who do not want to change their behaviour or, increasingly, may be men who have lost their wives, possibly to AIDS, who are fearful of taking another wife.

Sex tourism is an expression of the power of men from rich countries to purchase the sexual services of young women in developing countries. Asia is a favoured destination. The young women and their families are placed at grave risk of infection. Most data from Asia show higher levels of HIV infection in young women servicing this trade than in the general community. Similarly, studies show high rates of infection among prostitutes servicing military bases.

Geographic and social mobility

There is a high correlation in men between mobility and HIV infection; truck drivers, soldiers and traders in Africa have extremely high infection levels. Geographic mobility of young girls would also lead to increased risk. Again very few statistics are available but at least one study has shown that 70 per cent of rural to urban migrants are under the age of 25, and 40 per cent under the age of 16. Young girls under the age of 15 seeking schooling and employment predominate in rural to urban migration in many Latin American countries, in some African countries such as Ghana and Morocco, and in Asian countries such as Bangladesh, India, Indonesia and the Philippines. Studies of international migration show the increasing involvement of women, and of young women. A significant proportion of the young women who migrate to European countries from Asia and Africa end up in prostitution. Mail order brides are also another migratory group of young women at risk of infection.

Another particularly vulnerable group are women who live in conditions of civil unrest or war. In parts of Central and Eastern Africa, patterns of infection in women correlate with the movements over the last decade of soldiers and other military personnel.

Increased female education and increased employment opportunities for young women in developing countries have resulted in a trend towards later marriages, especially among urban, educated young women. While this may have the effect of lowering overall birth rates, it also results in an increased period of potential exposure to the risks of pregnancy and HIV infection. ▶

Poverty and homelessness

The group of young women most vulnerable to HIV infection are those who are homeless or living in poverty. UNICEF estimates that over 40 million young people in the world are living on the streets. Many of those have left home because of sexual abuse or poverty.

Studies from Africa, Latin America and North America show alarming rates of infection in this group. In Sao Paulo, Brazil, nearly 9 percent of 8,000 children tested in 1988 in state institutions were HIV positive. With an estimate of 7 million homeless children living on the streets in Brazil, authorities estimate that 146,000 children may already be infected. Child prostitution is common and girls of 9 to 10 work as prostitutes, often just for comfort, food or shelter. In New York City, in one 1988 study of more than 1,100 young men and women aged 16 to 21 living on the street, over 7 percent were HIV positive. Since almost none of them injected drugs, transmission would have occurred sexually. In Khartoum, a 1988 study of street boys aged 6 to 14 showed 7 percent of them to be infected.

Increasingly poverty is becoming a female phenomenon. More women are heading households or are their main financial providers; more women and their children are living in poverty. The coping options for women, young girls and children living in poverty are few, and none rival prostitution as an economic survival strategy. Nowadays, however, it is in many parts of the world a virtual death sentence for the woman and the children they love and support. Levels of HIV infection among women working as prostitutes in some Central and Eastern African towns and cities are as high as 80 or 90 percent. However

there is evidence of a decrease in new infections among these women as they organize to protect themselves and to educate and protect their clients. A growing number of non-governmental organizations, especially in Latin America, are assisting them with the education of their clients.

Even where women working as prostitutes adopt the use of condoms as a protective measure for themselves and their clients, they often fail to use them in their personal sexual relationships. This failure may arise from a belief that it is romantic love which distinguishes their commercial from personal sexual activities or from the subordinate relationship that so often exists between them and their pimps who are often their lovers.

INFECTED YOUNG WOMEN

Diagnosis of HIV infection in a young woman means not only the possibility of illness and death but also that choices about sexuality, motherhood, marriage, education and work become fraught with fear and pain. Infection too often means social isolation, loneliness and discrimination. It brings fear: the fear of losing one's job, housing, medical care and dental care; fear of losing family, friends and partner; fear for the future of one's children, both infected and not infected. Disclosure of one's infection status has a high price.

For a young woman, a diagnosis of HIV infection brings with it an anguished choice to forgo children or to risk giving birth to an infected baby. For young women in cultures where their social identity and acceptability is determined by their fertility, there may not even be this choice. The sexual expression of love may become difficult either for the infected woman or her part- ▶

ner. Relationships become difficult to enter and to maintain.

Infected young women with an infected child will need to cope with their own fatigue and sickness as well as the child's. It is estimated that infected women in sub-Saharan Africa have given birth to 600,000 children. Of these, about 200,000 become infected during pregnancy; the remaining 400,000 children, as well as the others that live, will have mothers that will sicken and die early in their lifetimes. One estimate is that, by the year 2000, 10 percent of children in 10 high incidence African countries will be without mothers as a result of this epidemic. Enough is known about the impact of protracted illness and death on households to be able to glimpse the impoverishment and suffering that will ensue for these children.

This is a sad picture and reflects the reality, but not its totality. An infected young woman has years, often a decade or more, of healthy life ahead of her after infection. She, and those around her, need to ensure that she can remain an integral part of the community of social and economic use. She, and they, will have special counselling and educational needs, and will require supportive programmes, including at a later stage childcare and household services to assist them.

THE PREVENTION OF HIV INFECTION IN YOUNG WOMEN

We have knowingly lived with this epidemic for a decade now. As we look back over our efforts we can identify a number of principles that have shaped our response to it.

Firstly, responsibility for prevention of infection by, or further transmission of the virus through, sexual or drug-using behaviour lies ultimately with the individual. Others, family, friends, governments, can only provide an environment which may assist individuals to change behaviour. They cannot change it for them.

Secondly, community-based organizations, that is, organizations drawn from or based within communities most at risk of infection, have a vital role to play in responding to this epidemic by:

—drawing up education and prevention programmes appropriate and acceptable to their own members;

—providing support, counselling and care to HIV-infected people and their partners, families and friends;

—providing information, support and counselling to communities to assist them to minimize HIV transmission, and lessen discrimination and stigma.

Thirdly, prevention and care policies and programmes can only be effectively implemented where the cooperation and trust of those infected or at risk of infection are maintained.

Our challenge now is to apply this understanding to the young women of our societies. We must acknowledge their vulnerability to infection. Not an easy task for parents, community leaders or governments. We must ensure that they themselves can acknowledge their vulnerability to infection. Maybe an even more difficult task.

Perhaps the task most difficult of all, once this awareness of vulnerability is created, will be to give young women the self-confidence and skills required to change their behaviour and to choose or create relationships based on mutual concern and respect. This freedom of choice depends on improving women's economic independence and on changes occurring in the ways societies construct gender, both masculinity and femin- ▶

inity, and sexuality. Otherwise, for young women, HIV infection will be a direct outcome of their social, personal and economic subordination.

Elizabeth Reid (Director of the Division for Women in Development, UNDP, New York, USA) as featured in Journal of the Society for International Development, *Development* 1990: 1, Young Women: Production/ Reproduction and Life Choices

Two of the bacterial infections that can lead to infertility, gonorrhoea and chlamydia, often do not produce clear-cut symptoms in women and girls, so they are not aware that they are infected. Chlamydia is the most common sexually transmitted infection in developed countries and may be responsible for 60–80 per cent of cases of tubal obstruction worldwide.[48]

One of the papers given at the October 1987 meeting on 'Better Health for Women and Children Through Family Planning' concentrates on the effects among young people:

Adolescents aged 15-19 years and young adults from 20-24 years bear a disproportionate share of the increase in reported cases of syphilis and gonorrhoea . . . A young woman may be rendered sterile before she has married or had a child. STDs can damage men also . . . partially or completely blocking the passage of sperm, and producing other health problems as well. Family planning can provide adolescents with information and counselling on sexually transmitted diseases and their long-term consequences. Some contraceptives, most notably condoms, offer protection against STDs.[49]

Women need much more education and information about STDs than they are getting now, and they must be accompanied by more ready access to diagnostic and therapeutic services. Men tend to seek diagnosis and treatment earlier because their symptoms are more obvious and because it is usually easier for them to go to the health facilities where treatment is available.

STDs in women take a heavy toll on children also. Reproductive tract infections put the unborn child at risk of low birthweight, congenital abnormalities, blindness, pneumonia, retardation and even death. In one country it is estimated that between 35 and 50 per cent of stillbirths are due to syphilis. In another, when maternal syphilis was reduced by 40 per cent over a five-year period, there was a two-thirds reduction in 'adverse pregnancy outcome'.[50] WHO, UNICEF and other international organizations and NGOs are working together to give higher priority to maternal syphilis control programmes and other STD prevention and treatment programmes.

OCCUPATIONAL HEALTH ☐ The games and songs of children may reveal more about our societies than is altogether comfortable:

**This is the way we wash our clothes,
Wash our clothes, wash our clothes.
This is the way we wash our clothes,
So early in the morning.**

The 'we' in this Anglo-Saxon ditty is certainly understood to refer to women, and 'early in the morning' is realistically when women need to (and are expected to) get started on their work.

One reason work can be hazardous to the health of women is that they do so much of it. The International Labour Organisation estimates that women put in two-thirds of the world's working hours. Studies from very different regions and countries invari-

ably find that women work, on average, one to three hours per day longer than the men in the same society, whatever the number of hours the men put in. Such long hours of work, whether at home or in the paid labour force, or both, leave women with little time for sleep or relaxation. This may lead to chronic fatigue and contribute to malnutrition, stress, premature ageing and other health problems. In many parts of the world, action plans to improve women's health start with steps to reduce their workload.

Women's health is affected by how *much* they work, to be sure, but also by the *kinds* of work they do. As mentioned earlier, smoke from biomass fuels such as dung endangers millions of women who cook for their families over open fires. At home or outside the home, women often have no choice but to do the work that no one else will do—heavy work, dirty work, monotonous, unpaid or low-paid work that involves long hours of standing, stooping,

bending, or carrying heavy loads. And they must continue working regardless of their physical condition.

A study in India found that 'there was a high incidence of stillbirths, premature births and deaths during the peak rice cultivation season. At this time when rice is being transplanted, everyone, including women whose pregnancy is almost full-term, are in the fields the whole day. The work involves squatting and bending for hours. Such physical strain and pressure in the uterus can lead to premature labour as well as stillbirths.'[51]

Women who work as agricultural labourers or plantation workers may be exposed to harmful pesticides used without proper safeguards. Each year, according to WHO estimates, 'more than 500,000 farm workers, pesticide plant employees and children become seriously ill, and about 5,000 to 20,000 people die from exposure to toxic insecticides'.[52]

Products that are banned or tightly con-

Women and work

A WOMAN'S WORK IS NEVER DONE

A day in the life of a typical rural African woman

20.30-21.30
Wash children and dishes

21.30
To bed

4.45
Wake up wash and eat

5.00-5.30
Walk to fields

18.30-20.30
Cook for family and eat

5.30-15.00
Work in fields

17.30-18.30
Collect water

16.00-17.30
Pound and grind corn

15.00-16.00
Collect firewood return home

trolled in industrialized countries are sometimes freely sold and used in developing countries. The warnings on the label about protective clothing, face masks, immediate access to washing facilities, training of operators, need for regular health check-ups . . . all those warnings are futile if they are ignored by the employer, or if the users are illiterate, unable to understand the language of the label, or simply fatalistic about

'The Third World uses 20 per cent of the world's pesticides but suffers half the poisoning cases and three-quarters of the deaths.'[53]

what happens to their own health and that of co-workers.

Women farm workers, usually poor, uneducated, and in desperate need of work, are not in a good position to protest against dangerous conditions even when accidents occur or they suspect that their health is

being affected. However, awareness of this problem is growing, and women's organizations, environmental groups, consumer unions and other groups around the world are pressing for action on the question.

Urban women face other types of health risks associated with their work, especially women at the lowest socio-economic levels. Typically they have few qualifications and few choices as to where they can work. They must take what they can get. Desperate not to lose their jobs once they have them, they put up with working conditions that expose them to a variety of dangers.

A study in Latin America found that as more mid-life women joined the work force, 'accidents were among the top five causes of death in women aged 50–59 in 11 out of the 18 countries surveyed'. In five countries this was true for women over 65 as well. The women were mostly working in textile, footwear, food production, electronics and handicrafts industries.

Excessive heat, light and noise added to the hazards, as well as exposure to toxic chemicals and radiation.[55]

Then there is the 'invisible' work force—women who do piece-work at home or who are self-employed in other ways. They do sewing, embroidery, rug-weaving. They are batik workers. Isolated from each other, not in a position to bargain, they earn very little for long, long hours of work. But that little may be critical for their families' survival, and in exchange for that they accept the inevitable eye problems, backaches, lack of sleep, stress and even more serious consequences. But in some instances these women, too, have joined together and are

JAMILAH

Jamilah was only eleven when she began work on a plantation. She did weeding, plucked and opened cocoa pods, sprayed pesticides and carried bunches of oil palm fruit to collecting points. When she was about 16 she often complained of pains in the abdomen and chest. The plantation paramedic dismissed her complaints as 'typical of most malingerers' and the most he would prescribe her were antacids. Before she reached 18, Jamilah died of a form of respiratory cancer.[54]

bringing about change, for example the Self-Employed Workers' Association (SEWA) in India.

Also in India is the Working Women's Forum. The Forum supports local initiatives like that of the lacemakers in Narasapur, who organized to oppose a private monopoly, or the migrant Tamil women workers in Bangalore who joined forces to resist exploitative pay scales.

An international network enables these local and national groups to exchange information and experience. The network has been one of the goals of Women Working Worldwide, a group of women in Britain who 'support the struggles of women workers through information exchange, international networking and public education'. They have gathered women workers' testimonies about dangerous or exploitative working conditions, concentrating especially on the clothing, textile and microelectronics industries because they employ so many women.[56]

Other types of action to help women avoid the health problems associated with work are:

• Reducing women's workload by promoting appropriate technology (more efficient stoves, making it easier to get water, mills to grind corn, and so on).

• Encouraging more equal sharing of the workload between women and men in all spheres, including child care, domestic chores and work outside the home.

• Supporting women workers as they organize to demand better working conditions from their employers.

• Getting women into positions where they can make their voices heard in the planning and management of work and the workplace.

• Pressing for passage and enforcement of labour laws and regulations that respond to the health needs of women workers, including reproductive health needs and the safety of unborn children.

There has been much debate on special protective measures for women and how such measures can be reconciled with equality of opportunity and treatment. A report from the International Labour Organisation observes: 'Many of these [countries] consider that, on balance, special protective measures for women workers are necessary. In others, the issues . . . give rise to controversy. Some countries have resolved conflicts between equality and protection by eliminating special protection or by defining some protection as essential to equality.'[57] A women's health collective approaches the issue from a different perspective. In reviewing company policies that bar women of 'child-bearing potential' from areas where they might be exposed to chemicals harmful to foetuses, it found that:

. . . the result is that women have lost access to jobs that were only recently opened to them. It is no coincidence that such policies do not exist in companies or institutions which employ a largely female labor force, such as hospitals or the electronics industry. When studies found that anesthetic gases cause spontaneous abortions, hospitals didn't ban women workers from

operating rooms. Instead they installed devices that eliminated the problem.

. . . exposures which may be harmful to a fetus are also harmful to an adult. Barring women from jobs instead of cleaning up the workplace diverts energy and attention from the real issue: the need to protect all workers from reproductive and other health hazards.[58]

WOMEN WITH DISABILITIES □ For both sexes, coping with disability can be a difficult enough task; but

. . . to be female and disabled in our society is a double drawback.

JO CAMPLING, UNITED KINGDOM[59]

If this is true for a disabled woman in one of the more affluent countries of the world, how much more true it is for women whose disability is combined with being poor, illiterate, malnourished, living in the rural area of a developing country, or being a refugee or migrant.

No one knows how many women there are with disabilities. The usual estimate is that one person in every ten has a significant disability. Probably more than half of them are women. This is because women live longer and experience the disabilities associated with old age, because they are subject to disabling complications from childbirth, and because certain disabling diseases (such as multiple sclerosis) and conditions (anaemia) strike women more often than men.

Another book in this series, *Women and Disability*,[60] contains many testimonies from women with disabilities and makes clear the great diversity in this group, in the type and degree of disability they have, in the circumstances in which they live, in the degree of independence they have been able to achieve. Yet one conclusion is common to all of them: having a disability will, in

the words of Ms Campling, 'mean a significant change in the way a woman sees herself and is seen by others'.[61]

Causes of disability □ Several of the causes of disability are *nutritional*. One hundred million people are thought to be disabled in some way because of nutritional deficiencies. This includes anaemia (that famous thief of energy and vitality), lack of iodine (which produces goitre and mental deficiency), and shortage of Vitamin A (which can lead to blindness and even death). Girls and women are, of course, more likely to experience nutritional deficiencies.

Accidents in the home, in the work place and on the road are a major cause of disability among women, and the toll is rising in developing countries.

Preventable childhood diseases such as poliomyelitis and measles still contribute to the numbers of disabled persons, although the proportion of disabilities arising from these diseases is declining as progress continues in the WHO/UNICEF Expanded Programme of Immunization and the NGO programmes that are co-ordinated with it.

Other causes of disability among women include pelvic inflammation, which may generate crippling back pain, and female circumcision. A mother's use of harmful substances during pregnancy or the complications of labour can result in children being born with birth injuries and permanent disability.

Effects of disability in women □ Each woman experiences disability differently. There are, however, certain common themes in the testimonies of disabled women throughout the world. Some examples:

• For women in traditional societies, disability may lead to complete isolation or abandonment. Where the causes of dis-

PHOTO: PETER KLEIN PEDERSON

ability are not understood and there is shame, superstition or stigma attached to it, the disabled person is often hidden away. This reduces the chances of being taken for treatment or rehabilitation, doubly so if the disabled person is female. Where marriages are arranged, the disabled young woman may not be considered 'marriageable', and thus the status, the social identity of being a wife and mother, is denied her. Though the process may be more subtle in less traditional societies, disabled women there report similar experiences—the expectations of society put obstacles in the way of their enjoying their sexuality and their right to marriage and motherhood.

- In countries where the opportunities for girls to be educated are limited, the chances of a young girl with a disability will be even fewer. Parents may be more reluctant to pay the fees or feel that they must keep their disabled daughter at home to protect her (an attitude widespread in all societies). Simple problems of mobility prevent many disabled girls from getting an education. If they do start school, disabled girls and women get less encouragement to go on with their studies. They are socialized, perhaps even more strongly than other women in their society, to conform to the stereotype of women as dependent stay-at-homes literally 'tending to their knitting'.

- Disabled women find that it is assumed that a disabled male should learn some skill or profession that will enable him to earn a living. The same assumption is not made about women with disabilities. Vocational rehabilitation programmes are generally male-oriented. Employment programmes for disabled people often have the same bias. A woman with a disability has to be twice as qualified in order to get in an employer's door.

- Disabled women are rather frequently victims of rape and violence, sometimes because they are assumed to be less able to resist, or in the case of women with mental disability because they are thought not to understand what is happening or be able to give credible testimony about it afterwards. Disabled wives who are victims of domestic violence are even less likely than other women to leave their abusive husbands, presumably because of their 'double dependency'.

- Universally, disabled women find the attitudes of society harder to deal with, and more disabling, than the disability itself. 'It isn't that one *is* disabled, but that one is *turned into* a disabled person by society.' 'Disability is not so much a physical condition as a psycho-social crisis.'[62] Women who have become disabled as adults describe the severe assault on their self-image as the world suddenly begins to treat them as if they were children (incapable of thinking for themselves), as if they were asexual, and as if their inability to do certain things, not the many abilities that they still have, was the most important part of their identity now.

Prevention of disability □ The measures that prevent disabilities are easy to describe but not easy to realize. They include many of the measures suggested elsewhere in this book for improving the general state of women's health: better nutrition; reduction of women's work-load; clean water and improved sanitation; prenatal care and trained attendants at childbirth; elimination of female circumcision; safety at home, in the work place and on

the road. More education for women would undoubtedly reduce disabilities in their children. If a disability did occur, having an educated mother would improve the chances of early detection and facilitate the rehabilitation process, keeping the impact of the impairment to a minimum.

But one familiar recommendation is basic to preventing disability and reducing its effects in the lives of women: a move on all fronts to improve the status of women.

Treatment and rehabilitation for women with disabilities □ The past decade has produced definite prospects for a better future for women with disabilities. The most important of these is undoubtedly the multiplication of *self-help* initiatives among them. In every region of the world disabled women are getting together in formal and informal groups, deciding what it is they need to accomplish and getting it done with independence and initiative. They work on their own and in cooperation with other associations of disabled and non-disabled women and men, nationally and internationally. Many women are active in Disabled People International.

Support for their initiatives has come from inter-governmental organizations and from NGOs of all types—women's groups, youth groups, development groups, and agencies working for and with disabled persons.

The International Labour Organisation has a project that will help disabled women to take part in developmental and skills-training programmes in Southern Africa so that they will be better able to earn a living. Mobility aids and a revolving loan scheme will supply the disabled women with the little extra support they need in order to participate. It is important to note that they will not be in a special programme but will be working alongside their non-disabled colleagues in programmes designed to

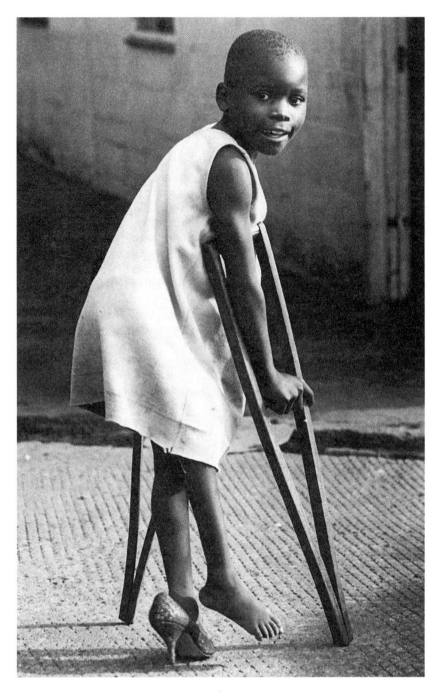

PHOTO: MIKE WELLS / UNICEF

increase income-generating capabilities. UNICEF targets both women and children in its immunization and nutrition work, as part of the drive for early detection and prevention of disability.

WHO and UNICEF support the exten-

111

sion of community-based rehabilitation (CBR). This concept is a positive development for women with disabilities, just as the PHC concept is good news for women in general, and for many of the same reasons. CBR is designed to make treatment accessible to all disabled people, in the communities where they live. This is important for women, who are often not allowed to travel any distance for treatment. CBR stresses community participation. Properly implemented, it empowers women in much the same way as PHC does, recognizing the work they have traditionally done in caring for the disabled. It gives women the knowledge and support they need in order to train people with disabilities and help them move towards independence. As in PHC, there is need for a secondary referral level with more sophisticated facilities and specialized personnel to support the workers at the primary level.

Many NGOs have led the way in introducing and promoting CBR and other programmes that have greatly benefited women with disabilities: Rehabilitation International; League of Red Cross and Red Crescent Societies; national and international associations for and of the blind. One particularly helpful contribution has been that of the World Association of Girl Guides and Girl Scouts. Their national and local affiliates have made a long, sustained effort to integrate girls with disabilities into their membership and see that they are really part of everything that goes on.

ELDERLY WOMEN □ The 'greying' of populations, a well-known phenomenon in the industrialized world, is fast becoming a feature of developing countries too.

The ageing of populations, once the 'privilege of comparatively few' societies, is now a prospect for more and more people throughout the world.

WHO FEATURES[63]

By 2020 the total population in developing nations is expected to increase by around 95 per cent, while the number of elderly persons will probably be 240 per cent greater than it was in 1980. The increase will be greatest in the oldest age group (over 80), the group where women will predominate for some time to come.

One effect of this increased longevity is to increase women's risk of chronic illness as they age . . . Although elderly men die at a higher rate, elderly women are most often disabled . . . partly because most of the common chronic diseases may persist for many years before they cause death, and women are more likely to live long enough to experience their disabling consequences. The chronic, non-fatal illnesses associated with aging include such potentially disabling problems as arthritis, hypertension, diabetes and osteoporosis. Also, the likelihood of encountering such age-related changes as diminished hearing and vision is greater among women as more of them live long enough to experience these problems.[64]

Not only health system planners, but planners in related social sectors, should be aware of the needs *and* potential contributions of older women. There are numerous examples in every society of the contributions older women make as health care providers or child care providers, as breadwinners (mostly in the informal sector), as workers in various community programmes, and as keepers and transmitters of the culture. Older women need good health in order to make these contributions. Conversely, for many of them, being able to contribute, to be active and giving, is vital to their psychological and emotional health.

There are some indications from research that while women live longer, men may

PHOTO: UNICEF/RUBY MERA

actually enjoy a longer 'active life', free from functional disabilities. Further research is needed on this. It is difficult to know how much of the difference between women and men of the same age is inherent in their sex and how much is due to early life history, the circumstances of women's old age, or even to the definition of what is 'functional'.

The combination of poverty, isolation and ill-health is seen in the lives of millions of older women throughout the world. It can be a deadly combination. The situation of older women varies from country to country for reasons linked to culture, the stage of development and social organization. At present, elderly women in rural areas of developing countries are likely to

be living with their families, although this is changing as young people emigrate to urban areas. In developed countries one finds a higher proportion of elderly women living alone.

> '... only 2% of those aged 60 and over in Fiji, Korea and the Philippines live apart from their families. Nearly a third of elderly Americans, however, live alone and nearly half of those aged 75 and over do so. In the United Kingdom, 80% of elderly people living alone are women.'[65]

At a meeting on elderly women in 1985 it was pointed out that being 'old' or 'aged' is relative. Interestingly enough, the elderly people present 'did not consider themselves old, regardless of their age, so long as they remained in good health; being old was only the point of view of others'.[66] One reason for the high value put on health is that it is the key to remaining active, which in turn allows older people to feel that they are participating meaningfully in society. 'Isolation means decline.'

It is hard to define 'health' in the elderly. What is illness and what is 'normal decline'? The ability to function in a given setting, physically, mentally and psycho-logically, can be measured, however, and much of the research on the status of health of the elderly has centred on this aspect.

In industrialized countries, at least, men tend to do better than women of the same age in tests of physical functioning. And because women live longer, as pointed out in the quotation above, they are at greater risk of being disabled at some point in their lives. Some of them will require increasing amounts of care and assistance as they grow older, whether it is provided in the family, in the community or in an institutional setting.

Most of the people who take care of them will of course be women. In the United States adult daughters provide nearly one-third of the long-term care for the elderly. In most cases the elderly parent lives with them. The daughters spend an average of four extra hours per day taking care of the older person, and for most of them it is a seven-day-a-week responsibility.[67]

Other differences are coming to light as more studies on the elderly collect data on women and men separately. A recent study in the United States found that, 'elderly women who had had heart attacks were five times as likely to develop Alzheimer's dis-ease or other dementias as other women of the same age. A similar connection was not seen among men . . . . Dementia was the most important serious illness that developed in men and women after the age

PHOTO: CHANG HONGEN

Reading 'The Road to Longevity' to grandma (China).

75, ahead of heart attacks, strokes and cancer . . . All dementias were three times as common among elderly women as among elderly men in the study.'[68]

These are preliminary findings, but if this link between heart attacks and dementia is confirmed, it is yet another reason for women to adopt the no-smoking, low-fat, plenty-of-exercise lifestyle that is recommended to prevent heart disease.

There have not been too many studies of the health of elderly women in developing countries, but the functional studies that do exist show results similar to those in industrialized countries. Women tend to have somewhat less ability to function adequately than men at the same age. But to a large extent circumstances define functioning and disability. In Indonesia it was found that the functional disability for women most strongly related to age involved fetching water—which was considered a normal part of 'women's work' and therefore was part of an elderly woman's ability to function.[69] If those women had lived in a house with running water or a tap nearby or if fetching water were 'men's work', they would not have been 'disabled'.

In a comprehensive study of mid-life and older women in Latin America and the Caribbean, Lee Sennott-Miller found that such women play a key role in both economic development and family stability. In spite of their subordinate position to men in these patriarchal societies, the older women serve as the economic and emotional mainstay of the family. They contribute to family income, care for grandchildren and sometimes their own elderly parents as well. They are:

. . . often the nucleus around which the entire family is organized. They sustain and are sustained by it. They fill the roles of provider, arbiter, caregiver, disciplinarian, housekeeper, cook,

repair person, family representative to the community, and often decision-maker as well. . . .

What are the implications of this complex situation for the women involved? One clear result of the need to reconcile many conflicting roles, strategies, needs, and demands is stress and the concomitant problems of anxiety, tension, and depression . . . the actual incidence of depression in midlife and older women is unknown [but] . . . apparently not of the epidemic proportions one might expect.

Physical illness occurs, of course, as well. Midlife and older women in Latin America and the Caribbean are afflicted, for the most part, with quite similar conditions as women in the same life stage in developed countries. With the exception of the high incidence of cervical cancer and the persistence of environmental and infectious illness in some areas, the major causes of death are cardiovascular disease, cancer, cerebrovascular disease, diabetes, and pneumonia, very much the same as for their counterparts in the United States and Canada.

Women's life expectancy is increasing in the Region and is expected to exceed an average of 71 years by the year 2000. This will be true despite a workload two to three times that of most women of comparable age in developed countries, as well as a probable history of multiple pregnancies, chronic anaemia, nonexistent preventive care, and inadequate medical services. The ability of midlife and older women in Latin America and the Caribbean to withstand the enormous physical and emotional pressures in their lives is one of the most interesting and heartening findings of the study.[70]

Older women are organizing themselves to work for improvements in their lives, just as other women are. Within the American Association of Retired Persons there is a Women's Initiative, which sponsors, among other projects, the Women's Health

115

PHOTO: JEAN-PHILIPPE DAULTE

Advocacy Project. One of its publications is a lively brochure entitled *Action for a Healthier Life*. The introduction sets the tone: 'Improved women's health means taking ACTION. The next few pages describe some simple steps every woman can take in the areas of Prevention, Detection, and Treatment'. The advice on the last page is to 'reach out', to stay active in the community, sign up for a class, become a volunteer, look around 'for the woman who needs someone to reach out to her'.

HelpAge International (a federation of national organizations of the elderly) supports projects for older women in developing countries and publishes a newsletter with practical tips for the elderly on how to preserve their health and make everyday life easier for themselves. Many articles focus on the needs and solutions to needs found by older women.

REFUGEE AND MIGRANT WOMEN ☐

Being uprooted from one's home is a stressful experience for most people. Even when the decision to go is voluntary and is made in anticipation of a better life ahead, the move to a new country and culture is almost always accompanied by a certain sense of loss and grieving for the family, friends and familiar surroundings left behind. For most uprooted people this is accentuated by the economic, social and psychological difficulties encountered in their new home. There is a potential, even in the best of circumstances, for this experience to have a major impact on the health of the people concerned.

But very few of today's migrants and refugees move 'in the best of circumstances'. Quite the contrary. Groups of refugees and migrants, and especially the women among them, are exposed to extreme physical dangers, psychological trauma and exploitation. Many women come through these difficult experiences with new-found confidence and strengths they had not previously known they possessed. But many suffer a great deal, and unnecessarily. There are measures that

116

A young Guatemalan, who has benefited from health and sanitation education while in exile, helps build a community for returnees in Guatemala.

could be taken to ease the difficulties of being uprooted.

Another book in this series, *Refugee Women*, explores this topic in depth.[71] Here we mention just a few health issues for refugee and migrant women that have not received the attention they deserve.

Many refugee and migrant women feel the double discrimination of being female and being rejected as 'outsiders'. Their deeply held traditions and values may be little understood or respected by the society in which they find themselves.

Another 'given' in the lives of most refugee and migrant women is total uncertainty about the future. 'When will we go back?' 'Will we go back?' For millions of women refugees or displaced persons, however, the basic question about the future is much starker: 'How can we survive today and tomorrow?'

There are currently at least 15 million refugees in the world, roughly 80 per cent of them women and children. If displaced persons and others in refugee-like situations are counted, the number is doubled. Being uprooted and forced to leave their homes represents a crisis for each one of these women; but it also represents an opportunity. For at least some refugee women, exposure to new ideas and experiences leaves them stronger, more self-confident and better informed. They are forced to find coping skills they never knew they had. For many the period spent away from home, difficult as it is, provides their first opportunity for health education, literacy training, and participation in community affairs.

To illustrate the health needs of uprooted women we will consider the health of refugee women in three different settings: during flight; in a camp or settlement in the country of first asylum; and in a resettlement country.

Flight ☐ There is a great need to give more attention to the physical protection of women during and after their flight from home. This is not easy. Most refugees today are fleeing from chaotic situations of conflict, guerrilla warfare and violence. Whole populations are subject to bombing, shelling, destruction of their villages and wholesale slaughter. Women are subjected to rape, torture and kidnapping. Even if they survive and escape, many carry physical and psychological scars for the rest of their lives.

There is greater awareness now of the psychological effects which often emerge later as 'post-traumatic stress syndrome'. Some excellent work is being done to help refugee women deal with the physical and psychological aftermath of their traumatic experiences. Several countries have centres to help victims of torture. There are counselling programmes for Vietnamese women and their families who have been attacked by pirates as they fled in boats. This has been most effective when the counsellors are themselves Vietnamese women, former refugees who have both psychological training and the essential thorough understanding of the culture.

Women unaccompanied by men, seeking refuge for themselves and their families, are sometimes exploited by border guards, soldiers and local officials, who demand sexual favours or bribes in exchange for allowing the women to pass or get the necessary papers. Young girls have been 'detained' by police for several weeks to cook, clean and serve as 'temporary wives' before being allowed to go further. These human rights abuses need to be brought to light and much more pressure needs to be put on those governments that allow them to continue.

Refugee women have exhibited amazing strengths, both in surviving their ordeals and in helping each other recover and build new lives. An Ethiopian woman who fled to Somalia tells of her experience:

PHOTO: L. TAYLOR / UNHCR

Somalia: Ethiopian refugees, Behin camp.

I left my homeland when I had one child. My mother was killed in front of me and many of my other relatives were also killed. I left without taking even one shilling with me. When I left home, I thought there was nothing left to live for, but we managed to survive. . . . A group of us meet every Thursday in one of the offices. We talk about the education of women and children, how to plough together, how to help the weaker ones who can't do anything for themselves, when and how to bury the dead, and how to help those who don't have children of their own by collecting something for them on a weekly basis when we get the rations.[72]

Migrant women usually have a much less perilous journey to their new home. However, if they are entering another country illegally or are travelling without male

members of their family, they too can be subject to the same forms of abuse and exploitation as refugee women.

Camp or settlement ☐ Obviously the conditions in refugee camps and settlements vary tremendously from place to place. To illustrate the impact of the refugee experience on women's health, we look at one example here: the situation of Afghan women in Pakistan. Many of them have been exiled from their homeland now for ten years. In general the level of health and nutrition in the camps is satisfactory. There is an extensive system of MCH clinics and Basic Health Units. The mud-walled huts and compounds are reminiscent of the villages that the Afghans left.

Yet there has been a drastic change in the lives of the women because they are much more confined than they were at home. The rules of purdah are applied more strictly than in Afghan villages because the men perceive the refugee camp situation as more threatening to the women. They feel they must protect them, and the family, from even the possibility of dishonour. Women are therefore allowed to leave the family compound only if heavily veiled and accompanied by a male relative.

This has made it more difficult for women and girls to take part in the various health, education, social service and income-generating programmes that exist in the camps. But Afghan women can be very strong-minded and have traditionally exercised considerable power within the family. In the refugee camps some women have found ways to participate in activities outside the compound, and some men's attitudes have changed.

The health status of the Afghan women refugees resembles that of millions of other women in developing countries, with the exception perhaps of certain stress-related disorders:

. . . hypertension, or high blood pressure, is unusually prevalent among the Afghan women. . . . Tuberculosis is common, especially among the new arrivals. It is reported to be more difficult to control in women than in men because of their heavy work load, poor nutrition, their confinement in crowded conditions, and the fact that they do not come regularly to health centers for treatment. Anaemia, too, is fairly widespread, and doctors report that the flowing robes and veils mask moderately severe malnutrition in some women. This is the result not only of the tradition of women eating last and eating what is left, but of overwork, frequent gastro-intestinal disorders and lack of knowledge about women's nutritional needs.

Added to that is a very high fertility rate. . . . It is not uncommon to have 6, 8, 10 or more pregnancies. There is a desire to replace those who have been lost in war and violence and to produce soldiers for the jihad.

One Afghan woman doctor said that refugee women come to her saying, 'I just cry all the time, I don't know why.' Anxiety and depression arise from many causes: the women's isolation in the camps and being cut off from their normal family and community support networks when they need them most; the bombings, violence and loss of family members that they have experienced; worry about absent members of the family; longing to go back to Afghanistan.

All of this is accentuated for women who are alone with their children because they are widowed or because their husbands are away working or fighting.[73]

For some women, life in exile has brought new opportunities. PHC programmes and health education programmes are touching the lives of Afghan women refugees. A few Afghan women have been trained to become health workers, who go about the community making home visits, reaching the women who need health information most—those who do not get out to the health centres.

'This represents a real breakthrough in view of the constraints described earlier. These trainees tend to be older women (40–60) who have a certain status in the community, who have the permission of the male members of their family, and who have the courage to stand up to the social pressures opposing this kind of activity for women. . . . These refugees will one day carry back to Afghanistan a new concept of health and a new awareness of what they themselves can do about it.'[74]

Resettlement ☐ For migrant women and for refugee women who resettle in countries and cultures very different from their own, the question of accessibility to

PHOTO: A. HOLLMAN / UNHCR

Health Education is of particular importance for refugee women.

health care looms large. Even where there is a comprehensive health care system, the needs of minority group women often go unmet unless deliberate steps are taken to facilitate their access to that system. Many women are unaware of the services that are available. There may be practical difficulties that keep them away, such as problems with the use of public transport, or having no one to stay with their children in their absence.

Sometimes refugee and migrant women would rather treat themselves than try to surmount the formidable language and cultural barriers between themselves and the health care system. Many a woman has described her panic at finding herself in the delivery room of a huge hospital, unable to communicate with anyone, and unable to understand what was being done to her with all that menacing-looking equipment wielded by masked figures. One refugee woman entering a hospital for surgery suddenly became very upset and was almost hysterical before the staff found someone who spoke her language. The problem turned out to be the fact that hospital personnel had taken the woman's passport, a life-threatening move in the eyes of a refugee whose very life had depended on having the right papers.

Lastly, resettled refugee women and some migrant women find that their concept of health and healing differs greatly from that of the society in which they are living. Certain South-East Asian cultures, for example, make no distinction between physical, mental and spiritual well-being. They are all seen as one, and their traditional healers would treat the whole person. This fact may be little understood by a Western-trained physician who, finding no physiological basis for a complaint, will dismiss it as psychosomatic, perhaps pre-

121

THE STORY OF GNIEP—A GIRL OF 11

I was born at Khum Dong, province of Battambang, Cambodia. My parents were farmers. Both of them went to work in the rice fields while I stayed home alone. I was the one who cooked the rice from the time I was just a little girl. I watched over the seedlings and the rice that was drying, so chickens and birds didn't come and eat them.

I left my mother three years ago to live with my aunt, who had been paralysed when she fell from a coconut tree. That was during the time of the Khmer Rouge regime of Pol Pot. Afterwards her condition got even worse when she was beaten with a stick. My father had left us to go to Nong Samet, a camp on the Thai border. He remarried there.

One day I went to Nong Samet with my aunt—the one who brought me up—to see my cousins. When my father saw me, he took me back to live with him. At Nong Samet my stepmother made me carry water to sell. My father, who was a soldier in the Cambodian resistance, was away fighting and didn't come back very often to the house. My stepmother didn't do anything, just ate and slept.

One day I was on my way to sell water to the rice merchants near the barracks of the Thai soldiers who guarded the camp. I did not follow the usual path, and I stepped on a mine, right near the camp. Some soldiers with motorcycles found me and took me to the Nong Samet hospital. The next day I was transferred to Khao I Dang refugee hospital in the interior of Thailand. There

they cut off my leg.

Four months later I returned to Nong Samet. I didn't have a prosthesis yet, but I went back to live with my father and stepmother, where I continued to do the same work as before. I worked around the house. I had a crutch made of bamboo, and I hopped along.

Then my aunt who was paralysed was hospitalised at Khao I Dang too. One day she came to Nong Samet to see me. I was alone in the house. She took me away with her, back to Khao I Dang. I was very happy that she took me with her. She's the one who brought me up, and I am more attached to her than to my own mother.

At Khao I Dang I was fitted with my first temporary prosthesis at the HANDICAP INTERNATIONAL workshop. It was made of bamboo. Later I got another one made of wood and leather. Now I can walk and play without crutches.

When I grow up I want to learn to make prostheses for myself. When I have a nice-looking prosthesis I would like to be a dressmaker, because I love beautiful clothes. I would really like to be a singer and dancer when I get my beautiful prosthesis. I know how to play drums, guitar, khmer violin, xylophone, and flute. But I don't like the flute.

I don't want to get married or have children.

Interview (translated from the French) from *Informations Handicap International*, no. 1, January–February 1984

scribing a tranquillizer. The basic cause of distress, which may be economic, or related to family relationships, will be unresolved. And the woman will not feel, or be, healed.

The strains on refugee families are great.

Sometimes the couple manage to stay united through the worst of their crises, only to have the results of all the anxiety and tension show up later, after they have been resettled and when they should feel safe and contented with the prospects for the future. Domestic violence at this stage is not uncommon. (At one shelter for battered women in Toronto, 40 per cent of the women are resettled refugees.) Certain refugee communities have recognized these problems and have organized counselling services and support groups for couples in difficulty.

On the previous page we offer the case study of a young Cambodian refugee who triumphed over physical disability; one wonders, however, if the psychological scars can be erased.

MENTAL HEALTH ☐ There are numerous mental health problems that affect women worldwide; only a few of the most salient can be dealt with here.

Depression ☐ Major depression is the most common serious mental disorder in women worldwide. Women also appear to be more prone to anxiety states. However, it is difficult to interpret or compare quantitative data on women's and men's mental health because of known differences in diagnosing and defining what is 'pathological' in each case.

In industrialized countries women are twice as likely as men to suffer from depression. They are also more often diagnosed as having anxiety (and neuroses in general). Several studies suggest that anxiety in women tends to increase with age and with decreasing socio-economic status.

Anxiety has been described as fear of anticipated loss—what might happen; depression is described as a reaction to perceived loss. 'Fear of loss of face, of esteem, respect, status, love, income, attachment of significant others, rejection, demotion, firing, retirement—all reinforce insecurity and a perceived inability to predict or control outcomes.'[75] Described in that way, anxiety may not be an altogether inappropriate response, given the life situations of many women. Freud considered 'inappropriate' anxiety to be a component of most neuroses, which he termed 'the price we pay for civilization'. 'If that is the case,' says one specialist in mental health, 'women's share of the price appears to be exorbitant.'[76]

It is difficult to draw conclusions about the mental health of women in the developing world because of the methodological issues just mentioned and because of lack of data broken down by gender. Nevertheless, it appears that there are few fundamental differences in the nature or prevalence of mental illness in developing countries as compared with the industrialized world.

In developing countries most studies, especially community surveys, show more women than men with some form of mental illness. However, many more men than women get treatment. There is an intriguing parallel here with findings in the United States and Great Britain that most women with mental disorders are treated by general practitioners, while men are more likely to be referred to specialized psychiatric services.[77]

What causes the higher rates of depression in women than in men? There is continuing debate on that question. Some feel the difference may be more apparent than real. Women may be more inclined to report emotional distress, to say they feel depressed, to seek treatment. There are also questions about how much diagnosis is influenced by cultural expectations and stereotypes of what is 'normal behaviour'. Several experiments have demonstrated that clinicians tend to evaluate identical symptoms differently in women and men. 'When a male was described as engaging in deviant behaviour under pressure of an impending examination, much less psychopathology was attributed to him than to a female behaving identically.'[78]

(See the earlier section, Minor Tranquillizers, pp. 90–93, for a discussion of discussion of how the attitudes of pharmaceutical companies and the medical profession towards women have tended to medicalize their problems, so that they get prescriptions for their 'illness' rather than encouragement to take action and change the situation causing the problem.)

Beyond that, it is likely that no single factor accounts for the higher rates of depression in women. Some researchers believe that biological or physiological factors play a role. And there is clearly a cultural component—women are treated differently by society. Different demands are made on them; they are expected to play several, sometimes conflicting, roles; the discrimination they encounter in various situations may make their problems worse (for example, in employment) or make them feel less able to cope with them. 'Every woman's mental health is affected by the way her society regards and treats unmarried or married women, childless women, mothers, poor women, assaulted women, divorced women, minority women, disabled women, widows, aged women or women with aspirations.'[79]

Other factors that have been found to put women at risk of depression include: infertility; an unhappy marriage; physical or sexual abuse; poverty; and isolation in old age. In industrialized countries full-time housewives are more likely to show signs of depression than women working outside the home, especially women with young children.

Certain changes in lifestyle also appear to increase the risk of mental health problems. A survey in Baltimore, USA found that among women heading one-parent households, emotional distress was more prevalent than in the population as a whole.[80]

Women of the Asia/Pacific region have come up with a succinct 'alternative analysis' of why women suffer more psychological distress than men. Here are their words:

- **The stress and strain of the added burden of work**
- **Frustration with sex role socialization and expectations**
- **Increasing awareness of rights and choices which affects adjustment within the family and marriage.**[81]

Suicide ☐ More men than women commit suicide. In North America the ratio is about three to one. But women *attempt* suicide much more frequently. In a study carried out in Paris, one in every six suicides attempted by men resulted in death, while for women the ratio was one in 29. Several theories have been advanced to explain this: women really do not want to die but are sending out distress signals (the same is said about young people, who also have a high ratio of attempted suicides compared to completed suicides). A second explanation is that when men attempt suicide they use more lethal means (for example, guns), while women are more likely to use slower, less violent methods such as an overdose of drugs, so that there is a greater chance that they will be found and saved. Third, women's desire to escape from an intolerable situation conflicts with their 'nurturing' role and their sense of responsibility towards the survivors.

In industrialized countries suicide rates for men are highest between the ages of 65–75, while the peak period for women tends to be about ten years earlier. One researcher concludes 'that for both sexes the risk is highest at the time of life when their valued roles in society are declining or removed . . . in countries where culture confers status on the aged, the Western pattern is reversed, with old men and old women having lower incidences of suicide than the young.'[82]

There are exceptions to the pattern of male suicides outnumbering those of women. A study of completed suicides in India found that more than half (54 per

PHOTO: ZAFAR / WHO

cent) involved women, and their average age was 28. These women tended to have a low socio-economic status, to be illiterate, with a rural background and a history of mental illness. Most were housewives.[83] In Bangladesh, the suicide rate for women is three times higher than that for men. The reasons given for suicide by women in both India and Bangladesh centre on family matters—physical violence or psychological abuse by the husband, problems with in-laws, the stigma of divorce or pregnancy outside marriage.[84]

Special needs □ There are several groups of women whose particular mental health needs have only recently been recognized. Among them are refugee women who have been tortured, women who have been sexually assaulted or who are victims of other types of violence, migrant and refugee women who are over-

whelmed by the move to a new culture, and mid-life and older women.

More research is being conducted now on the impact of these experiences on women. In many countries there are programmes or centres designed to provide the specialized therapy or support that is needed. The demand for such facilities and services far outstrips the supply at the moment, but the pioneer work done in these fields has demonstrated that sensitive, timely and culturally appropriate therapy and support can make a big difference to the mental health of women who have lived through these experiences. It can restore their self-esteem, help them deal with their anxieties and enable them to take control of their lives again.

In some cases family therapy is called for. Many refugee communities resettled in a foreign culture have organized their own family-oriented support groups, calling on their traditional ways of handling psycho-social problems as well as using the tech-niques of modern groups.

Professional therapy or counselling is sometimes supplemented by such groups, usually made up of people who have dealt with similar problems in their own lives or who, in any case, can listen with an under-standing ear. More often, however, profes-sional help is just not available or not sought, and the women concerned are left to their own resources or whatever help they can provide for one another.

Again, here are the words of women from the Asia and Pacific region who have studied this question:

Improving psychological and emotional health of communities is not generally a priority of health care systems of developing countries. . . . Psychological medicine and psychiatric treatment are usually one of the smallest services within the system. . . .

The idea of accepting that one is experiencing psychological stress, psychosomatic problems, or some form of mental instability, and then seeking treatment, is still a very new concept in the Third World. Counselling or psychotherapy as a strategy is very new and not generally understood as a possible intervention. Most people, including women, cope with their psychological problems using traditional cultural mechanisms such as religious healing, astrology, and spirit mediums.

Some government psychiatrists have been supportive of women's attempts to set up alternative services for women. In Malaysia, the Women's Aid Organization (WAO) for battered women, had two government psychiatrists as committee members of the first Protem Committee. They explained that psychiatrists in government health services were extremely busy helping women in acute crises and little time was available to talk with women let alone to initiate therapy. Women's and community organizations were encouraged to respond to women's emotional distress before the problem became complex, requiring long-term treatment or even hospitalization.[85]

WOMEN AS CONSUMERS OF HEALTH-RELATED PRODUCTS □

The alliance between women's groups and consumer groups on health issues would seem to be a 'natural'. They are often joined by development organizations. We saw this kind of alliance at work in the drive to promote an international code on the marketing of breast-milk substitutes, and in the efforts to reduce women's use of tranquillizers.

Women do most of the buying of health-related products and they consume most of these products, too. The three groups men-tioned above have a common interest in such issues as product safety, research, marketing practices and pricing, in all regions of the world. The health of millions of women and their families is affected by developments in these fields.

The issues are complex, however. Those who are concerned about them need to join forces in order to: 1. mobilize the necessary expertise; 2. generate political 'clout' where that is necessary; and 3. make sure that women and the public in general have the information and understanding they need in order to make wise choices.

When women go to market to buy fruit, most of them know a good apple, pear or papaya when they see one, or they will learn by trial and error. That should *not* be the procedure when they go out to get contraceptives and powerful drugs. But sometimes the situation of the consumer of health-related products is not too different from that. A former Commissioner of the Food and Drug Administration in the United States, writing in the early 1970s, observed that:

An American buying prescription drugs buys on faith what his doctor has

prescribed. He is like a child who goes to the store with his mother's shopping list, which he cannot even read. He is totally unsophisticated as to the workings of the $5 billion [1972 figures] industry to which he is contributing.[86]

Women make a very tempting market for companies manufacturing drugs and other health-related products:

- they represent a huge market, half the population of the world;

- women buy the drugs or remedies they use themselves and, as the main health care providers, they do much of the buying for other members of the family;

- women use more drugs than men, partly because of their reproductive health needs and partly, it would seem, because of the different criteria used in prescribing for men and women.

Not only do women use more drugs than men (in the United States, about two-thirds of all prescriptions are written for women),[87] but women worldwide use some of the most profitable drugs: oral contraceptives, injectible contraceptives and tranquillizers. No wonder drug companies target their advertising to women and feature women so much in the promotional material distributed to doctors. (See earlier section, Minor Tranquillizers, pp. 90–93.)

Oral contraceptives were introduced in the United States in 1960. By 1965 they accounted for 44 per cent of the total sales of one large pharmaceutical firm. The 'pill' has been described as '. . . a pharmaceutical company's dream: a product to be used, virtually daily, by perfectly healthy people'.[88]

Within a few years, however, questions had arisen about the safety of several contraceptive products and other drugs. (One

of the most dramatic cases concerned the sleeping pill, thalidomide, which caused thousands of severe deformities and deaths among children whose mothers had used the tablets during pregnancy. This tragedy did, however, lead to stricter regulations for approving and marketing drug products in several countries.) Women and consumer groups, and others concerned about these questions, met with powerful opposition from the pharmaceutical companies when they asked for tighter government controls, more openness about reported side effects, and the right to share the results of clinical trials.

As consumer resistance and government regulations resulted in shrinking markets in the industrialized world, the pharmaceutical industry turned its eyes towards the developing countries, where the potential market was enormous and government regulations were often non-existent or not enforced. In time there were initiatives within the NGO community and the United Nations, particularly in WHO, to promote safer, more rational use of drugs globally and to ensure that everyone could benefit from the advances that had been made in pharmaceutical products.

One way of doing this was to encourage the use of a smaller number of 'essential drugs' to replace the thousands of products that were being developed and promoted at great cost. The very number of products available (with new ones appearing daily) made it impossible for governments to test and regulate them, or for the prescribers, much less the patients, to be adequately informed about them.

Essential drugs are defined as those that are:

- necessary for the health needs of the majority of people in a country, and appropriate to that country's health system, socio-economic circumstances and environmental conditions;

- proven to be effective and safe under the conditions in which they will be used;

- priced so that the total cost of treatment is reasonable.

After extensive study and consultation, a panel of experts from both developing and industrialized countries, convoked by WHO, drew up a list of about 200 essential drugs that would generally meet those criteria. Such a list would have to be adapted, of course, to the conditions in each country, and every country was encouraged to develop its own list. Each national list needed also to be accompanied by measures to ensure its effective use: education of health professionals, patients and consumers; regulation of import, manufacturing and marketing practices; measures to ensure adequate supplies and distribution.

Because of the important role women play in safeguarding their own and their families' health, they need to be better informed about pharmaceuticals and all health-related products. They need to know how well their own government is doing in protecting the consumer from unsafe, ineffective or over-priced products. Every woman should feel free to ask her doctor or health worker about these things whenever she is given a prescription.

But few women are likely to do this until they are much better informed about the situation and aware of the dangers associated with the inappropriate use of drugs. Therefore women's organizations and networks have launched campaigns to tell women (and the general public) about the issues and spread the information they need

in order to feel more confident in asking questions and making decisions about health-related products.

For example, the *Women's Health Journal*, a publication of ISIS International Latin American and Caribbean Women's Health Network, recently launched an 'Information Campaign on Essential Drugs. The Policies of Pharmaceutical Industries and their Effects on Women's Health'.[89]

Another group dedicated to informing women on the issue is the Health Action International Group on Women and Pharmaceuticals. This group focuses on the highly complex questions surrounding fertility-related drugs, for example, the testing, use and distribution of contraceptives and the impact on women's health. They would like to see representatives of women and health groups more involved at all stages in the development and use of these products, and would welcome more dialogue with the manufacturers and health authorities.

Some observers believe that the pharmaceutical companies, or at least some of them, are ready to respond more positively to such demands now than they were in the past. There are signs of increased openness in providing information both to those who prescribe drugs and to the patients who use them.[90] Certainly if we do manage to bring about safer, more rational use of drugs worldwide, women will be among the major beneficiaries.

Reprinted on p. 129 is the editorial from a recent publication of the Women and Pharmaceuticals Group outlining their concerns about fertility-related drugs.[91]

WOMEN AND PHARMACEUTICALS: CURRENT CONCERNS

Women constitute about 50% of the world population. They are often caretakers of children, for whom they are likely to purchase medicines as well. This and their reproductive capacities make women a prime market for the pharmaceutical industry. In most developing countries women have little access to objective and understandable information on the safety and efficacy of pharmaceuticals, making them vulnerable to the often aggressive marketing practices of pharmaceutical manufacturers. The WEMOS/HAI International Group on Women and Pharmaceuticals aims at providing women with objective information on the proper use of pharmaceuticals, and at influencing policies in order to ensure a rationalization of the way in which pharmaceuticals are marketed and used in health care.

The group focuses on the use and distribution of 'fertility-related' drugs. Many of these drugs are distributed in commercial outlets such as pharmacies and drug stores, as well as government family planning clinics. The group is concerned about the use and distribution of contraceptives in family planning programmes, because these programmes are often target-oriented, aiming at reduction of fertility rates, and fail to respect a woman's right to a free choice out of a range of fertility regulating methods. This bulletin covers a number of current concerns of the International Group on Women and Pharmaceuticals.

OUT OF DATE DRUGS

The first general concern is the continued use of outdated drugs, such as diethylstilbestrol (DES), in Third World countries. DES is an example of a drug that is severely restricted in many industrialized countries, due to its serious side effects—among others a specific type of vaginal cancer in women whose mothers had used DES to prevent a miscarriage. It continues to be used for inappropriate indications in Third World countries due to a limited capacity of regulatory authorities to rationalize drug distribution, and lack of updated objective information on its safety.

The International Group on Women and Pharmaceuticals opposes such double standards in the marketing of pharmaceuticals and calls on manufacturers to apply the same standards in Third World countries as they do in industrialized countries. The group also calls for export controls which will support Third World governments in their attempts to regulate the pharmaceutical market. . . .

CONTRACEPTIVE TECHNOLOGIES

A second concern and major dilemma which confronts us in all aspects of our work is the question of how to meet conditions for proper use of contraceptives when faced with the reality of contraceptive needs and the harsh realities with which many women live.

The proper use of many techniques such as Norplant® and IUDs requires a good health care infrastructure—an infrastructure which simply does not exist in many developing countries, particularly in rural areas.

Should we conclude that because of this some technologies should not be made available and, if this is our conclusion, what are the implications for the rights of these women to choose?

In this bulletin a review of the development of Norplant®, a new long-acting hormonal implant, is given. Because of its provider-dependent and hormonal nature, problems in use are envisioned. Contraceptive vaccines— not yet ▶

on the market—are another example of a new, long-acting contraceptive technology. In an article on these vaccines the International Group on Women and Pharmaceuticals questions the need for such long-acting provider-dependent methods. The group calls for the development of methods which are simple to administer, which enhance women's autonomy and which can be used safely in sub-optimal health care infrastructures.

The abortion pill is a new contraceptive technology which is said to enhance women's autonomy. [During] a seminar organized by the International Group on Women and Pharmaceuticals . . . it became clear that at present use of the technology requires considerable guidance by health professionals. The extent to which this method can be used safely in sub-optimal health care infrastructures is questioned.

CONDUCT OF TRIALS
Much of the criticism of women and health groups regarding the safety of contraceptives can in fact be related to the limitations in the design of, and possibilities for interpretation of, clinical trials. The conduct of clinical trials is a third general concern of the International Group on Women and Pharmaceuticals. One of the limitations of clinical trials is that they are done in controlled settings. This means that the effects of the methods in less controlled settings cannot be assessed. Another limitation . . . has to do with the so-called inclusion and exclusion criteria, that are used to select a study population for the trial. The effect of the method on women who were not included in the trial cannot be extrapolated from the trial results. Examples of such groups are lactating women, adolescents, and malnourished women. Again, another limitation is that the trials rarely last longer than three years, thus long-term effects are not known. Indeed, most reproductive researchers argue that the best way to determine a new technology's safety is to test it in large populations as early as possible. The International Group on Women and Pharmaceuticals argues that before a new reproductive technology is tested in clinical trials and in post-marketing surveillance, its likely advantage over existing methods should be established.

The group stimulates debate on the pros and cons of new methods by organizing seminars in which researchers present the state of the art, and representatives of women and health groups review the me-thod. Ideally such discussion should take place at the country level if there are plans to introduce new contraceptive technologies. Discussion should take place at early stages of the development of the method, as only then is there a chance that women's perspectives can be incorporated into further development of the technology. Such discussion is urgently needed in the field of contraceptive vaccines. These methods are expected to enter the market in the coming decade.

The International Group on Women and Pharmaceuticals believes that women and health groups need to be aware of the standards for the conduct of clinical trials in order to critically assess the conduct of the trials that are being done in their countries.

HEATED DEBATES
New contraceptive technologies and the conduct of clinical trials in developing countries have been fuel for many heated debates among feminist health groups. Long-acting hormonal methods

such as Norplant® and Depo Provera have been opposed because of their possible health consequences and provider-dependent character. They are seen as instruments of neo-Malthusian population planners, concerned with control of population, and not with the meeting of women's reproductive needs. Often these stands take an 'anti-technology' character. Barrier methods such as condoms and diaphragms are put forward as appropriate alternatives. The WEMOS/HAI International Group on Women and Pharmaceuticals attempts to look at the new technologies from the perspective of women in varying social and cultural settings. While a diaphragm, for example, may be ideal for some women, this method may not be the most appropriate for women who do not have regular access to clean water and spermicides.

We are not looking for simple answers regarding the acceptability of new technologies, but we make a general call for appropriate reproductive health care for women. 'Family planning' should be approached in a more integrated manner, as a component of Primary Health Care programmes. Women's reproductive needs should be taken as the point of departure, not targets and fertility rates. There should be more stringent monitoring and supervision of the implementation of such programmes. It is in this context that the International Group on Women and Pharmaceuticals is developing guidelines for the distribution and use of contraceptives. These guidelines highlight the need for objective information on safety and efficacy of the methods, and emphasize the health care require-ments of the more complex technologies. It is hoped that such a 'reproductive health' approach can enhance the rational use of the new reproductive technologies, and will contribute to a climate in which women are given genuine choices and are empowered to control their own fertility.

*Anita Hardon—Women &
Pharmaceuticals Bulletin*, November 1990

1 A. Petros-Barvazian, report to a Workshop on Women's Health, at a meeting of the Task Force on Child Survival, March 1990, as reported in *World Immunization News*, vol. 6, no. 3, May–June 1990, p. 20.

2 Ibid.

3 Safe Motherhood Initiative, *A Programme of Operational Research*, booklet, Geneva, WHO, 1989.

4 S. K. Henshaw, 'Induced Abortion: A World Review, 1990', *Family Planning Perspectives*, March–April 1990.

5 J. Jacobson, *Worldwatch Paper 97: The Global Politics of Abortion*, Washington, Worldwatch Institute, 1990, p. 12.

6 Ibid., p. 42.

7 B. Dick, League of Red Cross and Red Crescent Societies, 'Preventing Death in the Act of Creation . . . Making Motherhood Safer—a Challenge for us All', background paper for the NGO Committee on UNICEF Forum, New York, April 1990, p. 5.

8 Jacobson, *Worldwatch Paper* op. cit., p. 32.

9 Ibid., p. 34.

10 Ibid., p. 49.

11 Ibid., p. 39.

12 WHO, *Safe Motherhood Newsletter*, no. 2, March–June 1990, p. 6.

13 World Bank, World Health Organization and United Nations Fund for Population Activities, *Preventing the Tragedy of Maternal Deaths: A Report on the International Safe Motherhood Conference*, Nairobi, Kenya, February 1987, p. 14.

14 WHO, *Progress*, Newsletter of the Special Programme of Research, Development and Research Training in Human Reproduction, no. 15, 1990, p. 1.

15 M. Carballo and A. Marin-Lira, *Patterns of Breastfeeding, Child Health and Fertility* (WHO/MCH/86.4), WHO, 1986.

16 O. Koso-Thomas, *The Circumcision of Women: A Strategy for Eradication*, London, Zed Books, 1987, p. 19.

17 Ibid., p. 29.

18 B. Raswork, 'Female Circumcision', *Maternal and Child Care in Developing Countries*, E. Kessel and A.K. Awan (eds), Thun, Ott Publishers, 1989 p. 25.

19 As quoted by L. Heise in 'Crimes of Gender', *Women's Health Journal*, no. 17, January–March 1990, p. 9.

20 Inter-African Committee on Traditional Practices Affecting the Health of Women and Children (IAC), *IAC Newsletter*, no. 7, March 1989, p. 4.

21 Ibid., p. 15.

22 WHO, *The Female Smoker: At Added Risk*, Information Kit published by the Tobacco and Health Programme of WHO for the World's Second No-Tobacco Day, 1989. The kit points out that in addition to the women who smoke commercially-produced cigarettes, women in many countries use tobacco in other, traditional ways. They chew it, smoke it through water pipes or hookas,

hold plugs of it in their mouths and smoke home-made cigars. All such practices carry serious health risks; however, these traditional uses are dying out, while the use of commercial cigarettes is increasing among women in developing countries.

23 Reprinted in *Contact*, newsletter of the Christian Medical Commission, World Council of Churches, no. 114, May 1990. Source: *Harper's*, published in the Bulletin of the Park Ridge Center, vol. 5, no. 1, January 1990.

24 *Women's Health Journal*, no. 17, January–March 1990, p. 52.

25 O. Ward, 'Alcohol Floods the Third World', *Health Now*, 9 May 1984, p. 4. The article cites a joint study by the United Nations Conference on Trade and Development (UNCTAD) and WHO, 'Alcoholic Beverages: the Dimensions of Corporate Power'.

26 'Minor Tranquillizers: The Solution or the Problem?', *Women's Health Journal*, no. 13, May–June 1987, pp. 25–33.

27 Ibid., p. 29. See also A. Chetley, *A Healthy Business? World Health and the Pharmaceutical Industry*, London, Zed Books, 1990, p. 27. Chetley cites a 1975 study that found 'women were 15 times more likely [than men] to appear in advertisements to doctors for mood-changing drugs'.

28 *Women's Health Journal*, no. 13, p. 30.

29 Ibid., p. 32, reporting on research done by the Centro de Informacion y Educacion para la Prevencion del Abuso de Drogas (CEDRO), Lima, Peru.

30 United Nations Environment Programme (UNEP) and UNICEF, *The State of the Environment 1990: Children and the Environment*, New York, UNICEF, 1990, p. 35.

31 *Stop Droga*, kit (in Italian) prepared jointly by the United Nations Inter-regional Crime and Justice Research Institute, the International Conference on Drug Abuse and Illicit Trafficking, Assessorato alla Sanita Regione Lazio, and the Istituto Internazionale per gli Studi e l'Informazione Sanitaria, Roma, 1989.

32 WHO, *World Health*, August–September 1989, p. 31.

33 M. E. Hurtado, 'Cancer, It's a Third World Problem Too', *Health Now*, 7 May 1984, p. 6.

34 *World Health Forum*, vol. 8, 1987, p. 116.

35 As quoted by J. Mackay in 'The Last Frontier: The Tobacco Industry in Asia', adapted from *Consumer Lifelines*, 17 August 1989, and reprinted in *Contact*, no. 114, May 1990.

36 'Control of Cancer of the Cervix Uteri', *Bulletin of the World Health Organization*, 64(4), 1986, p. 607.

37 Ibid.

38 Ibid., p. 608.

39 K. Stanley, 'Lifestyles and Cancer', *World Health*, November 1988, p. 25.

40 Ibid.

41 United Nations Centre for Human Rights, *Human Rights Newsletter*, vol. 2, no. 3, October 1989, p. 2.

42 WHO Global Programme on AIDS, 'The Health of Mothers and Children in the Context of HIV/AIDS', p. 1.

43 A. Petros-Barvazian and M. Merson, 'Women and AIDS: a Challenge for Humanity', *World Health*, November–December 1990.

44 R. Erben, 'The Special Threat to Women', *World Health*, November–December 1990.

45 Petros-Barvazian and Merson, 'Women and AIDS' op. cit.

46 R. Danziger, 'Women and AIDS', *World Health*, October 1989, p. 14.

47 WHO, *Progress* op. cit., no. 15, 1990, p. 5.

48 Ibid., p. 4. See also *WHO Features*, no. 152, December 1990.

49 P. Senanayake, 'Direct Effects of Family Planning on Adolescent Health', in *Basic Documents*, papers from the International Conference on Better Health for Women and Children Through Family Planning, Nairobi, October 1987, Abstracts 25.

50 WHO, unpublished document.

51 Asian/Pacific, *Health*, (op. cit., Chapter 3), p. 105.

52 WHO, *World Health*, May 1989, p. 26.

53 D. Bull, 'Pesticide Poisoning', *Health Now*, 17 May 1984, p. 11.

54 J. Zaini, 'Women in Malaysian Plantations: Health and Medicines', as reprinted in Asian/Pacific, *Health*, op. cit. (Chapter 3), p. 106.

55 L. Sennott-Miller, 'Growing Old in Latin America', *World Health*, April–May 1990, p. 13.

56 C. Hodgson, 'Women Working Worldwide: Our Experience of International Solidarity', *Women in Action*, 4/89, publication of ISIS International, p. 13.

57 International Labour Organisation, *Special Protective Measures for Women and Equality of Opportunity and Treatment*, Geneva, ILO (Doc MEPMW/1989/7), 1989, p. 37.

58 Boston Women's Health Book Collective, *The New Our Bodies, Ourselves*, New York, Simon & Schuster, 1984, p. 89.

59 J. Campling, *Better Lives for Disabled Women*, London, Virago, 1979, p. 2.

60 *Women and Disability*, prepared and compiled by E. R. Boylan, in the Women and World Development Series, UN/NGO Group on Women and Development, London, Zed Books, 1991.

61 Campling, *Better Lives for Disabled Women* op. cit., p. 2.

62 *Women and Disability*, op. cit.

63 WHO, *WHO Features*, no. 116, February 1988.

64 L. Sennott-Miller, 'Factors Influencing the Physical and Emotional Vulnerability of Older Women' in *Background Report on Elderly Women* (EGM/VW/1990/BP.4), paper submitted to the Expert Group Meeting on Vulnerable Women, Vienna, November 1990, by the American Association of Retired Persons and the International Federation on Ageing, Global Link for Midlife and Older Women, p. 26.

65 A. M. Davies, 'Older Populations, Aging Individuals and Health for All', *World Health Forum*, vol. 10, 1989, p. 302.

66 United Nations, *UN Decade for Women Bulletin*, no. 11, July 1985, p. 22.

67 P. Light, 'The Baby Boomers Enter their Golden Days—and Days of Crisis', *Macalester Today*, November 1990, p. 13. The data are from a study conducted by R. Stone, G. Cafferata and J. Sangl.

68 *International Herald Tribune*, 12 July 1990.

69 P. Doty, 'Health Status and Health Services Use among Older Women: an International Perspective', *World Health Statistics Quarterly*, vol. 40, no. 3, 1987, p. 282.

70 L. Sennott-Miller, *Midlife and Older Women in Latin America and the Caribbean: A Status Report*, Pan American Health Organization and the American Association of Retired Persons, 1989, p. 4.

71 *Refugee Women*, prepared and compiled by S. Forbes Martin, forthcoming in the Women and World Development Series, UN/NGO Group on Women and Development, London, Zed Books, 1991.

72 K. Hancock, *Refugee Women and Children in Somalia*, Mogadiscio, UNICEF, 1988.

73 P. Smyke, 'Afghan Refugee Children in Pakistan', *Transnational Perspectives*, vol. 14, no. 1, 1988, p. 29.

74 Ibid.

75 F. Paltiel, 'Women and Mental Health: a post-Nairobi Perspective', *World Health Statistics Quarterly*, vol. 40, no. 3, 1987, p. 239.

76 Ibid.

77 Ibid., p. 236.

78 Ibid., p. 234.

79 Ibid.
80 *New Internationalist*, July 1990, p. 16.
81 Asian/Pacific, *Health*, op. cit., p. 200.
82 Paltiel, 'Women and Mental Health', op. cit., p. 257.
83 Ibid.
84 Asian/Pacific, *Health*, op. cit., p. 198.
85 Ibid., p. 206.
86 Boston Women's Health Book Collective, *The New Our Bodies Ourselves*, op. cit., p. 566, quoting Dr James L. Goddard.
87 Ibid.
88 Chetley, *A Healthy Business?* op. cit., p. 28.

89 'Information Campaign on Essential Drugs. The Policies of Pharmaceutical Industries and their Effects on Women's Health', *Women's Health Journal*, no. 17, January–March 1990, p. 21.
90 See Chetley, *A Healthy Business?* op. cit., pp. 135–45.
91 A. Hardon, 'Editorial', *Women and Pharmaceuticals Bulletin 3*, Special Publication by the Women and Pharmaceuticals Group of Health Action International (HAI), in co-operation with HAI Europe, to mark the 6th International Women and Health Conference in Manila, Philippines, November 1990.

⑤ ACTION TO IMPROVE WOMEN'S HEALTH

'Unless you call out, who will open the door?'
Ethiopian proverb

This book is part of a call that has been growing stronger and more persistent for several decades: to open the doors that have been closed to women by discrimination, poverty, injustice and ignorance. That call began among a few women at the local and national level, it reverberates now at large international conferences and small community meetings alike. The pioneer women who first issued the call have been joined by other women, men, young people and children, indeed everyone concerned about justice, peace, human rights and development.

THOSE ARE GRANDIOSE WORDS, and the call would have remained at the level of a grandiose appeal had not women and men, girls and boys, joined together to turn that call into *action*. It is not enough to call out and wait for those on the other side of the door to open it. The progress made in these past decades came because women joined with each other and with like-minded men and young people to push open the doors that blocked their way.

This book is a call to action. It will meet its objective only when its readers take up that call, pass it on to others, and turn it into action in a thousand different settings around the world.

This chapter looks at actions that have been taken to improve women's health and what has been learned from the experience. The examples cited here and throughout this book show how many different types of activities are needed. We hope that every reader will find here ideas for the individual and/or collective action that is best suited to her or his circumstances.

There are opportunities for action at the international, national and local levels. At each level there is a contribution to be made by governmental or intergovernmental bodies and by non-governmental organizations, by structured associations and by informal groups or networks, through individual initiatives and through collective action. The priorities for action vary according to the key health issues for women in each place, the position of women in that society, the socio-economic and cultural context, and the particular interests and possibilities of the group taking action. Some groups work to improve the health of their own members or community; some work in partnership with others who need a little support in order to help themselves.

COMMON PRINCIPLES UNDERLYING EFFECTIVE ACTION □ But within this diversity, common principles underlie all effective action on women's health.

Attention to root causes □ Whether the objective is to meet a specific health need in one place, or to launch a broad programme of advocacy, health information and development education, everyone involved should recognize that one of the root causes for women's poor health is discrimination against women. In addressing any health issue, therefore, one of the first recommendations is invariably 'improve the status of women'. Whatever specific activity is undertaken, there must be a parallel concern for general improvement in the status

of women. Drawing attention to this link, helping people understand the mechanisms by which it works, should be part of any coherent advocacy/information campaign.

nformation/awareness-raising ☐

Information is power. Often women have not had access to the information they need in order to bring about change. Data on health problems and factors related to health must be broken down by gender and often by age group, in order to pinpoint problem areas for women and girls, understand the causes and find solutions. In situations where this information is not available from existing records, NGOs and local groups have collected it themselves in pilot studies and used the results to show the need for collecting the same information on a larger scale and routinely. Many community projects begin with simple, community-run surveys and community

discussions of the findings. These activities are in themselves effective awareness-raisers.

A cautionary note here: some projects never get beyond the information-gathering stage. As people begin to investigate a complex situation, they feel a never-ending need for more information. One must of course examine all the relevant factors in a situation, but at some point it is necessary to *act* and to keep on learning through action.

Knowledge is helpful only if people have the practical means of putting it to use. Information about family planning, for example, is of little use if the materials and services are not available to the people who want to use them. The most effective nutrition education programmes are not concerned solely with teaching about nutrition principles. They look at the practical problems of assuring food security for each household.

PHOTO: RAY WITLIN / UNICEF

What does *this* family need to be sure of enough food and a balanced diet for all its members? The answer may be seeds, tools, access to better land, credit or training for the woman farmer, or a change in the laws that govern women's right to own or inherit land. If those who organize nutrition education cannot work on all these fronts, they need to be in touch with other groups who can make sure that those related needs are met.

Intersectoral approach ☐ There is usually a need, as mentioned earlier, to involve many different sectors or parts of a community or nation in actions to improve women's health. If this is being done in the context of PHC, the intersectoral approach should be automatic. However, this needs monitoring to see how well women's needs are understood and taken into account in each sector, for example in the ministries or departments concerned with health, social welfare, agriculture and agricultural extension work, sanitation, transport, education, labour, commerce, foreign affairs, the legislative and judicial system.

It is not enough to tag on a few words at the end of a report, or to show one or two underfunded projects for women at the end of a budget. The mainstream activity in each sector, the work that takes up the bulk of the budget, has to be designed and implemented in such a way that it meets the needs of women as well as men.

Participation ☐ It is obvious that successful and sustainable action to improve women's health can only be carried out with the full participation of the women concerned. They have to express their own ideas about what their needs are and decide on the best ways to meet them. This can be more difficult than it sounds in cultures where women are not accustomed to speaking up. It may take time, a supportive setting and much patient discussion before there is a true meeting of minds.

This is especially true if women from different cultures and regions of the world are involved, or if, for example, women from urban middle-class or educated circles are working with village women or poorer urban women. Nevertheless, women *do* make it work. Through national and international women's organizations and networks these different groups of women have worked together successfully. And they have shared their experiences through various publications and information networks.

The panel overleaf, 'A Guide for Encouraging Community Participation', suggests ways to encourage women's participation in PHC. It is adapted from the World YWCA Manual, *Training for Primary Health Care*.[1]

Responsibility/resources ☐ One way of analysing the position of women is to look at the responsibilities they assume in a society and then look at the resources that are at their disposal to carry out those responsibilities. Think of resources not only in a material sense but in terms of time, knowledge, authority to make decisions, social support, respect for their views, and so on. It is clear that for the majority of women in the world their responsibilities outweigh their resources. Yet women have managed for the most part to cope with the responsibilities related to their various roles. They have done so well at this that women everywhere are identified as key 'agents of change' or 'target groups' for development programmes of all types.

PHC and health education programmes recognize women as health care providers and health educators. They are key persons for nutrition or family life education. They have more recently been recognized as essential people to include in water and sanitation projects and in efforts to protect the environment. Although the myth of the

A GUIDE FOR ENCOURAGING COMMUNITY PARTICIPATION (extracts)

BARRIERS TO WOMEN'S PARTICIPATION

From within communities

Women fear particular obstacles both from their circumstances in the community itself and also from the attitudes of community workers, as outlined below:

- Lack of time. Poverty and the fight for survival, including long hours of work every day. For women, this includes caring for children, the sick and the elderly, food gathering and preparation, collecting water, etc. Often there is little emotional or physical strength left for other activities.

- Cultural, social and religious limitations. Diversity of contexts and priorities due to social, religious, cultural or political groups.

- Attitudes of traditional or other leaders which favour personal interests over community development efforts.

- Attitudes of community members which favour personal interests over broad-based community development efforts.

- Attitudes of husbands and male relatives.

- Lack of sufficient skills in needs assessment, planning or leadership because of insufficient experience, education and confidence.

From community workers

- Resistance to change.

- Attitudes which tend to reflect a service mentality rather than a partnership approach towards community development. A 'we know best' attitude.

- Insufficient funds.

- Rivalries over who will take credit for a project if more than one person is involved.

- Individual or career interests.

- The independent ways organizations may operate.

ACTION

Approach the traditional leaders

- Find out as much as you can about them before you get in touch with them. Try to determine how much influence they have in the community, bearing in mind the divisions and conflicts which exist in any group.

- Determine their interests in community welfare, their attitudes towards women's participation and decision-making in community affairs.

- Focus on existing needs which have special bearing on the women, such as childbirth, breast-feeding, health care for the children. Emphasize the importance of speaking directly with the women about these concerns.

- Gain the leaders' approval and assistance for the assessment phase as well as the design and implementation phases of your work.

Also

- Find out about the existing and traditional ways of reaching decisions and solving problems (such as through chiefs or other authorities, open meetings, consensus, etc.).

- Find out about other informal but influential leaders (religious; educated, such as teachers; TBAs; wealthy; political). They may be helpful in deciding the most appropriate ways of obtaining information.

Approach the women

- Call meetings to set community priorities. Special attention should be given to seeking out vulnerable groups of women—single heads of households, the elderly, or other poor and marginalised women.

- Allow time for the women to express themselves, their problems, needs and what they see as solutions. Also, be sensitive to the fact that they may not be comfortable speaking in a group. Try and arrange to hear them alone if possible.

- You may need to find ways to gain the support of other men in the community.

What community participation is not

'We've got an idea and we want you to help make it a reality.'

WORLD YOUNG WOMEN'S CHRISTIAN ASSOCIATION (YWCA),
A TRAINING MANUAL FOR PRIMARY HEALTH CARE

PHOTO: JEAN-LUC RAY / AGA KHAN FOUNDATION

'male provider' lingers, there is growing awareness of how many families are completely or partially dependent on the earnings and production of women. Women are the target group for more and more income-generating programmes and programmes to increase agricultural productivity. Capable women are much sought after for community development projects.

These are positive signs: women's critical contribution is recognized and valued. But are women, as a consequence, in danger of becoming victims of their own advancement? Are we expecting every woman to become 'Superwoman'? Some NGOs have pointed out that even as we talk of reducing women's workload, we are adding new roles and responsibilities, without necessarily reducing the old ones or assuring additional resources and support. Where are women to find the time and energy to cope?

ADVOCACY/ACTION ☐ We talk about advocacy and action as two separate kinds of activity, but it is rare to find an effective programme on women's health that does not include the two to some extent.

Over the past decade, international NGOs and coalitions of NGOs have advocated successfully on women's health issues to bring about governmental or intergovernmental action (for example, promoting the Code on breastmilk substitutes). National NGOs have approached national legislators or government officials to obtain changes in laws or policies that affect women's health (for example, family planning policy or compulsory primary education). NGOs at all levels have used advocacy and awareness-raising techniques to mobilize their own members and to support them in action. Governments and intergovernmental agencies have used advocacy/awareness-raising techniques to rally non-governmental groups to act in support of government initiatives.

Five examples are given below of

advocacy/action programmes that involve co-operation between governmental and non-governmental bodies, and between groups at various levels—international, national and local:

'A happy birth-day' □ In 1987, after the Nairobi Conference on Safe Motherhood, the International Council of Nurses and the International Confederation of Midwives joined with WHO and UNICEF to prepare a kit entitled 'Help her have a happy birth-day'. The kit contains background information and a fact sheet on the problem of maternal mortality and morbidity worldwide. It describes the international Safe Motherhood Initiative and suggests ways that nurses and midwives can participate. There are ideas for raising awareness among nurses and midwives, other health professionals and decision-makers, and among the general public. There are suggestions for research and for direct action at the community level.

One passage from the kit, 'Challenges for nurses/midwives', is reproduced here. The kit was distributed to all national affiliates of the two NGOs, and to UNICEF and WHO country representatives.

CHALLENGES FOR NURSING/MIDWIFERY PERSONNEL

- training and supervising traditional birth attendants;
- identifying mothers at risk, early treatment of complications and timely referral;
- increasing access to maternity services and antenatal care;
- mobilizing and involving communities, particularly women themselves, in planning and implementing programmes so that their needs and preferences are taken into account;
- reaching women, men, children, communities, and leaders with information through culturally appropriate channels to change behaviour and strengthen family support systems;
- implementing an alarm and transport system to ensure that women in need of emergency care reach the referral facility in time;
- expanding family planning and family life education programmes, particularly for young people;
- meeting with decisions-makers in government to propose changes in laws, strengthen/upgrade referral facilities, improve educational preparation of nursing/midwifery personnel, and to allocate necessary resources, supplies and equipment;
- teaching women identified at risk in ante-natal clinics that delivery in a health facility is essential for their safety;
- carrying out studies to gain better understanding of the factors leading to maternal mortality and morbidity, and of the interventions of nursing/midwifery personnel to reduce maternal risks and improve maternal health services;
- updating nursing/midwifery curricula to reflect current health needs and new nursing/midwifery science;
- helping the community establish maternity waiting homes near health facilities for women with high-risk pregnancies;
- educating women, families and communities on specific risk factors.[2]

Safe motherhood and the role of midwives □ In January 1989 the International Confederation of Midwives (ICM), with the Ghana Registered Midwives Association as hosts, brought together teams from the Gambia, Ghana, Liberia, Nigeria and Sierra Leone in the first of a series of workshops on the role of midwives in the global effort for Safe Motherhood. Each team produced a detailed national implementation plan for bringing about needed change in their country, within the constraints of the conditions there.[3]

For each national plan the team had to decide on the major problems related to maternal mortality, for example lack of professionally trained midwives, or unsatisfactory distribution of them, inadequate referral system, lack of information and health data, and so on. The plan had to propose solutions to these problems that: 1. would not call for large new resources; and 2. would call for actions where midwives would play an active role.

The teams worked out specific objectives and strategies for achieving them, with time frames and specified persons or offices made responsible for implementation and monitoring. The teams also had to identify the positive and negative forces within each country situation that would affect actions to promote Safe Motherhood. The plans were put in finished form before the workshop ended 'to enable the teams, and in particular the midwives, to make formal presentations of quality to their own ministries or associations'. The progress reports from each country will be shared with midwives in other countries through ICM international headquarters.

Similar workshops have taken place in other regions, and before the next international Congress of ICM a special workshop on midwifery education was organized 'to develop an educational framework for midwives to reduce maternal mortality and morbidity'! Participants debated such questions as 'what will be taught, who will teach, how and where such learning can best take place and how such knowledge, skills or attitudes will be evaluated'.[4]

The fight to stop tobacco promotion
□ The Christian Medical Commission of the World Council of Churches used the May 1990 issue of its bulletin, *Contact*, to 'present some of the facts about tobacco, its slow destruction of health and life, and its promotion around the world, not only by companies but by some governments as well—for the sake of profit'.

The articles in this issue trace the links between politics and profits, as well as the relationships between tobacco consumption and development, including the impact on health, agriculture, environment and self-help efforts. One example given: 'In 1986, with the money it spent on cigarettes alone, Mali could have purchased 300,000 small plows for its farmers.'

The straightforward introduction to the issue calls on *Contact* readers to become active in the fight to stop tobacco promotion, especially in developing countries. To encourage group discussion and action, the bulletin offers a page of ideas and questions 'to help you examine and talk about tobacco and how it affects you and your country'. Here are some of the questions:

1. **What kind of image (for example, sportsman, rich businessman, romantic couple) is associated with the cigarette brands you know? Would you like to be in any of the situations that you see in these advertisements?**

2. **What are these advertisements telling you is the most important thing to have in life? Are these the things that you think are important in life?**

3. **Would you say that these cigarette brands are made to appeal to certain groups of potential buyers, for example young people or women? If so, how exactly do they do it?**

4. **How did you learn about the health risks associated with smoking?**

5. **In the tobacco advertisements that you see around you, is there any evidence that your government is trying to warn you of these health risks? Do you think that your government should be involved in this issue at all? If so, how?**[5]

Training for self-sufficiency □ Zonta International is an organization of women working to advance the status of women worldwide by supporting women in their efforts to get further training and

Do you know anyone who depends on tobacco for their living?

become self-sufficient. Zonta has provided financial support for co-operative projects with UNICEF, UNESCO, the United Nations International Research and Training Institute for the Advancement of Women (INSTRAW), and the United Nations Development Fund for Women (UNIFEM).

In co-operation with UNICEF, Zonta has supported a textile production project in Guatemala which includes a supply of supplementary food for the women and their families as well as training in the use of more advanced weaving looms. In Uruguay, Zonta supports a UNESCO-sponsored hostel for young mothers aged 13–21 and their babies. Through an integrated programme, the mothers are able to pursue primary and secondary education while at the same time learning about child and family welfare and acquiring skills to earn a living. The objective of the INSTRAW project was to involve women more effectively in water supply and sanitation programmes in Nigeria by mobilizing national women's organizations.

UNIFEM is a fund set up to ensure support for women's productive activities in developing countries, a development agency directed towards women and managed by women. Through UNIFEM projects Zonta has supported women in ten developing countries who are being trained in health promotion, nutrition, management and marketing techniques for agricultural co-operatives and other commercial enterprises, development of women's associations, and agricultural technology (with a revolving loan fund).[6]

A booklet addressed to Zonta members (women executives in business and the professions) urges them to support these local and international service projects that 'address a wide range of issues, including women's economic self-sufficiency, legislative equality, women aging, access to education and training, health and nutrition,

family planning—all considered basic human rights for women's development'.[7]

Maintaining effective communication ☐ Soroptimist International, a women's organization with affiliates in 87 countries, encourages its members to be 'an active influence for positive change in society through Awareness, Advocacy and Action'. Every four years a 'programme focus' is adopted, which is an outline of suggested topics for Soroptimist action in six programme areas (Economic and Social Development, Education, Environment, Health, Human Rights/Status of Women and International Goodwill and Understanding). Most of the topics are linked to specific paragraphs in the 'Forward Looking Strategies' developed at the 1985 Nairobi meeting on women.[8]

Soroptimist International has been particularly concerned about maintaining effective two-way communication between international agencies and NGOs at all levels. They look for ways to transmit the thinking and experience of 'grassroots' members to the international level, as well as making sure that members are aware of developments in international affairs. 'It is not only a question of raising consciousness amongst members but helping international agencies to identify NGO activities whose effect could be multiplied with technical assistance. In fact, improving the flow of information between NGOs and international agencies is essential to current thinking on "bottom up" development.'[9]

The case study that follows is based on two Soroptimist Programme Focus Reports, one from Cameroon and the other from the United Kingdom. They show similarities and differences in the way local Soroptimists translate the principles of 'Awareness, Advocacy and Action' into action, depending on the setting. The focus, 'AIDS awareness', was the same for both clubs.

CASE STUDY: SOROPTIMIST INTERNATIONAL—
ACTION ON AIDS

Reports from two local clubs

In Limbe, Cameroon, the AIDS Alert project was aimed especially at two target groups: young people and parents. Soroptimist members first visited the town's Youth Centres to discuss their plans with the young people. A loud speaker van that went around town before the scheduled talks helped to bring in a good audience. The young people listened intently and asked many questions. Some were learning about AIDS for the first time. Some were sceptical. Nevertheless, the talk given by a specialist from the local hospital, plus the facts and figures in the information materials that were distributed, helped convince them that the threat was real. At the same time they learned how they could avoid infection and found out about sources of help in the vicinity.

Local Soroptimists and speakers also visited all the post-primary education institutions in the area, giving talks and distributing information materials on AIDS. The Club sponsored a training programme on AIDS for the staff of local day care centres. Information on AIDS was incorporated in Soroptimist health, first aid and hygiene classes, with the Club's health co-ordinator responsible for follow-up.

The form on which Soroptimist clubs make their Programme Focus Report asks about the outcome of each project and recommendations. Under 'concerns, things to do differently', the Limbe Club made this observation: '. . . parents can be helped to do more to change the environment for their kids . . . we are concerned about the traditional taboos that make it almost impossible for parents to talk to their children about sex'. The Club will train day care staff and adult literacy instructors on teaching methods for adult learners, and help them to produce suitable teaching aids that include information on AIDS.

The Limbe Club, drawing on their experience thus far, has these recommendations for Soroptimists or other organizations doing similar work on AIDS: 'that more attention be paid to adult illiterates, to the poor and the young . . . greater effort to change the taboos that delay sex education . . . AIDS conferences at the regional, national or international levels should involve students/youth leaders and people who actually work at the grassroots. A lot of money is being spent on AIDS, but very little or nothing reaches the grassroots.'

In their future work in this field, the Limbe Club foresees more involvement of students in planning and carrying out activities. They want to motivate the student governing bodies to make their own plans for the continuing, permanent sensitizing of their peers. The Club intends to record or make a video tape of future activities.

In Falmouth, United Kingdom, the local branch of Soroptimist International organized an AIDS Awareness Seminar that brought together representatives of women's and men's service organizations, police officers, a Girl Guide Commissioner and the head of the local comprehensive junior school. Informal presentations were made by two specialists in AIDS Education from the Health Authority. According to the Programme Focus Report, they used 'audio-visual aids and a delightful touch of humour' to dispel the fear and misinform- ▶

ation that create barriers to understanding AIDS and its impact on an individual or a community.

Lots of time for questions, a coffee break that allowed people to get to know one another and share attitudes, group work on the advantages and disadvantages of being tested for HIV—all of these tactics helped people 'open up' and admit doubts or ignorance, and fears. Participants clearly grasped the message that AIDS must be a concern for *all* sectors of society and that it is a question of individual responsibility and collective action.

Although no specific recommendations for follow-up were made during the evening, there were several positive developments as a result of the Awareness Seminar. One of the speakers mentioned that the Health Promotion Department was having difficulty getting the AIDS education programme accepted in a nearby secondary school. A Seminar participant—from a service organization—called his organization's branch in the school district concerned and explained the situation. That branch in turn got in touch with the school authorities and it is likely that they will reconsider their position.

The Guide Commissioner who attended the Seminar asked for a similar 'awareness' evening for Girl Guides. Because one of the speakers reported that many young people were asking why they were not learning about the potential problem at a younger age, the local school system began to study the possibility of AIDS education for 12 and 13 year olds. The media course at the local College of Technology interviewed one of the speakers on Radio Falmouth and made plans to enlarge on the topic for World AIDS Day.

Based on Programme Focus Reports from Soroptimist International of Limbe, Cameroon, and Falmouth and District, United Kingdom, 1989

HEALTH EDUCATION ☐ From sophisticated television dramas to groups of village women gathered around a community health worker under a baobab tree . . . a large proportion of all activities to improve women's health would fall under the heading of 'health education'. The line between health education and the advocacy/awareness-raising activities just described is often blurred.

Health education programmes can vary enormously in form, method and content, but in general they focus on specific health problems with the objective of helping individuals acquire the knowledge and motivation needed in order to take action for their own health or that of their families and communities. Health education programmes of particular relevance to women have been carried out in formal or informal settings, in classrooms, workplaces, living-rooms and community meeting places. They may be systematically structured to transmit precise information, or they may concentrate on discussions and exercises that encourage women to ask questions and express their own beliefs and attitudes about health. Communication may be person-to-person or through printed materials, radio, video, television, theatre, puppets, music, and so forth.

Health education for young people

☐ Health education activities within the formal school system have increased greatly in the last few decades. Health curricula have been designed for children from pre-school age through secondary school. Sometimes health is regarded as a separate subject and is taught in regularly scheduled classes each week. In other systems 'health content' is integrated into the subject matter of other classes such as reading, mathematics, social studies, civics. Creative teachers get health and nutrition messages into early reading materials, games and group activities such as play-acting and puppet shows.

In mathematics classes children have learned how to make a graph by recording figures from a community PHC survey, or they may chart the average daily calorie requirements for people of different sizes, ages, levels of physical activity and, of course, gender, with a special category for pregnant and nursing mothers.

From the perspective of women's health, the important point about school-based health education programmes is to be sure they are relevant to local circumstances, that they recognize the specific health and nutrition needs of women and girls at different times of their lives, and that all topics are presented in a positive way that enhances the status of women. You might want to check, for example, and see how menstruation is handled in your local school system. Is it presented as part of the normal, healthy functioning of human beings who are female? Or is it treated in a way that makes women appear 'flawed', inferior or 'delicate'? Are old taboos and myths about uncleanliness perpetuated, perhaps by silence on the subject?

It is also important that the *same* health and nutrition information and family life education be given to both girls and boys, underscoring the joint responsibility of women and men in these areas.

There are programmes that encourage girls and boys, both in school and out of school, to become active health promoters in their families and villages. The Child-to-Child movement has helped prepare many children for this role, as have Red Cross and Red Crescent Youth groups and Boy Scout, Girl Guide and Pioneer programmes. These international movements are all committed to the principle of equal rights for women and men, girls and boys; but their leaders would no doubt admit the necessity to be sensitive to gender issues in health promotion and family-life education projects, and to pay close attention to what actually happens at local level.

Earlier chapters have mentioned the unmet need for health information among certain groups of young people, for example pre-adolescent girls, who need family-life education and information on STDs. Where school health education programmes do not meet their needs, or if they are not in school, NGOs have moved to fill the gap. The International Planned Parenthood Federation (IPPF) has encouraged special attention to out-of-school youth. Affiliates of the World Young Women's Christian Associations (YWCAs) and other women's organizations have been responsive to the needs of pre-adolescent and adolescent girls, especially those not in school. The programmes developed with this group often combine literacy training, skills training and health and family-life education. Among the intergovernmental agencies, UNICEF, UNESCO, UNFPA and WHO have become strong advocates for girls in this age group.

Health education for adults □ In discussing the need for health education among women, one must start with their need for more education of all kinds, not just on health. If women have been in school long enough to become literate, their access to health information, and all other kinds of information, is of course greatly increased. Many excellent printed health education materials exist for use at all levels, from the village to the university.

Sometimes language is a barrier. National NGOs have made a tremendous contribution by translating health education materials into national and local languages and adapting them to local conditions. UN agencies may provide support for this work. Some international NGOs have developed prototype materials expressly for translation and local adaptation. They deal with common health problems in simple, straightforward language, using illustrations that are not readily identified with a specific culture or leaving space for the work of local illustrators.

For non-literate adults there are many other ways to get the information needed for good health, starting with an exchange of ideas and experience in the community to identify their own needs and priorities.

PHOTO: MAGGIE MURRAY-LEE / UNICEF

Experienced health educators often warn 'outsiders' not to ignore the sizeable body of health information and health care experience that already exists in any community, particularly among the women.

Probably the most widely used method for health and nutrition education among illiterate women is to have a trained worker or volunteer, usually a woman, meet with small groups of women near their homes. Using a blackboard, wall-chart or other simple visual aids, these health educators convey essential health and nutrition information, keyed to local circumstances.

More importantly, they encourage the women to talk about their own health situation and to ask themselves why it is so and what they can do about it. There are rapid changes in health behaviour where adult education for women exists, even without

literacy, but especially if the content is focused on health. One expert in maternal and child health has commented: 'If you put information in a form relevant to women, it will be picked up and used. For example, home-based health records do work. . . . You don't have to wait for a generation to become literate before you can do this.'[11]

Radio programmes have also been widely used to get health information to non-literate audiences. They have been most successful when mixed with a little humour or drama, and when reinforced by community discussions or other types of follow-up. Television has proved to be a powerful medium for getting people to think about their health. In countries where a good proportion of the population can be reached by television, both 'spot messages' and longer programmes that dramatize health issues have had success in changing health behaviour.

Facts for Life □ With the zeal for health promotion and health education that followed Alma Ata (the conference that launched PHC), some families are bombarded with health messages from different sources—from the media, from schools, from the workplace, from health workers and community development workers, from NGOs, from government ministries. Ideally these messages should reinforce each other and not confuse people with contradictory advice; and the number of essential messages should be kept to a minimum. Because this was not always the case, three United Nations agencies—UNICEF, WHO and UNESCO—in partnership with more than 100· NGOs, undertook to get worldwide scientific consensus on essential child health information and publish it under the title *Facts for Life*.

It is addressed to 'those who influence or control the principal channels of communication in all societies'. It is presented as a

Marie F. was stunned when her doctor showed her the results of her recent mammogram and recommended surgery. But she recovered her composure quickly, grateful for the fact that she was at least somewhat prepared for this moment, thanks to Project H.E.L.P. Marie, along with many other Canadian women, had participated in Project H.E.L.P., the Health Education and Learning Project of the National Council of Jewish Women of Canada.

The objective of Project H.E.L.P. is 'to help women increase personal effectiveness in their own health care, specifically in relation to breast and gynecological surgical options'. The women who take part learn about the physiology of the breast and reproductive systems, about potential problems related to these systems, and treatment options, including surgical options. An evaluation of the project showed that participants gained in the ability to protect their own health and to 'feel more confident about their interactions with the health system'.

The project is funded by the Health and Welfare Department of the Canadian Government. Programme materials and leadership training techniques developed in Project H.E.L.P are to be shared with other organizations developing health promotion programmes.[10]

challenge to political leaders, educators, the media, employers, trade unions, the health professions and community health workers, development workers and voluntary agencies, women's organizations, youth movements, community organizations, traditional leaders, artists, writers, and entertainers.

Although the top ten health messages in *Facts for Life* are centred on children, most of them have major implications for the health and well-being of women as well (see box). *Facts for Life* is therefore of interest to people concerned about women's health, both as a tool for health education and because of the strategies for social mobilization that lie behind it:

- concentrate on a few basic ideas or messages;

- see that the same information comes from all sides, from all sources, for a long period of time;

- involve many different sectors of society in communicating these ideas, making clear why the outcome is important to them and how they can contribute.

FACTS FOR LIFE

'*Facts for Life* is a practical contribution to the evolving primary health care movement. Intended principally for the developing world, its national and international versions bring together today's essential family information on maternal and child health care. That information—about birth spacing, safe motherhood, breastfeeding, weaning and child growth, immunization, diarrhoeal diseases, respiratory infections, domestic hygiene, malaria and AIDS—could now enable most families in the developing world to make significant improvements in their own and their children's health. *Facts for Life* is therefore an aid to achieving the first level of primary health care—a well-informed community.'[12]

There is a companion volume to *Facts for Life* entitled *All for Health*. It 'distils what

has been learnt about the methods and pitfalls of health education in recent years and summarizes the essential "Twelve steps in health communication"':

1. **Define clearly what health behaviour you are trying to promote.**

2. **Decide exactly who in the population you are trying to influence.**

3. **Ask whether the new health behaviour requires new skills.**

4. **Learn about the present health knowledge, beliefs and behaviour of the target audience.**

5. **Enquire whether the health behaviour you are trying to promote has already been introduced to the community.**

6. **Investigate the target audience's present sources of information about health.**

7. **Select the communication channels and media which are most capable of reaching and influencing the target audience.**

8. **Design health messages that are easily understandable, culturally and socially appropriate, practical, brief, relevant, technically correct, and positive.**

9. **Develop and test your educational materials.**

10. **Synchronize your educational programme with other health and development services.**

11. **Evaluate whether the intended new behaviour is being carried out.**

12. **Repeat and adjust the messages at intervals over several years.** [13]

MEDIA ☐ The relationship between women and the media has changed dramatically in the past decade, reflecting a

Smart
Women
Don't
Smoke

The Female Smoker:
At Added Risk

World's 2nd No-Tobacco Day
31 May 1989

World Health Organization, Geneva.

Original design contributed by CHATA London. (33 Stillness Rd. SE23 1NG)

Biman Mullick

wider trend towards getting issues that women consider important into the mainstream. The March 1989 number of *The Tribune*, a Women and Development quarterly put out by the International Women's Tribune Centre, is entitled 'Women Using Media to Effect Change'. The introduction chronicles the evolution of the women–media relationship:

'Women Using Media to Effect Change' is the third issue of *The Tribune* to explore the topic of women and the media. Our first two issues, with the highly original titles of 'Women and Media, Part I' and 'Women and Media, Part II', began with the premise 'women are excluded, ignored, demeaned in the mainstream media so. . . .' The conclusion to that phrase and the jumping off point for both issues was '. . . so they need to create their own media'. We then explored the multitude of women's alternative communication activities ranging from street theatre to video to publication of periodicals. These 'alternative' communication modes are, in a very real sense, women's 'mass media' since, given women's higher rates of illiteracy, it is the type of media that is more likely to reach the majority, or 'masses', of women in many countries.

150

The underlying premise for this newsletter remains the same as the previous two issues, but we changed the ending to say '. . . so look at the skills and strategies we are using to change that media'. In groups large and small, in workshops, seminars and conferences, women are showing a determination to use the 'mainstream' media to move the issues we have identified as important onto the public agenda.

For people trying to get women's health issues onto the public agenda, this issue of *The Tribune* (no. 41) should be required reading. It is, as always, visually interesting, and very informative. It is full of examples of women using the media effectively, with many practical suggestions for getting results—how to write a press release, prepare a fact sheet, create a press kit, develop media contacts. (See Organizing for Group Action: Some Ideas, at the end of this section.)

In NGO and United Nations agency work on women's health issues, there is widespread use of both alternative and mainstream media. *Facts for Life*, for example, is aimed at communicators in both those sectors. Women's health networks (see pp. 170–72) have created their own alternative channels for communicating with one another, but they also make use of mainstream media.

NGOs have sensitized their members to the importance of media images of women. They urge audiences to react, to protest, when women are portrayed negatively or with stereotypes, as helpless victims, sex objects, fragile and dependent, unable to make a decision or have an opinion worth taking seriously.

Reacting against the negative, however, is only part of the solution. In a more positive vein, NGO action on women's health has included discussions or seminars

with female and male professionals in journalism, radio and television. The idea is to build up long-term relationships and sensitize these opinion moulders to women's health issues, providing them with both factual information and human interest stories. It means doing your homework on the issues and earning their professional respect. Many international organizations, as noted earlier, help out on this by preparing kits on different issues. The kits usually include fact sheets, sample press releases, short articles and photographs. Local branches can pass these materials on to their media contacts, adding information on a related local issue or event.

Women's media networks have sprung up in several regions: FEMPRESS in Latin America; DepthNews Women's Feature Service in Asia; the Association of African Women Professionals in Communication (APAC) in Africa. The addresses of these networks are given in *The Tribune*. There is also an international Women's Feature Service within the InterPress Service (IPS) (see box).

'The Women's Feature Service is centrally managed from Rome, Italy and regionally from Costa Rica, France, India, Jamaica, Philippines and Zimbabwe. It has a network of almost 150 journalists, editors, translators and managers from 60 countries.

The Women's Feature Service is also available as an English and Spanish bi-monthly bulletin, which is a selection of the service.

The Women's Feature Service can prepare custom made dossiers on the following issues and more: environment, health, community organizing, local movements, migration, changing values and norms, workers' rights, ethnic conflicts and refugees.'[14]

A few NGOs or coalitions of NGOs, as well as government agencies, have produced their own health-related materials for use by the mass media. Many of these productions are found in the field of family planning, a field where cultural sensitivity is especially important. One expert in this field stresses the link between traditional and modern means of communication:

Tradition can be used as a bridge to the future and should not be neglected. In order to get across the economic, population and family planning messages to the bulk of families, various traditional beliefs, practices and ways of communication could be used. The modern mass media, of course, have an important role to play, but [their] message must be acceptable to the personal norms and aspirations for well-being.[15]

This author feels that much more could be done to build on those aspects of tradition and culture that de-emphasize fertility. For example, 'In Ghana a mother is not expected to be procreating once her own daughters become mothers; her duty as a grandmother is [to assist] in the care of her grandchildren.' The media could stress this tradition when advising women to avoid late pregnancies. The traditional marriage ceremony in Ghana invokes ancestors and gods to bless the couple with many children. In a televised or broadcast drama a couple might express the view that having fewer but well-cared-for, healthy children gives greater honour to their ancestors than sheer numbers.

ORGANIZING/NETWORKING ☐ A distinctive feature of the 1980s was the extraordinary growth of networks and loosely linked self-help groups concerned with women's health.

. . . the universality of women's disadvantage has led to the rise of feminist leaders, institutions, and political movements in virtually every region of the world.[16]
Networks emerge when people are trying to change society.[17]

ORGANIZING FOR GROUP ACTION: SOME IDEAS

- *Appoint a Media Coordinator, but don't leave all the work to her.* Too often a group will appoint one person as their 'media person' expecting her to do all the work.

- *Assess your group's skills and interests.* Who among you has good writing skills? Involve her in writing press releases. Who likes to watch television or listen to the radio? Ask her to participate in a media monitoring project. Who enjoys reading publications from other countries? Ask her to keep her eye out for articles on what other groups are doing around your issue which you might use in preparing your own materials. Who among you has a keen political sense? Ask her to be alert to events or opportunities that you might take advantage of to get your issue into the media.

- *Identify one person to serve as your spokeswoman.* Give her all the necessary backup support required to move your issue onto the public agenda.

- *Know your issue.* Collect facts, statistics and examples of incidents in your own community that illustrate how your issue affects women around you. Organize your information systematically and decide on how you will communicate it to the press.

- *Know your opposition.* Know their position and the arguments that may be used against you. Anticipate in advance how you will respond.

- *Plan to spend time.* We must recognize that working with the media is not a one-shot effort, but an ongoing process.

- *Plan to spend money.* Be sure to budget money for postage, paper, printing, etc.

- *Develop a plan or strategy.* Then persevere.

- *Collaborate.* If there is an issue or project too large for one group to manage on their own, join forces.

THE TRIBUNE, NEWSLETTER 41, INTERNATIONAL WOMEN'S
TRIBUNE CENTRE

Many older NGOs and women's organizations perform some of the same functions as networks, but they differ from a network in that they have a more formal, stable structure, usually more centralized. Something different seemed to be needed for certain tasks and certain women. What was it? Here are a few attempts to define or describe a network:

- **A new word for an old idea.**
- **Networking is a verb, not a noun . . . the important part is the process.**
- **. . . a love affair rather than a marriage.**
- **. . . a fluid form of organization in which women and women's groups keep total independence regarding their priorities and strategies and have their own analysis of their situation; they are only committed to sharing information and supporting each other's struggle.**
- **This network is not intended to be an association; its purpose is simply to facilitate access to information and to each other.**
- **Whereas conventional organization charts have boxes arranged in some hierarchical order with a leader on top, a network looks like a 'badly knotted fishnet' with a multitude of nodes or cells . . . each linked to all others directly or indirectly.**[18]

Networks and loose coalitions seemed to suit many of the people who were organizing to become active on women's health issues in the 1970s and 1980s. A few examples will illustrate the geographic and cultural diversity of these collectives and the wide range of interests they represent:

- Bangladesh Women's Health Coalition.
- National Black Women's Health Project (USA).

- International Women's Health Coalition.
- Boston Women's Health Book Collective.
- DAWN, a network of Third World women promoting Development Alternatives for Women for a New Era.
- Women's Health Resource Information Collective (Canada).
- Women's Global Network on Reproductive Rights.
- Latin American and Caribbean Women's Health Network (ISIS—Latin America).
- ISIS International, 'an action-oriented resource centre and information service' supporting regional and national networks.
- The Asian and Pacific Women's Resource Collection Network.
- Gabriela National Women's Coalition (Philippines).
- Women Working Worldwide (United Kingdom).
- Women and AIDS Resource Network, New York.
- Global Link for Midlife and Older Women (GLOW).

If your group is preparing to act on women's health issues, you will find it worthwhile to contact NGOs, networks and resource centres such as those mentioned in this chapter. You might want to subscribe to one of their publications. You will learn more about what is already happening in your field of interest, and you may be able to increase your impact by joining forces with others. (See Annexe IV for useful names and addresses.)

WOMEN IN DECISION-MAKING POSITIONS □ It is commonplace to say that we will not have the needed

changes in health (or in education, or in government, or in development programmes) until there are more women in decision-making positions, that is women with the power or authority to make things happen to improve women's health.

Simply having a woman making decisions at a high level does not, of course, guarantee improvements in the lives of women generally. The essential is to have a person, woman or man, who understands the reality of women's lives, who is sensitive to gender issues, and who is committed to working towards greater equity between women and men. Being a woman does not automatically ensure all those qualities, but it helps.

What is our usual image of a woman in a 'decision-making position'? Perhaps it makes you think of a highly-qualified, determined woman in an executive suite or minister's office, briskly going through the papers on her desk, and dispatching aides to carry out the decisions she makes. That is one possibility, and some very capable women have contributed greatly to the health of their countries, and especially to women's health, in that way.

But consider some other images of 'women in decision-making positions' that might contribute just as much to women's health. We need to get millions of women into decision-making positions like these:

- *In the home*—participating in decisions about eating habits, family size and spacing of births; deciding how to manage family income; deciding what crops to plant; deciding when to take a daughter to the health clinic for medical attention.

- *In the community*—deciding with the rest of the people in the village where new water wells should be located; deciding whether to build 'waiting facilities' for mothers-at-risk; asking whether the health needs of older women (those beyond the MCH stage) are adequately met.

- *In the schools*—women and young girls must help decide what should be in the health curriculum and general curriculum, how the pre-adolescents can be informed about STDs, AIDS and other health issues important to them, what can be done to bring down a high drop-out rate among girls.

- *In the workplace*—women having a voice in decisions about working conditions, promotion policies, salary scales, maternity leave, parental leave, child care, pension funds and retirement policies.

- *In the nation*—deciding on candidates, casting their vote and bringing into office people who are prepared to give higher priority to the things that are important to women's health.

Wherever women are, whatever they are doing, they need to be in 'decision-making positions'.

Women who are sensitive to gender issues and who have risen to responsible offices are able to do a great deal to change the picture of women's health. Two examples:

- The National Institutes of Health in the United States recently created an Office of Research on Women's Health to see that women are no longer excluded from research studies as they have been in the past: 'From now on, scientists proposing to study only men will have to justify that decision on scientific grounds.' Three women in the US Congress were instrumental in getting this legislation through.[19]

- The woman who was Executive Director of the American Veterans' Committee discovered in the late 1970s that the US Veterans Administration (VA) published

154

PHOTO: P. ALMASY / WHO

107 different categories of information on the veteran population but that none of it was broken down by sex. An important study of VA hospitals in 1977 said in its preface, 'In this study only male veterans are considered because the female veterans amount to less than 2%.'

- Nevertheless, that two per cent were entitled to comprehensive health care, like the men, which they could not get because the VA hospitals did not have gynaecological services or adequate facilities for women. Again it was circular: because the hospitals were not set up to handle women's health problems, women veterans did not go there; because they did not go there, administrators argued that there was no demand for such services and therefore no need to change.

But the situation was changed when the Executive Director of the American Veterans' Committee, with the support of her own (almost all-male) organization and some influential Congressmen, demanded change. The data collected now by the VA are broken down by gender, and the VA has recognized the right of some two million women veterans to have the same comprehensive coverage in health care that is available to men veterans.[20]

In many other countries and regions of the world, qualified, capable women leaders are making their mark in large and small ways. They are heads of government and intergovernmental agencies, they direct health and health-related ministries, they serve in legislative bodies and in all kinds of private organizations dealing with health issues.

The increased participation of women in decision-making at all levels and in all spheres of activity is surely one of the more positive developments of the last decade. But in all countries, there *is* a long way to go.

CONCLUSION ☐ One cannot review the state of women's health today without profound concern. The age-old underlying causes of women's ill-health— discrimination, poverty, ignorance—seem to be as alive and irrepressible as ever in many places. However, if the preceding chapters have left you with that impression only, please go back and re-read the short profile of Aba at the end of Chapter 2.

There *are* 'more and more like her' today, and their numbers are growing. But there could and should be millions more. There is a ferment of activity among women in all parts of the world as they take initiatives to improve their own health and that of their families and communities. There are literally thousands of small and large groups, collectives, coalitions, networks, organi-

zations . . . all taking action on the health issues that are priorities for women.

This is reason to reaffirm the cautious optimism of the 1981 Kit on Women and Health. Even more, the UN/NGO Group on Women and Development hope you will see it as reason to become active yourself, in whatever way is open to you, in support of this drive to make the world a healthier place for women, for all.

1 From the manual, *Training for Primary Health Care*, produced by the World YWCA (Young Women's Christian Association), Geneva, 1989. As featured in *Common Concern* (quarterly publication of the World YWCA), no. 63, September 1989.

2 *Help Her Have a Happy Birth-day*, Information Kit jointly produced by the International Council of Nurses, International Confederation of Midwives, UNICEF and WHO, 1987.

3 International Confederation of Midwives (ICM), *Planning for Action by Midwives*, report of a workshop on 'Enhancing National Midwifery Services', Accra, Ghana, January 1989; London, ICM, 1989.

4 International Confederation of Midwives, draft programme for pre-Congress workshop, Kobe, Japan, October 1990.

5 *Contact*, newsletter of the Christian Medical Commission, World Council of Churches, no. 114, May 1990.

6 Zonta International, *1988–90 Z Club Program Packet*, Chicago, 1988.

7 Zonta International, *1988–90 Biennium*.

8 The 'Forward Looking Strategies (FLS) for the Advancement of Women' came out of the 1985 Nairobi Conference to review and appraise the achievements of the just-ending UN Decade for Women. The Forward Looking Strategies have been described as 'a tool and guide for achieving vital changes in issues of concern to women'. The International Council on Social Welfare has produced an excellent publication, 'Women: Their Vital Role in Development, Some Observations of ICSW on the Forward Looking Strategies for the Advancement of Women'. It reviews the issues addressed in the FLS and shows how they are being used to stimulate study and action within ICSW.

9 S. Heptonstall, personal communication to the author, 7 January 1990.

10 National Council of Jewish Women of Canada, 'Surgery, a Necessity or a Choice?', report on the Health Education and Learning Project (H.E.L.P.), Ontario, Canada, September 1989.

11 Intervention at Expert Group Meeting on Family Planning, Fertility Decline and Child Survival, UNFPA, New York, May 1990.

12 UNICEF, WHO and UNESCO, *Facts for Life—A Communication Challenge*, nd.

13 UNICEF, WHO and UNESCO, *All for Health—A Resource Book for Facts for Life*, nd. Both *Facts for Life* and *All for Health* can be ordered from UNICEF, New York.

14 Announcement about the Women's Feature Service appearing in *Development*, 1990: 1, p. 47.

15 M. Greenstreet, 'Education and Reproductive Choices in Ghana: Gender Issues in Population Policy', *Development*, 1990: 1, p. 44.

16 B. Gaberman, Ford Foundation, as quoted in Chetley, *A Healthy Business?*, London, Zed Books, 1990, p. 27.

17 V. Hine, anthropologist, as quoted by J. Naisbitt in 'Networking: One of the New Directions Transforming Our Lives', *Communities in Action* (WHO), Newsletter 16, 1985, p. 17.

18 Definitions taken from the Naisbitt article (n. 17), from the IBFAN (International Baby Food Action Network) Kit on Breastfeeding, and *Women's World*, no. 21–2, 1989.

19 *International Herald Tribune*, 12 September 1990.

20 J. Willenz, *Women Veterans: America's Forgotten Heroines*, New York, Continuum, 1983.

ANNEX I CASE STUDY

Policy Planning for Women's Development at Provincial Level – The Case of Rajasthan[1]

Sudhir Varma,* a member of SID Rajasthan, one of SID's most active Chapters in the area of women in development, describes women's status in India at both national and local level. He argues for a much stronger recognition of women's needs in development, particularly at the local decision-making level.

THE NATIONAL PICTURE

The issues relating to women in development which began to take shape in the early 1970s have by now assumed proportions which cannot be ignored by policy planners and administrators anywhere in the world. Governments have responded in a wide variety of ways to the exhortations made from time to time to create national machineries to meet the needs of women in development. In most of the third world countries, 'patch-works' have resulted both at the policy and implementation levels. Projects have been prepared—many in a great hurry—with women as a target group. More often, a 'women's component' has been tacked onto many an ongoing programme with indifferent results.

The Indian response to the World Plan of Action 1975, drawn up at Mexico, was quicker than most of the other developing countries. There were two reasons for this: firstly, a Prime Minister who was sensitive to women's issues, and, secondly, a report

had just been submitted by a Committee on the Status of Women in India, set up in 1971 under pressure from international agencies, to the Indian parliament, to coincide with the International Women's Year.

Unfortunately, the Indian Planning Commission in the draft Sixth Five Year Plan 1980–1985 included a separate chapter on Women and Development without integrating its many important suggestions into the mainline chapters which contained detailed programmes and financial allocations. The same approach continued in the Seventh Five Year Plan 1985–1990, with the result that most of the ideas remained on paper—due principally to a continued lack of strong and sensitive machinery at the central and provincial levels to handle women's issues.

In India there has not been a serious attempt to respond administratively to the suggestions made by the United Nations. The concern at the provincial level was even less.

RAJASTHAN

The State of Rajasthan in Western India is one of the most backward regions in the country. Its entire socio-cultural setting has a feudal background with 'purdah', widows suffering from a fate worse than an animal, a history of 'Sati' and 'Jauhar', child marriages, growing distances for collection of fuel-wood and water owing to geographical reasons as well as natural calamities, and female literacy failing to improve while the birth rate increases. There continues a highly adverse sex ratio and reports of female infanticides. The majority of women toil unpaid in single-cropped, small pieces of land.

STATUS OF WOMEN IN RAJASTHAN

The health status of a woman in rural Rajasthan is extremely poor. The state has

* Sudhir Varma is Secretary to Government of Social Welfare, Women and Child Development, Rajasthan, Jaipur, India.

the highest crude birth rate in the country —39.7. The total fertility rate is also high at 6.0 compared to 4.8 in the country and the Infant Mortality Rate in rural Rajasthan in 1985 was 114 compared to 107 in rural India. The improvement in Infant Mortality Rate has been one of the slowest in the country. The rate for the Scheduled Castes is much higher than the average. For example, in 1978, when the rural average Infant Mortality Rate was 139, it was 188 for Scheduled Castes. The expectation of life at birth is lower for a female (59 years) than for a male (59.6 years) and will continue to be so till the turn of the century. Maternal mortality is also one of the highest with 9 out of 10 births being attended to by untrained *dais*. The mean age at marriage for girls is also the lowest in the country at 16.09 years along with the highest proportion of married children in the 10–14 years age group at 18.31 per cent for girls compared to 6.59 per cent in the country. The sex ratio, with 919 females for 1,000 males, is also much lower than the Indian average of 933—the lowest being 830 in the rural areas of Districts Bharatpur and Jaisalmer —both notorious for reports of female infanticides. The state is far away from the objective of 'Health for All' laid down for 2000 A.D.

In the field of education also, the female literacy rate is only 11.31 per cent but it is as low as 2.59 per cent for Scheduled Castes and 1.2 per cent for Scheduled Tribe women in the State. The enrolment ratio of girls at primary level was only 30.4 per cent in 1985. For Scheduled Caste girls it was lower at 22 per cent and for Scheduled Tribe girls 23.3 per cent. With a very high drop-out rate of 58.2 per cent for girls at the primary level, the enrolment ratio becomes irrelevant. The work participation rate in the state for females in 1981 was only 9.3 per cent compared to an average 14 per cent for the country; 85.8 per cent of these workers are in the agriculture sector and the percentage of total workers in the organized sector is only 2.1, the figure having remained more or less constant for the last few years. The impact of poverty alleviation programmes for women is also not satisfactory.

There is a wide divergence between status in Indian States (see Table on p. 160) which suggests that a single national policy may not be of much relevance in a country the size and diversity of India. The raising of women's status as a whole has to be a sum total of efforts in individual states requiring regional policies and micro level solutions.

GENDER BLINDNESS IN POLICY PLANNING

As in most of the countries of the world, policy planning in the sectors of health, education, and employment in India has been generally gender-neutral. Although at the national level some change has occurred, policy-making for women has not been at the state level. The state governments have always looked to the central planning process to devise programmes. With a drought-ridden economy, Rajasthan, in particular, has always depended on centrally-sponsored schemes in these areas. From its own resources it has not been able to touch the State's high rate of illiteracy, ill health and poverty. The Sixth Five Year Plan of Rajasthan, unlike the National Plan document, did not even think to include a separate chapter on women's development. The International Decade for Women also by-passed the region where women badly needed intervention. Gender-neutrality continued even in the State Plan objectives of raising the living standards of the weaker sections. Though Scheduled Castes and Scheduled Tribes, rural artisans, small and marginal farmers, agricultural labourers were mentioned, women were not.

Thus, at the national level there have

A RANGE OF INDICATORS IN VARIOUS REGIONS OF INDIA

	India	Rajasthan	Gujrat	Tamil Nadu	Kerala
Crude birth rate (1985)	34	39.7	33	24.7	23.3
Total fertility rate (1984)	4.8	6.0	4.2	3.5	2.4
Infant mortality rate (Rural) (1985)	107	114	112	95	32
Mean age at marriage (Girls) (1981)	18.32	16.09	19.51	20.22	21.85
Sex ratio (1981)	933	919	942	977	1032
Literacy rate (Female) (1981)	28.5	13.4	36.9	39.4	73.4
Enrolment ratio (Girls) 5–9 Years (1981)	32.2	16.28	39.4	54.6	75.1
Work participation rate (Female) (1981)	14.0	9.3	11.0	22.4	12.8

Source: Census of India, 1981

been some signs of bringing women into the mainstream of development, but in Rajasthan even these signs are missing. Rajasthan has never attempted a policy document on public health. The State government has blindly followed the central government's policy of expanding medical services under a formula not suitable to the State geographically and socially, especially not for women. The State has refused to shoulder the burden of health care and most of the programmes are implemented only as centrally-sponsored schemes under strict guidelines laid down by the Government of India. With the central expenditure also being very low—expenditure on health as percentage of expenditure in the public sector from the First to the Seventh Plan being 1.9 and on family welfare 1.5—the central schemes have not had any impact.

The State on its part has spent on an average only 2.7 per cent of its total plan expenditure on health and nothing on family welfare, which covers most of the programmes on women's health. Most of this expenditure has gone towards salaries and establishment costs. These meagre resources have also gone primarily for men. Women have by and large been left out of the health care delivery system especially in the difficult tribal, hilly and desert areas of the state, as revealed by the sex-based data of outdoor and indoor patients of rural dispensaries and hospitals.

It is well known that most of the members of a household are not interested in the health of the woman of the house unless her condition is near to death. Neglected by the State, a strange sense of well-being has developed among rural women. During a survey of rural areas of Rajasthan, the author found that women considered themselves healthy if they were able to work at home or on the farm and felt satisfied with their nutritional intake if they got enough food to keep them working. Although their health parameters were extremely poor, most of the women felt they were in good health and were eating sufficient food.

GIRLS' EDUCATION

Nor has there been a separate policy on education even though the literacy rates for women are extremely low. Although anxieties about the low enrolment ratio and high drop-out rates have been expressed from Plan to Plan, the basic causes for the low literacy rates, which can be rectified only at the state level, have not been attended to. The central government tends to blame the State governments for being a major obstruction to the growth of literacy rate in the country but has never taken seriously their need, as regions, for focused attention and financial support. Politicians at State level must bear some of the blame for not understanding the role of girls' education and for having put pressure on governments to convert most of the proposed girls' primary and upper primary schools into boys'. Like health, resource constraints at the State level have been a major obstacle in the path of universalization of elementary education. For example, in the ongoing Seventh Five Year Plan, Rajasthan could put only 4 per cent of its total outlay into the field of elementary education. This was slightly higher than the 2.8 per cent put into the Sixth Plan, but was insignificant in comparison with the need. Except for mentioning girls' education as a priority area, State governments of northern India have done almost nothing to devise a strategy for micro-level planning and implementation of programmes of education and have been procrastinating on the universalization of elementary education.

It is at the provincial level that one realizes the stark contrast of women's poverty to men's. Government employment programmes must therefore differ from place to place, from region to region, to ensure that women are reached. Similar programmes for all the regions administered by the central/federal governments are of little use. In the sector of health there are many areas which can be corrected only at the provincial level. For example, all appointments of doctors and paramedical staff are made at that level and to give more weight to women doctors and paramedical staff can only be done at that level. In the field of education, opening and maintaining schools for girls at the primary and upper primary levels could be more effectively done by a strong provincial administration. In the matters of finance also, it is only a strong provincial policy which can provide more money in the health and education sectors for women.

THE GOVERNMENT ORGANIZATION FOR WOMEN IN INDIA

Despite the great need, the Women's Bureau in India is one of the weakest in the world in proportion to the size of the country and the poor status of women. It is weakly structured and ill-defined, particularly at the State level. In most of the States in India there is no separate department for women and children. By and large the State departments of Social Welfare look after women's issues also. Most of them still have the 'welfare approach' and are oblivious of the developments in the field of women's issues in the world or even within the country.

In Rajasthan, which is, however, one of the very few States to have a separate department for women, the concept of a Bureau has still to take shape. It has been for the last four years a programme-oriented department and is unable to shepherd a movement to raise the status of women. The State Social Welfare Advisory Board, which is expected to play the role of an apex body for non-governmental organizations at the provincial level, is dormant. It has little or no authority to initiate programmes suiting the needs of women at the regional level. Its budget is also very paltry. Unlike some developed countries, no provincial level statutory advisory council has been set up.

Another problem is the approach of officials towards women's issues. It has been noticed that State-level departments —other than the Department of Women— are much more gender-blind than their counterpart departments at the central level, requiring much more vigorous conscientization efforts. This is probably because the officials at the central level have a much better knowledge than the state officials of what is happening in other countries.

Therefore, while training officials, efforts need to be made at the provincial (State) level to sensitize officers of other departments and agencies (such as credit institutions) through workshops and seminars and publicity.

In addition to strengthening the main department handling women's issues, the approach to women's issues by provincial departments such as Medical, Health and Family Welfare, Education, Labour, Industries, Science and Technology, Agriculture, Animal Husbandry, Cooperatives, etc., need to be changed. It can be noted that at the State level, some of the departments like home and labour have not yet adopted a developmental approach and are therefore unable to prepare plans of action which will integrate women into development.

In conclusion, for women to truly be part of the development process in India, the States must be integrated into all areas of local government policy—education, health, labour and policy planning. Only with a strong State programme recognizing women's special needs, and involving women at all levels in development will India be responding to the worldwide call for women's fuller participation.

---

1 Journal of the Society for International Development, *Development* 1990: 1, Young Women: Production/Reproduction and Life Choices.

ANNEX II

DEFINITIONS

OF KEY TERMS

amniocentesis a technique used to draw amniotic fluid from the uterus of a pregnant woman to determine the sex of the foetus, or to screen for chromosomal abnormality.

anaemia a condition in which the blood is deficient in haemoglobin or red blood cells. May be caused by lack of iron, folic acid or other vitamins and trace elements in the diet, or be the result of malaria, hookworm, and other infections.

anorexia *or* **anorexia nervosa** prolonged and severe loss of appetite, refusal or inability to eat.

bulimia condition characterized by bouts of compulsive overeating followed by self-induced vomiting, purging or fasting.

carcinogen a substance or agent producing or inciting cancer.

cardiovascular relating to the heart and blood vessels.

cirrhosis a chronic disease, especially of the liver, with hardening caused by excessive formation of connective tissue.

dementia deteriorating mental capacity, often marked by memory loss and confusion.

ectopic pregnancy a pregnancy where the fertilized ovum (egg cell) is implanted and develops outside the uterus, usually in one of the fallopian tubes.

fallopian tubes pair of tubes that carry the ovum (egg cell) from the ovary to the uterus or womb.

FAS (foetal alcohol syndrome) the defective development of the foetus as a result of the mother drinking alcohol during pregnancy—cause of physical and mental impairments.

fertility rate *or* **general fertility rate** the number of live births per 1,000 women aged 15–49 years in a given year. **total fertility rate** the average number of children that would be born alive to a woman over her lifetime if she were to pass through her child-bearing years conforming to the age-specific fertility rates of a given year.

FLS ('Forward Looking Strategies for the Advancement of Women . . .') see n. 8, Chapter 5.

gishiri cut a traditional procedure found in northern Nigeria whereby the vagina of a woman in prolonged obstructed labour is cut, usually with a razor blade, in an attempt to relieve the obstruction. Also used to 'treat' menstrual disturbances, infertility and other problems.

GNP (gross national product) the total domestic and foreign output claimed by residents of a country.

hypertension abnormally high blood pressure.

incidence rate the number of persons contracting a disease as a proportion of the population at risk, per unit of time.

life expectancy the average number of additional years a person would live if current mortality trends were to continue. Most commonly cited as life expectancy at birth.

mammography X-ray examination of the breasts.

maternal death 'the death of a woman while pregnant or within 42 days of termination of pregnancy irrespective of the duration of or the site of the pregnancy' (WHO).

maternal mortality rate number of maternal deaths per 100,000 live births in a given year (WHO). (Sometimes defined as 'number of deaths of of women due to pregnancy and childbirth complications per 100,000 live births in a given year.')

MCH maternal and child health.

morbidity the prevalence of disease and illness in a given population.

ovulate to produce or discharge eggs from an ovary.

pelvis the basin-shaped structure of bones in the lower body.

perineal tissue tissue in the area between the anus and the posterior part of the external genitalia, especially in women.

PHC (primary health care) 'essential health care based on practical, scientifically sound and socially acceptable methods and technology made universally accessible to individuals and families in the community through their full participation and at a cost that the community and country can afford' (WHO).

prevalence rate the number of persons having a particular disease at a given point in time per population at risk.

schistosomiasis an endemic parasitic disease transmitted to humans via vector snails; causes blood loss and tissue damage.

STDs sexually transmitted diseases.

toxaemia *or* pre-eclampsia a serious condition in pregnancy in which abnormally high blood pressure is combined with oedema (water retention) and protein in the urine; requires immediate medical attention.

urethra the duct by which urine is carried off from the bladder and discharged from the body.

uterine prolapse a condition in which the muscles of the pelvic floor weaken and allow the uterus to descend into the vagina.

VVF vesico-vaginal fistulae (see Chapter 4, Maternal morbidity).

ANNEX III

A GUIDE TO EDUCATION AND ACTION

IN THIS ANNEXE, the UN/NGO Group on Women and Development would like to suggest ways in which this book can be used by groups that wish to deepen their understanding of women's health issues as a prelude to advocacy and action.

Because of the diversity among the readers of this series, not all these suggestions will be relevant to every group. You may be using this book in a development education group, or in connection with an action programme in your community. The members of your group may all be women, or a mixture of men and women, older and younger generations. You may be in an academic setting with formal classes or in an informal discussion group that meets in someone's living-room. You may belong to an established international agency or NGO, or to an embryonic women's health collective.

Whatever your situation and your objectives, we trust you will be able to adapt some of these ideas to your needs or that in reviewing them you will be inspired to come up with other, better ideas for your group. Your group must come to its own conclusions regarding its priority issues, the causes and consequences of women's ill-health in your area of concern, and the opportunities for action that are open to you.

In the suggestions that follow the phrase 'your area' appears frequently. Interpret this broadly. It can mean: your locality or region where your group operates; your area of concern or interest; your sphere of action (local, district, national, regional or international). In short, it refers to what-

ever constitutes the 'arena for action' of your group.

SUGGESTIONS AND QUESTIONS FOR YOU AND YOUR GROUP TO CONSIDER

- Review Chapter 4, select a *few* key issues—the ones that are most important to the women in your area or to the members of your group, or the issues where you have the best opportunities for taking action and bringing about change—and concentrate on those. Perhaps after discussion you will decide that Chapter 4 does not include the key issue that is most important for your group. Identify and define your own key issue(s).

- To find out what the major health issues are for women in your area, consult them. You could also contact your local public health authorities or the personnel of health facilities. Identify the major causes of illness and death for women. Perhaps someone from the public health department or from a health facility could come and discuss the issues with your group. If the data you need about women's health are not available, then you have another kind of challenge. (See the beginning sections of Chapter 2 and Chapter 5 about getting the information you need.)

- When you have decided on the key issue or issues you want to address, review Chapter 3, Factors Influencing Women's Health. In your area, which of these background factors—poverty, status of women, policy decisions, demography, local customs, and so on—are at work in the issues you are addressing?

- Discuss what it would take to bring about change in the issues you have identified, or in the background factors that contribute to the women's health problems you are concerned with. Who needs to act? Is it the women directly concerned? Is it policy-makers or decision-makers in related areas? How can your group stimulate the action that is required?

- Review Chapter 5, Action to Improve Women's Health. Which of the examples of action given there and in other chapters would be appropriate for your group in connection with the health issues you want to work on? Talk about the strengths and weaknesses your group would have in undertaking each type of action. Where might you get help, information, support? Locally, from a national or international organization or network? (See Annexe IV for a list of relevant organizations.)

- Find out who else is doing what in connection with the health issues that interest your group. Are other groups working on some of the same issues locally, nationally or internationally? What kinds of activities are they engaged in (for example, advocacy, lobbying, media campaigns, health education programmes, community self-help projects, support groups)? Are the women most directly concerned aware of the issues and involved in the action? If not, could your group bring them together? Discuss whether there are 'gaps' that your group could fill. Would you be more effective by joining forces with other groups? What are the pro's and con's of that approach?

- Could your group make use of the material in any of the Information Kits mentioned in this book, most of them produced by international organizations and networks? Could you take the international material and tailor it to the needs of your members or your community?—Perhaps translate sections into local languages? Or could you combine these materials with local information, photographs, statistics and testimonies of local women and health workers? A reminder of a few of the subjects covered in these kits: safe motherhood; what nurses and midwives can do to promote safe motherhood; preventing heart attacks; breast-feeding; women and AIDS; women and smoking; and so on.

- If your group decides to do something in the area of advocacy/awareness-raising, you could centre a discussion or seminar on the points raised in Chapter 5, including the different examples of health education, social mobilization, advocacy and awareness-raising in relation to AIDS, smoking, maternal and child health, and so forth. Does your group have contacts with the media? Do you have a publication where you could present information or questions that would stimulate discussion on the issues you have chosen? How would the '12 steps in health communication' (from the book *All for Health*) apply to the action your group is planning?

- You could have a revealing discussion by looking carefully at the case study on Rajasthan in Annexe 1 and relating it to Chapter 3, Factors Influencing Women's Health. Which factors are at work in the situation described in the case study? What are some of the author's suggestions for change? How is this case similar to and different from your situation? In your country is there a difference between official policy at the national level and what actually happens at the state or provincial level? Make sure the discussion does not stay at a superficial level where the participants may be misled by apparent differences. Several of the root causes at work in this case stu'dy are to be found to some degree in *all* countries of the world. Do you recognize them?

• Have everyone read the article on AIDS by Elizabeth Reid in Chapter 4. How many of the factors described in Chapter 3 are instrumental in the spread of the HIV infection among young women? Talk about how these factors can affect young women and put them at risk. What changes in policy would help young women avoid exposure to AIDS? What changes in attitudes? Who could bring about these changes and how?

• Review the first part of Chapter 4 and have a discussion on the right to reproductive health. What is the maternal mortality rate in your community, or in a community that your group is working with? What are the immediate causes of the deaths and ill-health related to child-bearing? What root causes play a role? What reproductive health needs are unmet? Do infertile couples get help? Are family planning services adequate? Do young people get full and timely information on sexuality, STDs for example?

ORGANIZING A SEMINAR*

Several of the suggestions listed above could be the basis for all or part of a seminar organized by your group. If you decide to have a seminar, you will want to examine the list of suggestions for organizing a seminar reprinted below. It was drawn up by the Asian and Pacific Development Centre in Kuala Lumpur. Many groups have found it extremely useful.

The list of suggestions about organizing a seminar is followed by a 'typical' five-day seminar schedule and programme that includes both plenary and small group sessions.

SEMINAR CHECK-LIST

1. Be sure about the purpose of the seminar.

2. Organize speakers/experts well in advance to give them time to prepare for the seminar and their papers on particular topics.

3. Arrange advance media coverage if you wish to have the purpose of the seminar made publicly known. Invite the media to cover the seminar if you want the message and outcome made known to a wider audience.

4. Select a skilled chairperson who can gauge when to adjourn or to break up into group discussions.

5. Identify resource people who can act as group discussion leaders, and *Rapporteurs* who will write down the main ideas. In the absence of skilled *Rapporteurs* some advance training is recommended to ensure that group discussions are adequately reflected in the plenary session or in the final report.

6. Select participants according to the objectives of the seminar. Ask them to bring their experiences in written form, in pictures or on tapes, for use in the workshop sessions.

7. Choose an environment appropriate to the seminar topic, for example at the village level if related to the rural poor.

8. Provide basic facilities and ensure adequate working space as well as secretarial and clerical support for participants.

---

* Asian and Pacific Development Centre, Kuala Lumpur, Malaysia.

9. Consider the use of audio-visual material—tapes, slides, charts—as tools to provide the focus for discussion.

10. Have a definite schedule prepared to present to participants and stress that the goals should be achieved within that timescale.

11. As an introduction, arrange an informal session to allow participants to become acquainted. This will encourage a relaxed atmosphere and free exchange of views.

12. At the commencement of the seminar, make the purpose clear to the participants.

13. The organizer should have some idea of the anticipated outcome and be prepared to intervene and state this.

14. Do not overtax participants, particularly on the first day. Allow adequate time for private study and social activities.

15. To maintain interest and alertness, plan a range of approaches—practical exercises, simulated games, 'brainstorming', breaking into small groups, and so on.

16. Ensure ongoing evaluation and feedback to participants.

17. Allow flexibility according to what evolves in the course of the seminar and do not rule out any alternatives.

18. Try to overcome cultural barriers through observation and sensitivity.

19. Follow up the seminar with analysis and evaluation.

A TYPICAL SEMINAR PROGRAMME

Obviously this is a prototype that needs to be modified to fit the subject matter and the objectives of your group in holding a seminar. The programme given here assumes that the seminar is centred on one of the key issues in Chapter 4 (for example, safe motherhood), and that the objectives are: to increase awareness about the issue among members of your organization and among other target audiences; and to bring about changes in laws, policies or attitudes that will eliminate some causes of the problem (for example, higher minimum age for marriage, more educational opportunities for women, better pre-natal coverage).

This format would be appropriate for a regional seminar organized by an international NGO with a national affiliate as host. It assumes about 30 participants from six countries, plus four or five resource persons and staff of the seminar secretariat. The expected outcome is a plan of action for each of the six national affiliates represented, which will also be the basis for the seminar report. The programme includes plenary sessions and work in small groups. In this case each working group is made up of the team from one country. Participants from each country might include the secretary-general, president, information officer and person responsible for health in the national affiliate, plus someone from the national health system, the media or another sector whose collaboration is vital.

The purpose of the small groups is to allow topics to be discussed in greater depth or in more specific terms than is possible in a plenary, and to bring in a range of viewpoints. The groups must understand before they start exactly what their task is and what is expected from them in the way of reporting.

This programme assumes that participants will have received a background paper prepared for the seminar. It could draw on Chapter 4 of this book (one of the key issues), Chapter 3, Factors Influencing Women's Health, and Chapter 5, Action to Improve Women's Health. Its contents must of course be 'customized' to fit the needs and potential of your organization in the region concerned.

PLAN FOR A SEMINAR

In planning the schedule below, it is assumed that participants would arrive in the evening before the first day, when they would also register and attend a 'Get Acquainted' reception as a prelude to the following day's activities.

	FIRST DAY	SECOND DAY	THIRD DAY	FOURTH DAY	FIFTH DAY
MORNING	**Plenary session** Welcome—host organization Keynote speaker— overview of issue Organizer— objectives of seminar, group work (*Pause—coffee, tea*) Audio-visual presentation Discussion/questions	**Plenary session** Panel: root causes • cultural • status of women • socio-economic • political Discussion (*Pause*) What can be done? Presentation(s) by persons who have worked on the issue Discussion/questions	**Working Groups** Evaluation of ideas for action • what are strengths and weaknesses of organizations in each type of action? • what external factors would help or hinder our action? • whose collaboration is needed? (*Pause*) Continue as above, decide on priorities for action	**Working Groups** Complete preliminary outline of plan of action *and* Budget	**Plenary** Brief oral presentation of each Working Group report (written copy of national plan outline distributed) (*Pause*) Questions Discussion of national plans of action
AFTERNOON	**Working Groups*** Dimensions of problem in our country; how many affected, who, where? Consequences (*Pause*) Is needed information available? How much awareness exists now? *The resource persons (people who addressed the plenary, panelists, representatives of international agencies, specialists on the issue) can rotate through Working Groups as they meet.	**Working Groups** Root causes in our country, which background factors are at work? (*Pause*) Working Groups: 'Brainstorming'— • ideas for action on the issue in our country	**Working Groups** Develop preliminary plan of action for national organization • objectives • actions required— what, where, when? • who is responsible for each step? • how measure progress, evaluate? (*Pause*) Continue work on plan of action for national orgnization	**Visit to local health facility, project or community dealing with the issue** *and/or* **Drafting of Working Group reports** by *Rapporteurs*, Group Moderators and others asked to help	**Working Groups** Amend national plan if needed (*Pause*) **Plenary session/ closing** Summing up— highlights of seminar and action plans Arrangements for follow-up and exchange of information on national progress Closing (Hand in questionnaire on evaluation of seminar)

ANNEX IV
LIST OF
ORGANISATIONS

SOME OF THESE ORGANIZATIONS are solely concerned with women; many of the others have special departments, standing committees, working groups or other units that deal particularly with women's issues.

INTER-GOVERNMENTAL ORGANIZATIONS

(Many of these organizations have national and regional offices that are also sources of information on women and health.)

Council of Europe, BP 431 R6, 67006 Strasbourg, France.

International Fund for Agricultural Development, 107 via del Serafico, 00142 Rome, Italy.

International Labour Office (ILO), 4, chemin des Morillons, 1211 Geneva 22, Switzerland.

International Research and Training Institute for the Advancement of Women (INSTRAW), P.O. Box 21744, Santo Domingo, Dominican Republic.

Office of the United Nations High Commissioner for Refugees (UNHCR), PO Box 2500, 1211 Geneva 2 Dépot, Switzerland.

Pan American Health Organization (PAHO), 525 Twenty-Third St. NW, Washington DC 20037, USA.

United Nations Centre for Social Development and Humanitarian Affairs, Division for the Advancement of Women (UNOV/CSDHA), Vienna International Centre, PO Box 500, A-1400 Vienna, Austria.

United Nations Children's Fund (UNICEF), 3 United Nations Plaza, New York NY 10017, USA; and Palais des Nations, 1211 Geneva 10, Switzerland.

United Nations Development Fund for Women

(UNIFEM), c/o UNDP, 1 United Nations Plaza, New York NY 10017, USA.

United Nations Development Programme (UNDP), 1 United Nations Plaza, New York NY 10017, USA; and Palais des Nations, 1211 Geneva 10, Switzerland.

United Nations Education, Scientific and Cultural Organization (UNESCO), 7 place de Fontenoy, 75700 Paris, France.

United Nations Environment Programme (UNEP), PO Box 30552, Nairobi, Kenya.

United Nations Population Fund (UNFPA), 220 East 42nd Street, New York NY 10017, USA.

United Nations Volunteers, Palais des Nations, 1211 Geneva 10, Switzerland.

World Bank, 1818 H Street NW, Washington DC 20433, USA.

World Food Programme, via delle Terme di Caracalla, 00100 Rome, Italy.

World Health Organization, Avenue Appia, 1211 Geneva 27, Switzerland.

NON-GOVERNMENTAL ORGANIZATIONS, GROUPS AND NETWORKS

African Medical and Research Foundation (AMREF), PO Box 30125, Nairobi, Kenya.

Appropriate Health Resources and Technologies Action Group (AHRTAG), 85 Marylebone High Street, London W1M 3DE, England.

Asian and Pacific Women's Resource Collection Network, Asian and Pacific Development Centre, Kuala Lumpur, Malaysia.

Associated Country Women of the World (ACCW), Vincent House, Vincent Square, London SW1P 2NB, England.

Association of African Women for Research and Development (AAWORD), BP 3304, Dakar, Senegal.

Boston Women's Health Book Collective, 240 Elm Street, Somerville MA 02144, USA.

Christian Medical Commission, World Council of

171

Churches, 150 route de Ferney, 1211 Geneva 2, Switzerland.

DEPTHNEWS ASIA Women's Features, DEPTHNEWS ASIA, PO Box 1843, Manila, Philippines.

Development Alternatives with Women for a New Era (DAWN)/APDEC, Pesiaran Duta, PO Box 12223, Kuala Lumpur, Malaysia.

Family Health International, Research Triangle Park, North Carolina 27709, USA.

Foundation for Women's Health Research and Development (FORWARD), 38 King Street, London WC2E 8JT, England.

Global Link for Midlife and Older Women (GLOW), American Association of Retired Persons (AARP) and International Federation on Ageing (IFA), 1909 K Street NW, Washington DC 20049, USA.

Health Action International (HAI)-Europe, J. Lennepkade 334T, 1053 NJ Amsterdam, The Netherlands; HAI-Asia/Pacific, c/o IOCU, PO Box 1045, 10803 Penang, Malaysia; HAI-Latin America, c/o IOCU, Casilla 10993, Sucursal 2, Montevideo, Uruguay.

HelpAge International, St James's Walk, London EC1R 0BE, England.

Inter-African Committee on Traditional Practices Affecting the Health of Women and Children (IAC), c/o Economic Commission for Africa, ATRCW, PO Box 3001, Addis Ababa, Ethiopia; and 147 rue de Lausanne, 1202 Geneva, Switzerland.

International Association for Maternal and Neonatal Health, 22 avenue Riant-Parc, 1209 Geneva, Switzerland.

International Baby Food Action Network (IBFAN). Three regional service centres: IBFAN Penang, c/o IOCU, PO Box 1045, Penang Malaysia; IBFAN Geneva, c/o GIFA, CP 157, 1211 Geneva 19, Switzerland; IBFAN Minneapolis, c/o Action, 3255 Hennepin Avenue S, Minneapolis MN 55408, USA.

International Confederation of Midwives (ICM), 10 Barley Mow Passage, London W4 4PH, England.

International Council of Jewish Women (ICJW), 19 rue de Téhéran, 75008 Paris, France.

International Council of Nurses (ICN), 3 place Jean-Marteau, 1201 Geneva, Switzerland.

International Council on Social Welfare (ICSW), Koestlergasse 1/29, 1060 Vienna, Austria.

International Council of Women, 13 rue Caumartin, 75009 Paris, France.

International Organization of Consumer Unions (IOCU), Emmastraat 9, 2595 EG Amsterdam, The Netherlands; Regional Office for Asia and the Pacific, PO Box 1045, 10838 Penang, Malaysia.

International Planned Parenthood Federation (IPPF), PO Box 759, Inner Circle, Regent's Park, London NW1 4LQ, England.

International Union for the Conservation of Nature and Natural Resources (IUCN), avenue Mt Blanc, 1196 Gland, Switzerland.

International Union for Health Education, c/o Institut Santé et Développement, 15–21 rue de l'Ecole de Médecine, 75270 Paris, France.

International Women's Health Coalition, 24 East 21st Street (Fifth Floor), New York NY 10010, USA.

International Women's Tribune Centre, 777 United Nations Plaza, New York NY 10017, USA.

InterPress Service/Women's Feature Service, Via Panisperna 207, 00184 Rome, Italy.

ISIS International and ISIS International Latin American and Caribbean Women's Health Network, Casilla 2067, Correo Central, Santiago, Chile.

ISIS–WICCE Women's International Cross-Cultural Exchange, 3 chemin des Campanules, 1219 Aire-Geneva, Switzerland.

League of Red Cross and Red Crescent Societies, PO Box 372, 1211 Geneva 19, Switzerland.

Medical Women's International Association

(MWIA), Herbert-Lewin-Strasse 5, 5000 Cologne 41–Lindenthal, Germany.

NGO Working Group on Refugee Women, c/o ICMC, 37–9 rue de Vermont, 1211 Geneva 20, Switzerland.

Society for International Development (SID), Palazzo Civiltà del Lavoro, 00144 Rome, Italy.

Soroptomist International, 87 Glisson Road, Cambridge CB1 2HG, England.

WEMOS/HAI International Group on Women and Pharmaceuticals, PO Box 4263, 1000 AG Amsterdam, The Netherlands.

Women's Global Network on Reproductive Rights, NwZ Voorburgwal 32, 1012 RZ Amsterdam, The Netherlands.

World Association of Girl Guides and Girl Scouts (WAGGGS), Olave Centre, 12c Lyndhurst Road, London NW3 5PQ, England.

World Federation of Public Health Associations, PO Box 99, 1211 Geneva 20, Switzerland.

World University Service, 20 Compton Terrace, London N1 2UN, England; and chemin Iris 5, 1216 Cointrin-Geneva, Switzerland.

World Young Women's Christian Association (YWCA), 37 Quai Wilson, 1201 Geneva, Switzerland.

Zonta International, 557 West Randolph Street, Chicago IL 60606, USA.

ANNEX V
RESOURCE
GUIDE

THE LITERATURE AND AUDIO-VISUAL resources on Women and Health are vast. This list is intended only to suggest the range of materials available and to indicate sources for further information on the subjects you are interested in. Many of the organizations mentioned below issue publication lists and audio-visual lists periodically. The journals and newsletters are also good sources of information on the latest materials related to women and health. The addresses of the organizations listed here can be found in Annexe IV, List of Organizations.

BOOKS

American Association of Retired Persons and Pan American Health Organization (1989), *Midlife and Older Women in Latin America and the Caribbean*, Washington, AARP and PAHO.

Asian and Pacific Women's Resource Collection Network (1989), *Asian and Pacific Women's Resource and Action Series: Health*, Kuala Lumpur, Malaysia, Asia and Pacific Development Centre.

Boston Women's Health Book Collective (1984), *The New Our Bodies, Ourselves*, New York, Simon & Schuster.

Chetley, Andrew (1990), *A Healthy Business? World Health and the Pharmaceutical Industry*, London, Zed Books.

International Women's Tribune Centre (1987), *It's Our Move Now: A Community Action Guide to the UN Nairobi Forward Looking Strategies for the Advancement of Women*, New York, IWTC.

Kelley, Ninette (1989), *Working with Refu-*

gee Women: A Practical Guide, Geneva, International NGO Working Group on Refugee Women.

Kessel, E. and Awan, A. (eds) (1989), *Maternal and Child Care in Developing Countries*, Proceedings of Third International Congress for Maternal and Neonatal Health, Lahore; Thun, Switzerland, Ott Publishers.

Koso-Thomas, Olayinka (1987), *The Circumcision of Women: A Strategy for Eradication*, London, Zed Books.

Royston, Erica and Sue Armstrong (1989), *Preventing Maternal Deaths*, Geneva, WHO.

Seager, Joni and Ann Olson (1986), *Women in the World: An International Atlas*, New York, Simon & Schuster.

UNICEF, WHO and UNESCO (nd.), *Facts for Life: A Communication Challenge*, Benson, Oxfordshire, P & LA (available from UNICEF).

Werner, David (1983), *Where There Is No Doctor: A Village Health Care Handbook*, London and Nigeria, Hesperian Foundation, Macmillan.

Williams, Glen (nd.), *All for Health: A Resource Book for Facts for Life*, New York, UNICEF.

World Federation of Public Health Associations (1986), *Women and Health: Information for Action*, Geneva, WFPHA.

Wells, Troth and Foo Gaik Sim (1987) *Till They Have Faces: Women as Consumers*, Penang, International Organization of Consumer Unions and ISIS International.

World Young Women's Christian Association (1989), *Training Manual for Primary Health Care*, Doreen Boyd and Derek Williams, Geneva, World YWCA.

PERIODICALS AND OCCASIONAL PUBLICATIONS

Association of African Women for Research and Development (AAWORD), *Echo*, quarterly newsletter, Dakar.

Christian Medical Commission, World Council of Churches, *Contact*, a bi-monthly publication, Geneva.

Danida, Department of International Development Cooperation, Ministry of Foreign Affairs (1989), *A Strategy for Human Health: Plan of Action for Integration of Environmental Considerations into Danish Development Assistance*, Copenhagen.

Foundation for Women's Health Research and Development (FORWARD), *Sisterlinks*, quarterly, London.

Global Link for Midlife and Older Women (GLOW), *Network News*, newsletter, Washington.

International Organization of Consumer Unions, *Circular Letter on Consumer Issues Related to Women* (issue no. 4, 1989, on health), Penang.

ISIS International, *Women in Action*, quarterly.

———, Latin American and Caribbean Women and Health Network, *Women's Health Journal*, bi-monthly, Santiago.

ISIS–WICCE, *Women's World*, bi-annual publication, Geneva.

International Planned Parenthood Federation, *People*, a quarterly review of population and development.

International Women's Tribune Centre, *The Tribune: A Women and Development Quarterly*, New York.

Society for International Development, *Development*, Journal of SID, with frequent articles or special issues on women in development, for example, 'Young women', 1990: 1, Rome.

United Nations Children's Fund (UNICEF), *State of the World's Children*, annual publication with much information on women.

——— (1990), *The Girl Child: An Investment in the Future* publication of the UNICEF Programme Division.

——— (1987), *UNICEF and Women: The Long Voyage*, by Virginia Hazzard, UNICEF History Series, Monograph VII.

United Nations Population Fund (UNFPA), *Investing in Women: The Focus of the '90s*, by Dr Nafis Sadik, occasional paper (nd.).

———, *Population*, UNFPA newsletter, monthly.

———, *Populi*, quarterly journal.

———, *The State of the World Population*, annual report.

Women's Global Network for Reproductive Rights, *Newsletter*, Amsterdam.

Women's Global Network for Reproductive Rights and Latin American and Caribbean Women's Health Network/ISIS International, *Maternal Mortality & Morbidity: A Call to Women for Action*, special issue for International Day of Action for Women's Health, 28 May 1990.

World Bank, World Health Organization and United Nations Fund for Population Activities (1987), *Preventing the Tragedy of Maternal Deaths*. Report on the International Safe Motherhood Conference, Nairobi, Kenya, February 1987 (available from World Bank, Washington).

World Health Organization, *Communities in Action*, newsletter on community health, PHC.

———, *Safe Motherhood Newsletter*, quarterly.

———, *Women and Breast-feeding*, illustrated booklet.

———, *Women, Water and Sanitation*, illustrated booklet.

———, *World Health*, official illustrated magazine of WHO, bi-monthly.

———, *World Health Forum, World Health Statistics Quarterly, WHO Features*.

——— (1986), *Cancer Pain Relief*, booklet.

——— (1985), 'Women, Health and Development: A Report by the Director General', WHO Offset Publication no. 90.

World Health Organization and UNICEF (1986), 'Health Implications of Sex Discrimination in Childhood: A Review Paper and an Annotated Bibliography', S. Ravindran, Geneva, WHO.

———— (1989), *Protecting, Promoting and Supporting Breast-feeding: The Special Role of Maternity Services*, a joint WHO/UNICEF Statement.

World University Service and Third World First, Links 27 (nd.), *Knowing Women: Women and Educational Alternatives Worldwide*, London.

World Young Women's Christian Association (YWCA), *Common Concern*, quarterly newsletter on women and development, PHC, community action.

Worldwatch Institute (1990), *The Global Politics of Abortion*, Worldwatch Paper 97, Jodi Jacobson.

★ ★ ★

For the other books in the *Women and World Development Series* and for a wide selection of publications on women's issues in general:

Zed Books Ltd.	Zed Books Ltd.
57 Caledonian Road	165 First Avenue
London N1 9BU	Atlantic Highlands
United Kingdom	New Jersey 07716
	USA

INDEX